# THE FILMS OF
# CARY GRANT

# THE FILMS OF CARY GRANT

by DONALD DESCHNER

*Introduction by Charles Champlin*

THE CITADEL PRESS   Secaucus, New Jersey

First edition
Copyright © 1973 by Donald Deschner
All rights reserved
Published by Citadel Press
A division of Lyle Stuart, Inc.
120 Enterprise Avenue
Secaucus, New Jersey 07094
Manufactered in the United States of America by
Halliday Lithograph Corp., West Hanover, Mass.
Designed by A. Christopher Simon

Library of Congress catalog card number: 73-84151
ISBN 0-8065-0376-9

# ACKNOWLEDGMENTS

Grateful acknowledgment is made to the many individuals and organizations named and unnamed who aided the author in preparation of this book.

The staff of the Library of the Academy of Motion Picture Arts and Sciences, Actor's Equity (New York office), *America,* Gene Andrewski, Bennett's Book Shop, the British Film Institute, Elizabeth Kastanotis (Boston Public Library), *Catholic World, Canadian Forum,* Dorothy Chamberlain, Philip Chamberlain, Charles Champlin, Cherokee Book Shop, David Chierichetti, Cinemabilia, *Citizen News,* Columbia Pictures, Inc., *Commonweal, Cue,* the Cecil B. deMille Trust, Michael Druxman, Eddie Brandt's Saturday Matinee, Larry Edmunds Book Shop, Inc., Fairfield Grammer School Staff, A. Wymer Gard, *Films and Filming, Films in Review, Manchester Guardian, Hollywood Reporter, Hollywood Spectator,* Jim Harmon, Walter Hampden Memorial Library, W. S. Haugh, Alfred Hitchcock, Peter Hanson, Hollywood Book Service, Kenneth Lawrence's Movie Memorabilia Shop, Library of Congress, *Literary Digest, Library Journal, Life,* *Look,* Los Angeles County Museum of Art, *Los Angeles Daily News, Los Angeles Times, Los Angeles Examiner, McCall's,* Clifford McCarty, Paul Mayersberg, Metropolis Book Shop, Metro-Goldwyn-Mayer, *Mirror News* (Los Angeles), *Motion Picture Herald,* Joseph Musso, *Nation, New Republic, The New York Times, The New Yorker, Newsweek,* Quigley Publications, *Redbook, Rotarian,* Gunnard Nelson, Chester A. Nelson, Paramount Pictures, Inc., Gene Ringgold, Casey Robinson, RKO-Radio Corp., Michael J. Santoro, Screen Actor's Guild, *Spectator, Scribner's Commentator, Saturday Review, Scholastic* magazine, Mr. Richard Russell, St. Louis Public Library, State Historical Society of Wisconsin, *Theatre Arts Magazine, Time,* Times Newspapers Ltd. (London), 20th Century-Fox Corp. Theatre Poster Exchange, Inc., Library of the University of Michigan, Sidney Huttner (Regenstein Library, University of Chicago), W. H. Crain (University of Texas Library), Universal Studios, United Artists, Inc., United States Marine Corp., *Views and Reviews, Variety,* and Warner Bros.

# CONTENTS

# THE FILMS OF
# CARY GRANT

Cary Grant

# INTRODUCTION

*by Charles Champlin*

The commissary at Shepperton Studios on the fringe of London. A raw and wind-whipped day outside. A pleased and excited burble of lunchtime conversations inside. An Academy Award-winning actress lunches with her director and with her young co-star, who would soon have an Academy nomination of her own. Nearby sits the male star of a phenomenally successful American television series.

Shepperton is in full swing—the storm before the lull of the late Sixties—and in the commissary is an almanac's-worth of the famous and near-famous from both sides of the camera.

Suddenly a wave of silence, as tangible as a draft, moves forward from the door. The Oscar-holding actress stops in mid-sentence. The debonair television star stares at the visitor like a bleacherite at a Hollywood premiere.

Cary Grant, the well-silvered hair touseled by the wind, collar up against the chill, an untidy folder of business papers under his arm, a secretary scurrying to keep up, has popped in to see an associate.

He strides through the room, trying to be unaware of the paralyzing effect he has had on all other activity, giving half-embarrassed smiles and nods to familiar faces, looking for all the world like a Hitchcock hero on the lam and bluffing his way through a party he's crashed in hopes of eluding pursuers. He joins his friends, and the lunchtime murmurations resume. But he doesn't stay long, and another watchful hush follows him to the door and out into the gray English winter afternoon.

The memory is indelible, because no other actor could have had anything like so stunning an effect on an audience of fellow professionals who had, after all, watched many a star rise and wane and many a talent blossom and fade.

There is another memory. A warm summer night at Malibu. The designer Jean Louis and his wife Maggie are giving a party for their house guests, Rudolf Nureyev and Dame Margot Fonteyn. The guest list ranges from Anouk Aimee to Loretta Young. The Rolls-Royces if laid end to end would have stretched halfway to Santa Barbara, and, as I remember, they did.

Toward three in the morning, Shirley MacLaine is frug-

Fairfield Grammar School, Bristol

A page from the program for *Golden Dawn*

ging with Nureyev to the four-piece rock group. Cary Grant and Dyan Cannon wander in from a stroll on the beach (they plunged into matrimony a few days later) and pass through the rooms amidst a cone of awed silence and turned heads. They watch the dancing.

"I don't know," says Grant, grinning. "When I dance with a girl, I like to hold her. I mean, that's the pleasure of it." He gazes at the floor space between the dancers and lifts his eyebrows in the look of startled, innocent disbelief which generations of light comic actors have tried hard to duplicate.

"Uhn-uhn. Don't like it," Grant was saying. "And another thing. Bucket seats. Bucket seats are an abomination." His hands measure the vast, incommunicable gulf between bucket seats. "I don't know what the world is coming to." He grins again, wraps his arm around Miss Cannon and they move off to say good night to their hostess.

It is a Philip Barry moment—an urbane, amusing, romantic encounter in the world of the rich and beautiful.

That memory is indelible, as well, because you sensed that Cary Grant was himself aware that art and nature had in that brief instant come close together, and that he was being the figure he has so often played. The grin was gently self-mocking, not displeased.

Every actor who becomes a star and then a superstar endures because he embodies better than anyone else a particular life-style. He is a charismatic individual, vivid and unforgettable, and his is also a more general figure—a type—embodying a set of attributes and qualities which are the projections of the audience's wishes and dreams.

Cary Grant, more than any other actor, has perfectly and totally embodied the idea of the debonair romantic hero, moving with ease, assurance and charm, with quick wit and swift resourcefulness, through a world which has most often and most successfully been urban and contemporary, moneyed and literate.

He can be a dramatic actor of very great power, as he proved so eloquently in *None But the Lonely Heart* in 1944, when he was a poor young man inspired by Ethel Barrymore to escape the blighting darkness of a life of crime. It is in fact probably our loss and his that he has not been asked more often to stretch himself with more urgent and compelling dramatic material.

He has also acted the traditional robust action hero, as in *Gunga Din* and *Destination Tokyo,* and in so thickset an enterprise as *The Pride and the Passion,* which created little of either.

But neither he nor Hollywood have had any doubts about where his real strength lies. For what distinguishes Grant from such fellow superstars as Gable and Cooper, Stewart and Wayne and Bogart and Fonda, is his special mid-Atlantic (really almost stateless), classless, romantic, articulate, freewheeling, free-spirited, worldly yet oddly naive and idealistic charm.

There used to be an Ivy League joke to the effect that a Yale man walked into a good saloon as if he owned it, a Princeton man as if he knew the owner, and a Harvard man as if he didn't give a damn who owned it. Grant in his most memorable moments has projected a kind of rakish insouciance which embraces all three attitudes.

The Grant character owes much of its appeal to the several paradoxes it incorporates. That matchless accent, for example, is English but it owes a good deal more to Bristol (or Bow Bells) than to the BBC and Oxford. It is cosmopolitan and capable of great elegance but it is not stuffy, Tory or harmfully upperclass. It is smart, engaging and mobile.

Mobility looms large in the Grant persona. Thinking back over all the bright roles, you somehow remember him as footloose but, paradoxically, not irresponsible—a swinging bachelor who, however, would never let a lady down and who has clearly only been waiting for the right girl to come along. He is agile, not Alfie.

Grant, like his accent, has seemed essentially classless: comfortable and welcome among the working-stiffs, yet not nervous or out of place in the marble halls of the super-wealthy (unless, as in *Holiday,* the script asked him to be). He has also worked the neat trick, like such rougher-cut diamonds as Steve McQueen, of exerting a massive romantic appeal on women without rousing men to anger or contempt, and indeed while keeping their respect and admiration.

The other paradoxes which have surfaced in the Grant characterizations over the years include his special blend of worldliness and naivete and his ability to mix polish and pratfalls in successive scenes. Grant is also, refreshingly, able to play the near-fool, the fey idiot, without compromising his masculinity or surrendering to camp for its own sake. His ability to play off against his own image as the strong and handsome romantic hero-figure is, as a matter of fact, probably unique among the superstars. No one else comes even close to mind who could similarly toy with his own dignity without losing it.

It seems very likely that there is a kind of hierarchical ranking even among our dream-figures and our fantasies. Dreams of athletic glory are one thing, dreams of swashbuckling heroics are another and probably even more wistful thing. But very possibly the most potent dreams of all—because they are both the nearest to hand but also the most maddeningly elusive—are the dreams of social grace. To be the man who knows what to say and do and be in any social situation, and most particularly to be able to move with assurance through the world of the successful, is enviable beyond price, and the charm of a figure who can do it is immense.

And what may well, therefore, give Cary Grant his special place among superstars, his ability to roll a ripple of appreciative silence across a crowded commissary, is that what he is and does excites the envy of us all (man and woman alike) so powerfully. He is, perhaps, the man more of us would be in dreams than any other, the man more women would have had their lover be than any other. And not least, he shows an almost miraculous ability to defeat time, and thus enacts the most powerful dream of all for us.

With Virginia Cherrill

With Virginia Cherrill

3

up around the movies that the superstars are bad actors or worse, who get by simply by playing themselves. The truth is that being natural in front of a camera does not survive the first two takes, and the performer who is merely trying to play himself is, by the twentieth reading of a line, a sweat-eyed wreck with his stomach knotted like a gourd.

Superstars may or may not have begun with the element of stagecraft in hand (Grant did), but if they survive and prosper they become very gifted actors indeed—or they are crafty enough to work with directors who have enormous patience and cunning.

Grant had obviously learned a lot about presence during the days of his music hall apprenticeship, and it's been his good fortune to work with some of the most perceptive directors in the business, most notably George Cukor, who extracted the first screen performance (in *Sylvia Scarlett*) with which Grant was fully happy and who, in *Holiday* and *The Philadelphia Story,* helped Grant add further luster to the high-polish romantic comedy style he had developed while working with Howard Hawks and Leo McCarey.

Unfortunately, even Hollywood itself (as reflected in its Academy Award choices) is less impressed by the difficulties of doing comedy than of chewing the scenery in dramatic roles. But the truth is that Grant quickly became and has remained one of the ablest actors in the movies. The further truth is that light comedy is actually the heaviest and most difficult discipline of them all (as anyone painfully knows who has watched a comedy fail to work). Grant's glossary of grins and grimaces, the lifting eyebrows, the earnest bafflement, the dawning awareness that something has gone terribly, terribly wrong, the panicky suspicion that the lady's intentions are dishonorable and perhaps even carnivorous, the double-takes for openers, the falls and cowerings and the blithe assurance which precedes the fall, are all the hallmarks of an extremely skilled actor who has never stopped learning.

But if Grant is an uncommonly fine comic actor, he is also, of course, an incomparable romantic actor, and it is hard to say whether history will more honor the bright comedy or the idealized romance (or feel it necessary to isolate the two).

By now, more than four decades after his astonishing career in the movies began, Cary Grant has peopled the dreams of uncounted millions of us everywhere in the world. He has helped define the aspirations and shaped the dialogue and the deportment of many of us in ways that neither he nor we recognize. He is, in fact, one of the last of the great consciousness prototypes who arose in the golden age of the movies and who are unlikely to arise there again—certainly not with the positive attributes of wit, charm and romantic idealism which belong, incomparably, to Cary Grant.

With Virginia Cherrill

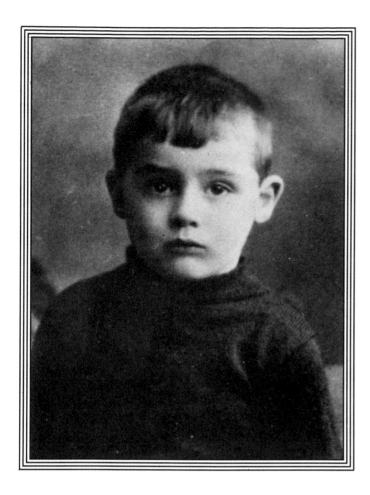

# CARY GRANT

## BIOGRAPHY

On January 18, 1904, a son was born to Elsie and Elias Leach in Bristol, England. He was named Archibald Alex Leach. Years later he would become world-famous as Cary Grant. But in his childhood there was little indication of the future that awaited him. His father worked for a local clothing merchant. His mother ran the home in a capable and fairly strict manner. Archibald attended Fairfield School in Bristol, receiving a sound basic education.

When Archie was twelve, his mother suffered a severe nervous breakdown and was placed in a nursing home. Adult explanations are not always satisfactory to the mind of a young person. That day he came home from school and she was gone. Echoes of his feelings of that moment and the next few days, must have remained with him for a long time. His father asked another woman to take care of Archie and the house; but despite her efforts to help the boy, she could not replace his mother.

At the age of thirteen, he ran away from home and joined Bob Pender's Troupe. When he was discovered missing, his father searched for him, found him, and brought him back home. Elias felt that his son was too young to be on his own.

About a year and a half later Archie again left home and rejoined the Pender Troupe, which specialized in eccentric dancing, stilt-walking, clown routines and pantomime work. Thus began his grounding in theatrical work that would lay a firm foundation for his career. This time, seeing the boy's determination and realizing that the Penders would provide a good home, Elias permitted his son to stay. The Pender Troupe played the vaudeville theatres in London and the provincial circuit throughout England.

In 1920 the Pender Troupe had an offer to come to the United States, and Archibald decided to come with them. In July of that year they set sail from Southampton on the *Olympic*. Landing in New York City, they found a crowded but adequate apartment with a number of rooms on one floor in a "walk-up."

Under contract to Fred Stone, the Penders played their special acts in the Hippodrome Theatre in a musical called *Good Times,* which was produced by Charles Dillingham and opened on August 9, 1920.

The following year Archibald worked on the Keith vaudeville circuit, performing in Chicago, Philadelphia, Cleveland, Boston, and other eastern cities. During the

The Bob Pender Troupe of stiltwalkers. Cary Grant, then still Archie Leach, is the third tallest figure.

Grant in *Boom Boom* on Broadway in 1927.

summer of 1922 he worked as a stilt-walker at the Steeplechase Park at Coney Island for George Tilyou, manager of the park. Late that year and well into 1923 he played on the Pantages circuit traveling across the United States to the West Coast and into Canada as well. Don Marlowe, famous as one of the stars of the *"Our Gang"* comedies, remembered Archie Leach playing the vaudeville circuit: "The future of Cary Grant looked very bleak indeed when he played the Lyceum Theatre in Duluth, Minnesota, during Christmas week in 1922. He was working as an audience plant with a mind-reading act."

These were not easy times for Archie Leach. For the next three years he remained mostly in New York City, finding occasional work, but often finding none. Almira Sessions, a famous vaudeville star and later a character actress in films, remembers encouraging Archibald and helping him find work. He did not forget this help, and when she later came out to Hollywood, she was often offered jobs in his films.

By the late 1920s his career was developing successfully. He began to appear regularly in major Broadway productions in worthwhile roles. In 1927 the new Hammerstein Theatre was completed by Arthur Hammerstein. For the premiere production, he selected *Golden Dawn,* with book and lyrics by Otto Harbach and Oscar Hammerstein II and score by Emmerich Kalman and Herbert Stothart. Louise Hunter and Paul Gregory were the leads. Archie Leach was hired to play the role of Anzac. Although the book had weaknesses, the musical score was praised and the lavish production was pleasing to most of the critics. *Golden Dawn* opened on November 30, 1927 and ran for 184 performances.

During the next season, he played the role of Reggie Phipps in *Boom-Boom,* a musical with Jeanette MacDonald and Frank McIntyre. The book was by Fanny Todd Mitchell, with music by Werner Janssen. Produced by the Messrs. Shubert at the Casino Theatre, the show ran for 72 performances.

For the fall of 1929, the Shubert Brothers planned a spectacular production of *Die Fledermaus* using the original music of Johann Strauss but with the book rewritten by Fanny Todd Mitchell. Archibald Leach was hired for the leading male role, to play opposite Gladys Baxter. The musical, retitled *Wonderful Night,* opened at the Majestic Theatre on October 31, 1929. Unfortunately this was two days after the stock market crash which ushered in the Great Depression. Advance ticket sales slowed down and then fizzled out. The show closed after 125 performances.

J. J. Shubert was General Productions Manager for the Municipal Opera Company in Saint Louis. He hired Archie Leach to perform in the outdoor bowl during the summer of 1931. The season opened Friday, May 29, with *Three Little Girls*. There were twelve productions which ran for a total of 87 performances, ending late in August. As listed in the program and in newspaper reviews, Archie Leach appeared in *Three Little Girls, The Street Singer, Music in May, Nina Rosa, Countess Maritza, The Three Mus-*

keteers, *A Wonderful Night, Irene,* and *Rio Rita.* The other two shows were *Rose Marie* and *The Circus Princess.* In the newspaper preproduction write-ups as well as the reviews, most of the space was given to descriptions of the productions and summaries of the plots; they contained little comment on the performances. However, this 1931 season was so successful that it not only paid for itself, but was able to wipe out the debt incurred by the previous year's unsuccessful season.

Returning to New York City, Archie Leach began rehearsal for a musical play, *Nikki,* written by John Monk Saunders and starring his wife, Fay Wray. Based on a magazine serial and also a film, *The Last Flight,* it was produced by William Friedlander, and opened at the Longacre Theatre on September 29, 1931. The critics didn't like the show, and it closed after thirty-nine performances.

Paramount, at this period, was making films in New York as well as on the West Coast. Sound was now used for most films, and the stars of the New York stage could easily appear in films without interrupting their stage work. In addition, short films were needed to fill out programs. These shorts usually consisted of sketches by comedians like George Burns and Gracie Allen, Jack Benny, or Eddie Cantor, or two or three numbers sung by performers like Ethel Merman or Rudy Vallee. Chinese character actress Anna Chang starred in a ten-minute, one-reel film called *Singapore Sue.* Archie Leach in his first film appearance played one of four American sailors visiting her cafe. This was one of several shorts written and directed by Casey Robinson, who later recalled:

"I needed a leading man to play an American sailor. Among the young men brought to see me was Archie Leach, who had never been in front of a camera. I liked him and cast him without hesitation."

Another scene from *Boom Boom.*

On the set of *Ladies Should Listen,* director Frank Tuttle chats with Charles Ray while Grant reads

"This young actor, Archie, so impressed me during the filming that I wrote a note to important executives at Paramount, none of whom I knew at the time, urging them to screen the short, not for my work but for that of a young actor whom I felt to be a sure-fire future star." However, for some reason this film was not released until the middle of the following year.

Archibald Leach decided to drive across the country to Hollywood. Having signed a contract with Paramount, he changed his name to Cary Grant, and began working in feature films. He completed seven films in his first year in Hollywood. *This Is the Night* was premiered on April 8, 1932. Directed by Frank Tuttle, the cast included Lili Damita, Charlie Ruggles, Roland Young, Thelma Todd and Grant. The next film, *Sinners in the Sun,* was his first with Carole Lombard. It was a typical romance film with elaborate modernistic settings of the period. *Merrily We Go to Hell,* his third film, starred Sylvia Sidney and Fredric March, both of whom he would perform with in later films.

Playing the mad captain of a submarine, Charles Laughton virtually stole the show in *The Devil and the Deep.* Cary Grant and Gary Cooper were crewmen and Tallulah Bankhead played the captain's wife. It was a story of jealousy leading to tragedy. Next came the showy but not too successful von Sternberg production, *Blonde Venus,* which gave Grant star billing along with Marlene Dietrich and Herbert Marshall. Even with the beautifully photographed settings and the lavish nightclub production numbers, this story of a marriage' that failed and then finally was saved did not seem to have adequate appeal. Nancy Carroll and Randolph Scott appeared with Grant in *Hot Saturday,* the story of a small-town romantic misunderstanding. In his last film that first year, Grant played Lieutenant Pinkerton to Sylvia Sidney's Cho-Cho San in *Madame Butterfly,* based on the famous opera and play. It was presented as a realistic film, although Grant did sing at the end.

With Wesley Ruggles and Isabel Jewel (1936)

With Katharine Hepburn and director George Cukor on the set of *Sylvia Scarlett*

During filming of *Wings In the Dark,* Sir Charles Kingsford Smith, having just completed a record-breaking flight from Australia, talks with Cary Grant and Myrna Loy

In his second year in Hollywood, Cary Grant made six films. The first was *She Done Him Wrong* with Mae West, who, while she didn't discover him as has often been claimed, certainly gave his career a boost. Grant plays a mission church minister who keeps a watchful eye on Lady Lou, played by Mae West. Based on the play *Diamond Lil,* the film contains such famous lines as "Come up and see me sometime," and "I'm doing a job that I never did before."

*The Eagle and the Hawk,* a bitter film about World War I flyers co-starred Fredric March, Jack Oakie, and Carole Lombard. The first film to give Grant top billing was *Gambling Ship,* which was released in June of 1933. Later that year he again co-starred with Mae West, this time in *I'm No Angel.* For the Paramount all-star production of *Alice in Wonderland,* Cary Grant played the Mock Turtle.

On February 10, 1934, Cary Grant married Virginia Cherrill at Caxton Hall in London. Just three years before, she had gained fame playing opposite Charles Chaplin in *City Lights.* She continued to appear in other films during this time, but in a few years completely gave up her film career. Grant appeared in four films released in 1934: *Thirty-Day Princess, Born to Be Bad, Kiss and Make Up,* and *Ladies Should Listen.* On December 4, his wife of less than a year filed for separation. On December 19, the Paramount Publix Corporation bankruptcy was settled by reorganizing the company, and a new company emerged, Paramount Pictures, Inc.

Four Cary Grant films were released in 1935. *Enter Madam, Wings in the Dark,* and *The Last Outpost* were Paramount productions. The RKO production was *Sylvia*

*Scarlett,* directed by George Cukor, and was Grant's first film with Katharine Hepburn. As a change of pace from playing clean-cut leading men, in this film Grant played a petty scoundrel. Recently director Cukor discussed the production problems, the plot weaknesses, and the studio re-editing that kept this film from being successful; but he remembered and particularly praised Grant's performance.

Virginia Cherrill was given a divorce, on March 26.

On May 5, 1935, Grant made his first appearance on the *Lux Radio Theatre* in the play *Adam and Eve.* He would appear several times on this show over the next twenty years, often under the direction of Cecil B. DeMille. There would be other guest appearances on radio shows in the late 1930s and through the 1940s on such programs as *Groucho Marx's Kellogg Show,* the *Eddie Cantor Show,* and an early talk show, George Faulkner's *The Circle.*

In 1936 there were four films: *Big Brown Eyes* and *Wedding Present,* both with Joan Bennett, *Suzy* with Jean Harlow, and *Romance and Riches,* also known as *The Amazing Quest of Mr. Bliss,* the first film that Grant made in England. Perhaps if this film had been more successful, he would have remained in England making pictures there, but such was not the case. Including the last-mentioned film, Cary Grant had made twenty-five motion pictures during his first five years in the film business. Twenty-one of these films had been made for Paramount. In his ensuing career, he would return only twice to that studio, once in 1955, and again in 1958. Most of his work in the late 1930s and through the 1940s would be either for Columbia Pictures or RKO, with an occasional picture for Warner Bros. or Metro-Goldwyn-Mayer.

Grace Moore was his co-star in *When You're in Love,* his first picture for Columbia. The other films for 1937 were *Toast of New York, Topper,* and *The Awful Truth.* The latter, co-starring Irene Dunne and Ralph Bellamy, directed by Leo McCarey, was one of the finest comedies of this period.

Grant would make five films with director Howard Hawks. The first was *Bringing Up Baby.* In this film, Grant played Huxley, a paleontologist who falls in love with Susan, played by Katharine Hepburn. (Baby is a pet leopard.) *Holiday* was his second film in 1938; again his co-star was Hepburn. Grant traveled to Europe in the fall, returning to the United States on November 25, 1938.

Three films were issued in 1939. *Gunga Din,* a George Stevens spectacular set in India, but filmed entirely on the California desert and in Hollywood studios, presented Grant, along with Douglas Fairbanks, Jr., and Victor McLaughlin as happy-go-lucky British soldiers who are forced to fight a villainous, mad thuggee leader who threatens British rule. Sam Jaffe gave a fine performance as the Indian in the title role. The two other films that year were *Only Angels Have Wings* and *In Name Only.*

On September 1, 1939, Hitler invaded Poland. So began World War II. On September 3 both Great Britain and France declared war on Germany. While the United States

On the set of *When You're In Love,* with Co-director Robert Riskin, Grace Moore, and producer Everett Riskin

With director Leo McCarey on set of *The Awful Truth*

Co-directors Robert Riskin and Harry Lachman and Cameraman Joseph Walker watch as Cary Grant and Grace Moore film an intimate love scene in *When You're In Love.*

With director George Cukor and Doris Nolan on location rehearsing a scene for *Holiday*

Cary Grant, Howard Hawks and Noel Coward watch Thomas Mitchell and Jean Arthur rehearse a scene for *Only Angels Have Wings*

Grant slices a birthday cake presented to him on the set of *Only Angels Have Wings* with Thomas Mitchell, Jean Arthur, producer-director Howard Hawks, and members of the camera crew watching

Director Howard Hawks discussess a scene with Cary Grant while Thomas Mitchell and Richard Barthelmess watch

With Sargent Kahanamoku in Honolulu

Grant returns from European vacation on the Ile De France (1939)

would not join the actual fighting for another year, Franklin D. Roosevelt led this nation in sympathizing with the Allied cause and in offering aid to the British and others in their fight against Germany. Just as thousands of ordinary citizens did, many members of the motion picture industry also offered help to the Allies. Grant flew to Washington and talked to the British ambassador, who suggested that British stars remain in Hollywood, continue making films, and give their time and money to projects that would promote the British cause.

In 1940 three Grant films were released: *His Girl Friday, My Favorite Wife,* and *The Howards of Virginia.*

*The Philadelphia Story* with Katharine Hepburn and James Stewart, based on the successful Broadway play, was released early in 1941. In April *Penny Serenade* with Irene Dunne opened. During the summer Grant and some friends went to Mexico, where he and Barbara Hutton enjoyed a pleasant holiday free from reporters. Mid-November saw the release of *Suspicion,* Grant's first film with director Alfred Hitchcock. Together they would make four films. Based on the novel *Before the Fact, Suspicion* was to end with the villain, played by Grant, mailing a letter which, unknown to him, would accuse him of the murder he had just committed. The studio bosses said no! The audience, they decided, would not accept a star playing such a character, so a happy ending was made for this film, completely changing the characters and the point of the original story. Were the producers wrong? This was the only Hitchcock-Grant film that did not gross over $4,000,000 to become a top box-office money-maker. Even a director like Hitchcock would have to wait another five or ten years before he could control his productions, and this only after the great studios had been weakened by television and foreign films.

In mid-October, Frank Capra brought to Hollywood several members of the original Broadway cast of *Arsenic and Old Lace,* including Josephine Hull and Jean Adair. When Bob Hope turned down the lead role of Mortimer, Cary Grant accepted it. Although Capra often used improvisational methods while shooting, the work was intense and the film was completed by December. But the Japanese had attacked Pearl Harbor and the American people were thrown into a frenzy of war activities. The war and a contract holding back the film until the play closed on Broadway, would prevent the film from being released for theatrical showing until 1944, although our troops in North Africa would see the premiere behind the lines in 1943.

To sell bonds for the war effort, in March of 1942 a number of Hollywood stars made a three-week whistle-stop tour across the United States. Cary Grant traveled with this group. While he played some routines of his own, Grant often appeared as the straight-man opposite Bert Lahr in his famous "Income Tax" scene. The train usually arrived in town in the morning, there might be a parade of stars or guest appearances, and then in the evening a gala stage presentation.

For his work in *Penny Serenade,* Grant received his

first Academy Award nomination for best actor, but Gary Cooper won it that year for his performance in *Sergeant York*.

On June 26, 1942, Cary Grant legalized his name and became an American citizen before a judge in Los Angeles. On July 8, he married Barbara Hutton in a simple six-minute ceremony at the Lake Arrowhead home of his business manager, Frank Vincent. *Talk of the Town* with Ronald Coleman and Jean Arthur and *Once Upon a Honeymoon* with Ginger Rogers were his two films for 1942.

Work began at Warner Bros. on a big war film. Director Delmer Daves recalls the making of *Destination Tokyo:*

"As a writer I had been working at sea in submarines on the background to *Destination Tokyo* in 1943. Warner told me he liked the script very much and that the technical details fascinated him. He was worried, however, that he would have to send the director, whoever he might be, to sea on order to understand fully the meaning of the details in the script. Then he told me that he would

With Anita Princeps at a preview of *His Girl Friday*

With Howard Hawks and Rosalind Russell on set of *His Girl Friday*

Grant demonstrates a scene to Morrie Ryskind who adapted *His Girl Friday* from the original play by Ben Hecht and Charles MacArthur

On set of *His Girl Friday* with Ira Uhr, casting director, and Howard Hawks

13

like me to direct the picture. Now I didn't actually want to direct the picture, although when I started out in the motion picture business as a property boy I did have visions of becoming a director eventually. But by this time I had been a writer for fourteen years and I enjoyed it so much that I wasn't sure about the change. But he said, 'Just do this one,' and of course that was the beginning of my career as a director. But it wasn't as simple as having Mr. Warner sign me to direct the film. I had to be approved by the star, who was Cary Grant. The producer was Jerry Wald. Well, Cary Grant called to say that he approved the script. He asked who the director was going to be, and Wald with fear and trembling, because he knew that Cary had approval or rejection of any director, said, 'Delmer Daves.' Cary hesitated for a bit, thought it over and said, 'Why, yes, Delmer would make a fine director.' When he asked who the cameraman was and was told it was to be Bert Glennon, a man with whom he'd worked before, he said, 'Excellent. I'm looking forward to doing this picture.'

"So Jerry Wald called Warner and told him that Cary had approved me as a director. Then about ten or fifteen minutes later the phone rang. It was Cary's agent. He said he'd received word that Cary wanted to do the film *Destination Tokyo* and he wanted to know who the director was going to be. But this time instead of enthusiasm we got nothing but shock and horror. He said, 'Delmer Daves has never directed a picture in his life! What do you mean he's going to direct Cary Grant? Let him practice on somebody else before he deals with my star!' Well, Jerry Wald stammered a bit and said, 'Have you talked to Cary?' and the agent said, 'I don't care what Cary says. I'm handling his affairs and I refuse to let a new man, who's never directed before, direct him.' So Jerry then says, 'Okay,' and calls Warner to tell him what the agent said. That seemed to be that. But then the agent calls back to say that he's talked to Cary who had told him that he wouldn't do the picture with anyone else but Delmer Daves.

"Later on I asked Cary Grant what had inspired this very definite approval. He told me that when the agent called and rebuked him for taking a chance on a new man he recalled to the agent that once upon a time Mae West had pointed to him and said, 'I approve that young man. I think he'll be my new leading man,' and as a result a career was born. Cary, knowing me as a friend and having seen and liked many of the pictures I had written, felt that I would make a director and so why not be the first man to say, 'I have faith in Delmer Daves.' So that's how it started. It was the combined faith of Cary Grant, Jerry Wald, and Jack Warner."

*Destination Tokyo* was released in January of 1944 and was very successful. *Arsenic and Old Lace* which had been held back three years was finally released. The two other films that year were *Once Upon a Time,* a fantasy about a caterpillar; and *None But the Lonely Heart.* The latter was from a screenplay by Clifford Odets based on a best-selling novel of the same title by Richard Llewellyn. Odets also directed.

With Virginia Field, attending a press review of *The Howards of Virginia*

Rehearsing *The Howards of Virginia* with director Frank Lloyd and Cedric Hardwicke

With Forrest Tucker and Martha Scott on location filming for *The Howards of Virginia*

Grant plays backgammon with Paul Mertz, musical advisor, between takes on *Penny Serenade*

With director George Stevens and Irene Dunne on set of *Penny Serenade*

With cinematographer Joseph Walker and Irene Dunne on set of *Penny Serenade*

With Ronald Colman, Irene Dunne, and director George Stevens comparing the model and the set for *Talk of the Town*

Director George Stevens shows
Grant how to play a scene in *Talk of
the Town*

With Howard Hughes, A. C. Blumenthal and President Miguel
Aleman at the National Palace in Mexico City (1947)

With Barbara Hutton at a benefit
premiere of *Talk of the Town*

With Barbara Hutton (1944)

With Barbara Hutton and Randolph Scott

Brian Aherne visits Grant on set of *Once Upon A Time*

With Alexander Hall, director of *Once Upon A Time*

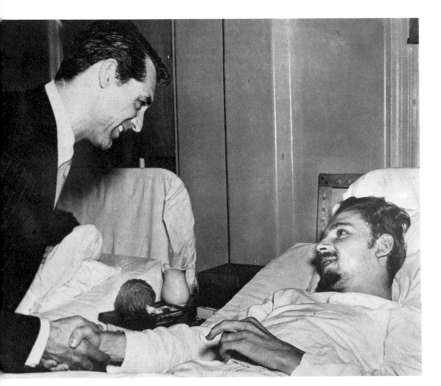

During World War II, visiting a wounded Marine

On August 16, Grant and Barbara Hutton separated, but they made a public announcement of reconciliation on October 3.

In the spring of 1945 Grant received from the Academy of Motion Picture Arts and Sciences his second nomination for best actor for his performance in *None But the Lonely Heart*. But the Oscar that year was won by Bing Crosby for his very popular performance as a parish priest in *Going My Way*.

*Night and Day* was the only film Grant made in 1945. It was loosely based on the life of Cole Porter, whom Grant played. Although it had a poor story—really a screenwriter's fantasies of a composer's life—the many fine Porter songs made it a pleasant and very successful film. On August 30, lawyer Jerry Giesler led Barbara Hutton into the courtroom of Superior Judge Thurmond Clark in Los Angeles and in about ten minutes obtained an interlocutory decree of divorce.

July 1946 saw the release of *Notorious,* in which Grant co-starred with Ingrid Bergman, directed by Alfred Hitchcock. The film dealt with a German spy ring in Latin America. Grant also made a guest appearance in *Without Reservations,* which starred John Wayne and Claudette Colbert.

In 1947 he performed with Shirley Temple in *The Bachelor and the Bobby Soxer,* and with Loretta Young and David Niven in *The Bishop's Wife.* During the summer he flew to England to discuss plans for films to be made with Alexander Korda, but unfortunately nothing came of these hopes.

*Mr. Blandings Builds His Dream House,* based on a humorous best-selling book which recounted problems and adventures in buying and building a house in the country, was Grant's new film. The other film made in 1948 was *Every Girl Should Be Married,* in which his co-star was Betsy Drake.

Grant's only film in 1949 was his third under the direction of Howard Hawks. *I Was a Male War Bride* was made in Germany and England. During actual shooting, and delaying work on the film, Grant became ill with jaundice and was hospitalized for a time. He was found to be in excellent health after a medical examination later that year in Baltimore. On Christmas Day he and Betsy Drake were married near Scottsdale, Arizona.

In 1950 he made *Crisis,* which was directed by Richard Brooks, who recalls how Grant helped him:

"All the time I was working with producer Mark Hellinger in the late forties as a writer I didn't have a contract, only an agreement. At MGM, of all people, Arthur Freed, who loved musicals, wanted to see some of my pictures, and wanted me to come over to MGM. I wouldn't go over to them unless they gave me a contract which allowed me to direct as well as write. They said that if they didn't let me direct the first picture they'd let me direct the next, and if I didn't direct that I could leave and break my contract. The first was a picture I wrote, *Any Number Can Play.* They cast Clark Gable, and he or someone didn't feel

Fred Allen visits set of *Once Upon A Time*, seen here with Grant, Janet Blair, Ted Donaldson and director Alexander Hall

A scene from *Once Upon A Time* is played for the camera. Director Alexander Hall and James Gleason watch Ted Donaldson, Janet Blair and Cary Grant

Visiting the set of *Having a Wonderful Crime,* 1945. Pat O'Brien, Grant, Carole Landis and George Murphy

With Mary Brian (1946)

Grant's suit of armour is shined before he steps before the camera for a scene in *The Bachelor and the Bobby Soxer*

With Janet Thomas and Frank Morgan at a party given by Veronica Lake (1946)

20

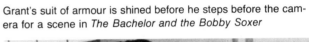

Visiting with actor Will Byffe at Shepperton Studio, September 1947, while in England to discuss a film with Alexander Korda

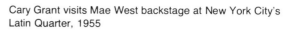
Cary Grant visits Mae West backstage at New York City's Latin Quarter, 1955

While in Bremerhaven in 1948 to make *I Was a Male War Bride*, Cary Grant and Ann Sheridan visit with Joseph Cotten and Orson Welles who are working on *The Third Man*

With Betsy Drake

With Betsy Drake on steps of the portable dressing room during filming of *Room For One More*

I was competent to direct him. So Mervyn LeRoy directed the picture. Then I wrote another, and that was *Crisis.* Cary Grant was the one who said, 'If he can write it why can't he direct it, because he must know as much as anyone about making pictures?' He was very kind and I learned a great deal from him. I was very lucky, because with José Ferrer and Cary Grant, I was with very professional people.

"I wanted to do a story of this kind and I did not want a woman in it. Originally, the way I wrote the story was that Cary Grant was a surgeon, a widower. He had a little girl of about nine years of age, and he never had a chance to be with her, so he took her on a vacation to South America, and what happened to the child made a much stronger story than what happened to his new bride. But MGM at that time felt, well, if you've got Cary Grant, why d'you want to have a kid in it? You've got to have a dame in it. And you're rather new just now, you haven't done so many pictures. Anyway, a woman materialized in the picture.

"When they saw the picture, they said, gee, that's pretty serious. Cary in a serious picture, that could be a disaster. So they advertised the picture, "Carefree Cary on a Happy Honeymoon" all through the States, and of course no one went to see it at all. It played in England, and I think it played in France and Canada. It was banned in all South America, Central America and Mexico. It was banned in Italy because the dictator in it was hanged by his heels; so was Mussolini.

In regard to the Cary Grant part, "he is a man of habit, regardless of where he is. He's being kidnapped but still at four or five in the morning when people usually brush their teeth, he has to brush his teeth, even if he has to borrow some tequila from a native on the train. As he says later, to the dictator's wife, yes, he'll do the surgery, but he wants his fee. I wanted it to build up to the point where you would accept someone who, no matter what, may dislike something but goes ahead and does it because it's a matter of routine and principle with him. . . . I've never thought whether Grant was meant to be liked. My intention, and he went along with it, was that he should be a man of modern times, that he, as a man of ethics who has had many of the humanities subdued in him because of his career, has to put his life on the block. In other words, he has to make decisions under primitive conditions, away from his own world, the civilized world of the hospital where everything is worked out very nicely for him, where someone can pay a fee or can't pay a fee. Suddenly he is put in the real world of making a decision. Here, whether he likes it or not, it isn't a matter of routine, but whether he would get out of this alive. The whole point was whether he would do this job and what he would do afterwards, having done it. How does he act as a scientist and how does he act as a man, both in the same human being? As a matter of fact, it didn't cross my mind whether he should be liked or not."

In 1950 Cary Grant made an unbilled guest appearance on a television show which was built around the character "Charlie Weaver" as created and played by Cliff Arquette. Grant played a hobo passing by.

Grant returned to comedy in 1951, but to comedy of an unusual and perhaps serious kind. The film, *People Will Talk,* was written and directed by Joseph L. Mankiewicz and told the story of an individualistic doctor whose main interest is in helping people even if he must use unorthodox methods. A jealous colleague on the same university staff begins an investigation in order to disqualify the doctor and ruin his reputation, but ultimately the hero is exonerated when all is told, and the inquisitor must slink into the darkness. Written and produced at a time of political fear, at a time when many men thought it wiser to be silent than to speak out, this film had serious things to say in a pleasant manner, things that were quite timely.

*Room for One More* and *Monkey Business* were his two films in 1952. The first, in which he co-starred with his wife, Betsy Drake, was a comedy about a woman who wants to adopt all the children and pets she sees, and a husband who attempts to keep things under control. The second film was under the direction of Howard Hawks, and had Ginger Rogers, Marilyn Monroe, and Charles Coburn in the cast. The following year Grant made *Dream Wife,* with Deborah Kerr. In 1954 he made no films.

In 1955 he again played under the direction of Alfred Hitchcock; his co-star was Grace Kelly. *To Catch a Thief* was a suspense film about jewel thievery on the Riviera.

The following year no Grant films were released; but in 1957 there were three. The major one was *The Pride and the Passion* with Sophia Loren and Frank Sinatra. This Stanley Kramer production told the story of a large gun that the Spanish people were able to save and use most successfully in their fight against Napoleon's army. The other two films that year were *An Affair to Remember* and *Kiss Them for Me.*

When interviewed by Richard MacCann that year, Grant expressed great dissatisfaction with current writers. He said he missed the skill and the finely polished scripts of writers like Philip Barry, Frederick Lonsdale, and Bernard Shaw. Since many writers were very well paid for stories of violence which were easier to write, they didn't bother to work on harder-to-write comedies. In the same interview Grant suggested that after working hard to achieve success, it was wonderfully rewarding "just to examine everything around."

*Indiscreet* and *Houseboat* were the two films for 1958. That year he and Betsy Drake separated.

*North by Northwest,* the successful Hitchcock film, was released in 1959. Based on several ideas that had interested Hitchcock for some time, the film is in a sense an anthology of typical Hitchcockian situations. A classic study in suspenseful build-up is found in a scene that takes place in broad daylight at an intersection in the middle of cornfields. In this setting, a number of incidents seem to indicate danger, but turn out to be ordinary aspects of daily life. Then danger suddenly comes from an unexpected source, and in his attempt to escape alive, the character played by Grant accidentally leads his enemy into a spectacular and flaming death. The pacing and editing of this sequence is representative of Hitchcock's best work. Grant was chosen for his role because Hitchcock said that he felt that Grant was one of the few actors who could make this character believable.

*Operation Petticoat* was the other film Grant made that year. It was about a disabled submarine in the Pacific during World War II. Tony Curtis, Joan O'Brien, Dina Merrill, and Arthur O'Connell were in the cast of this pleasant comedy. In an interview, director Blake Edwards recalled the making of this film. "From the standpoint of making money, this was the most successful film that I've made. It was one of the biggest grossing films that Universal has ever had. As a whole I thought it was a good film. I had some bad experiences on it, but I learned a great deal about personalities and politics. I locked horns with Mr. Grant immediately. I was there by virtue of the fact that Cary Grant had agreed to give this newcomer a break. I was really in great jeopardy of being off the film before I got started and I had to, at one point, sit down and really examine myself. I learned something about myself —that I didn't have to go quite that hard to prove my point. Although I'm still very determined, I'm more objective about it now."

*The Grass Is Greener* with Deborah Kerr, Jean Simmons, and Robert Mitchum was made in 1960. The next year Grant made no films. In 1962 *That Touch of Mink*, a comedy with Doris Day and Gig Young was released. On August 14, 1962, Grant's third marriage ended when Betsy Drake won her divorce. *Charade*, a murder mystery with Audrey Hepburn, opened on Christmas Day, 1963. In 1964 in *Father Goose*, Grant played a bearded loner living on a South Pacific island until World War II interrupts his solitude. His life is changed when a group of young girls under the charge of Catharine (played by Leslie Caron) are forced to live in his quarters.

Cary Grant married Dyan Cannon on July 22, 1965 in Las Vegas. Having met her some time before, when she was suggested for a part in a film he was contemplating, he began to date her and they decided to marry. During the summer of 1965 a very successful retrospective showing of Grant's films was held in New York City. In 1966 he made *Walk, Don't Run*, a romantic comedy set in Japan at the time of the Olympic games and filmed on location in Japan. Having so long wanted a child, it was a great delight for him when a daughter was born in 1966. She was named Jennifer. Regrettably, the marriage did not last, and on March 21, 1968, Dyan Cannon won her divorce.

Having made no films since 1966, Grant has kept busy, spending more time on several business ventures. He makes a point of enjoying as many hours as he can with Jennifer. For all practical purposes he has retired from film-making; however he has indicated that if "interesting" scripts should turn up, he might make one or two more films.

As an appropriate climax to his career, he was given a special honor by his colleagues in the motion picture

Grant dances with Sophia Loren between takes while on location in Spain to film *The Pride and the Passion*

industry. On the evening of April 7, 1970, the Academy of Motion Picture Arts and Sciences bestowed upon Cary Grant a special Academy Award, praising him for the high quality of acting throughout his career and for the pleasure he has brought to so many moviegoers throughout the world.

## MYTH AND REALITY

The name of Cary Grant is known throughout the world. One can talk about him with a local inhabitant in Red Cloud, in Marseilles, in Bonn, in Sydney, in Tokyo, or in Rio de Janeiro, and the listener will know whom you are talking about, and will probably have seen at least two or three of his films. Grant is one of a number of major stars who have been in Hollywood films over the past several decades, and who because of personality, image, acting talents, and the promotion of their names have become the property of the whole world.

In film history, the star did not come first. In the beginning only the subject or type of film was of interest. Then for a time the producer, director, or owner of the company had top billing. However, Adolph Zukor began advertising "famous players" when he released a Sarah Bernhardt film for distribution in the United States. By the late 1910s, name players were on the scene—players whose names alone sold a picture, players whose names brought in the audience. Douglas Fairbanks promised exciting adventure. Mary Pickford promised drama or comedy involving a young lass. Chaplin promised a certain kind of comedy and William S. Hart a certain kind of western. The developing studios found their fortunes written in the names of

With Tony Curtis watching a scene being filmed for *Operation Petticoat*

With Doris Day and crew on set of *That Touch of Mink*

At London Airport with Betsy Drake, leaving for Monaco to visit Prince Ranier and Princess Grace in March 1961

With Audrey Hepburn during the filming of *Charade*

Grant visits Joan Crawford, producer-director William Castle and John Ireland on set of *I Saw What You Did,* 1965

With Dyan Grant and their 3½-month-old daughter, Jennifer

With Dyan Cannon

25

the stars. Gradually the Hollywood film industry became formed around the star.

Yet while the star was the most important element, he was also caged by studio controls and the demands of the general public. An image of each important star was created, packaged, and promoted by the studio in order to sell that star to a vast audience. In some cases the image and the person were the same; in other cases there was a great divergence. This was not without its effects on both star and audience. Two popular beliefs arose. In one case the image and the man were thought to be precisely the same. In the other case, it was thought that the image and the real person were contrary to one another, that the actor was really a Jekyll and a Hyde.

Myths grow from reality, but they are not necessarily factual. Rather they are generalizations. But to many, the myth becomes more important and takes on more reality than the truth of the matter. It is the job of the actor to create another personality, another character in a performance so that you may know and understand and feel with that character. That is the actor's work. But when he is not working, then he is just like you or me in being a human being.

The silent film, because it eliminated the voice of the actor, created a more universal image. Perhaps the most serious effect that the coming of sound had on motion pictures as a whole was the effect upon audiences of hearing the actual voices of favorite stars. Several careers were ended because the voice did not match the image. Even the sudden rash of voice coaches brought to Hollywood at this time could not solve all the problems. It was precisely at this point in film history, especially the period between 1928 and 1933, that many of the most popular and lasting stars began their film careers. Most of them came having trained their voice in stage work. Naming just a few and suggesting the variety of performers, there were Fredric March (1929), Spencer Tracy (1930), Ginger Rogers (1930), Clark Gable (1931), Bette Davis (1932), Mae West (1932), Katharine Hepburn (1933), and Claire Trevor (1933).

Cary Grant also entered film-making at this time. Under his real name, Archie Leach, he had appeared on the stage, first as an acrobat and stuntman in England and then in the United States. For about seven years he worked with little reward on the Keith and Pantages circuits. Gradually he began to get roles in plays as well as musicals. His roles became larger and more important. His name began to appear on programs and billboards while working for the Shubert Brothers in the late 1920s, but reviewers seldom paid any attention to him, and his expanding career could in no way be considered impressive. Finally he made a short film for Paramount Studios in New York and was given a five-year contract.

Cary Grant became his new name. He came to Hollywood and immediately began working. After several films and by the end of his first year he was playing leads. For the next forty years he would continue to be a major star, a big money-maker, and one of the most popular film personalities.

One might ask how and why he became a star so quickly. For one thing, Paramount was a studio that kept its contract players constantly working. A new film every two or three months with Grant in it meant that he was being seen by the public and by the studio heads; it also meant he was quickly developing his screen technique. Certainly he brought his stage training to use, and he got along with his coworkers. And the public responded to him. Although he played other roles, he was from the beginning the well-dressed, very handsome gentleman, a very appealing image. Even when he played a gangster, he retained a certain finesse in the character that would not be there if James Cagney or Edward G. Robinson were playing the role. Grant's image became so stratified as the well-dressed gentleman that there was some concern as late as 1964 when, in *Father Goose,* he played a roughly whiskered and carelessly dressed recluse living on a South Sea island. However, it didn't seem to affect his audience, for the film was successful. Perhaps by this time, audiences were used to seeing a favorite star in an unusual characterization. But in the 1930s such liberties were not allowed to be taken with the image. Grant performed either in romances opposite popular actresses like Sylvia Sidney, Marlene Dietrich, or Jean Harlow; or in comedies like *I'm No Angel* and *Thirty-Day Princess.* And yet he also was seen in serious and dramatic roles capably performed in films such as *The Eagle and the Hawk* or *Blonde Venus.* As a matter of fact, throughout his entire career he played a wide variety of roles, and he can be categorized as one kind of actor only by ignoring certain important films. When one looks at the career of an actor, one should not be deceived by simplified descriptions or labels. As a matter of fact, to be limited to such concepts is to be unfair to the actor and his craft.

Another danger in dealing with celebrated personalities is idolatry. The star becomes an idol, and is accepted not in any human sense, not in any rational sense, but as a god of some kind. Perhaps this is not the danger it once was, for today celebrities are often downgraded. This can happen to royalty and elected officials as well as to movie stars. But in the film industry, there seems to be an integral necessity to sell the star. The means used are not always pleasant and kind to the star himself. Crude publicity and the most obnoxious fan magazines were accepted if they aided in selling a particular star or a particular film. It is a credit to Grant that he has been most selective of the films in which he has appeared. While this indicates his good business sense, it also indicates his respect for his audience.

There is a tendency to regard an actor or a director as all good or all bad, regardless of the facts. There are those who make lists of "best" directors and actors. As popularity polls or lists of one's favorites, these may have some value. As film history or as film criticism they become nonsense. One who wishes to discuss the film work of

Cary Grant with his estranged wife Dyan Cannon, leave New York's Biltmore Theatre where she was starring in *The 90-Day Mistress* in November 1967

In London, November 1970, to appear in charity gala to aid the World Wildlife Fund

Four-year-old daughter Jennifer accompanied by a nannie at Heathrow Airport, February 1970.

Grant at Heathrow Airport, London, accompanied by an airline stewardess in February 1970

Cary Grant must examine all the work that Grant has completed, evaluate it on several levels, and then make an honest judgment of its weaknesses and its strengths. This is the only way to avoid the clichés and failures of understanding that lists are likely to create.

There is one serious difficulty with film criticism in that the films themselves may not be available. So we judge an actor on the basis of a few films which may not be representative of his work, and which may not even show his best work. Or even worse, we turn to printed references with no corrective comparison, especially the kind that is found in cult magazines. When most people think of the films of Cary Grant, they think of those of the late 1930s and the 1940s. But there are some interesting aspects to his later films, too. And if one begins consideration with films from 1937 on, one has already eliminated one-third of his work and is missing such key films as *I'm No Angel* and *The Eagle and the Hawk*.

Many of the great silent film comedians were acrobats or dancers. Such training was essential to the type of performance they gave, as when Keaton or Chaplin worked in the purely visual style so appropriate to silent film. The coming of sound made drastic changes. Chaplin had to change, although in his first sound film, *City Lights,* there was no spoken dialogue, only a sound and music track. Later, when Chaplin spoke in films, some critics questioned whether he should have. But when Chaplin made *Limelight,* he clearly proved he had mastered the sound film as well. Cary Grant, with his well-trained stage voice, came into films after sound had arrived. Unfortunately, he made no silent films and so never used his acrobatic training in films the way Keaton had. Once Al Jolson sang, content, styles, and format all began to change. *It Happened One Night,* starring Clark Gable and Claudette Colbert, came out in 1934. It was a very successful and popular film and set a trend in comedy that would develop into Grant successes like *The Awful Truth*. What a contrast these films are to Chaplin's *Gold Rush* or Keaton's *Navigator* or *College*.

In the late 1930s Hollywood made some fine achievements in its special kind of comedy, and the development of sound had much to do with this. It was often not the cleverness or wit of the text as much as the technique and skill of the delivery. One can point to Katharine Hepburn for her manner of speaking her lines rather than to the lines themselves as they might coldly appear on a printed page. Grant was also a skilled player in the manner of his delivery. He often raised the material above its innate value. On a single viewing of these films, one is seldom aware of the effort, so skillful, so polished is his presentation. One of the great achievements in acting, as Bogart once commented, is the ability to hide all the machinery necessary for a good performance. That is when the viewer is no longer aware of the acting because the actor has so involved him in the content that there

is no time to consider the method. In films like *The Awful Truth* and *His Girl Friday,* Grant achieves that kind of a fine performance.

Because it often looks so simple, some people consider acting easy work. But it is a difficult and demanding craft. A rich and active imagination is a necessity. Some native understanding of human emotions is needed. It is much more than just memorizing lines; one must be able to deliver the line in the right manner, in the right tempo, with the right tone in response to another voice. The line must be given the correct meaning in terms of the plot and characters involved, and it must be delivered in such a way that the audience clearly understands it in this context. The actor must have certain skills of speaking and using his body to express and project these concepts. He must not overdo the action or the words, for then the audience will find it too exaggerated to be suitable; on the other hand, he cannot underplay to the degree that the audience will miss the meaning. While some of the situations in his films seem exaggerated, as often happens in good comedy, Grant's playing of these moments is usually extremely well controlled.

In this book you will find a record of the films of Cary Grant, representative stills, and contemporary criticism for perspective, but it is the film itself in the final analysis that must be examined. An actor can be judged only by his acting. An actor's work must be seen in the context of other acting at the same time as well as before and after him. Some background information on the industry and the historical period may help us better understand these films. Look at the films of Cary Grant whenever and wherever you can find them. Enjoy them for the values you find in them. Then if you wish, examine and evaluate them. In this way you will see the unique position that Cary Grant holds in the story of the American film.

Grant visits Keith Baxter and Anthony Quayle backstage after a performance of *Sleuth,* April 5, 1971

# THE FILMS

# THIS IS THE NIGHT

1932

With Thelma Todd

**CREDITS:**

Produced and distributed by Paramount Publix. *Director:* Frank Tuttle. *Screenplay:* Avery Hopwood from *Pouche* by Rene Peter and Henri Falk. Dialogue and lyrics by George Marion, Jr. *Cinematography:* Victor Milner. *Music:* Ralph Rainger. *Release date:* April 8, 1932. *Running time:* 80 minutes.

**THE CAST:**

| | |
|---|---|
| *Germaine* | Lily Damita |
| *Bunny West* | Charlie Ruggles |
| *Gerald Grey* | Roland Young |
| *Claire* | Thelma Todd |
| *Stephen* | Cary Grant |
| *Jacques* | Irving Bacon |
| *Chou-Chou* | Claire Dodd |
| *Studio Official* | Davison Clark |

**SYNOPSIS:**

Charming Stephen, a famous javelin thrower, has signed a contract as a new Paramount player. When he returns home, he finds his wife Claire in the arms of Gerald Gray, a wealthy Parisian bachelor.

Plans are made for this group to go to Venice. Bunny West hires Germaine to pose as Gerald's new wife, so as to deceive Stephen.

Stephen falls in love with Germaine, while the same thing happens to Bunny and Gerald. However, Gerald is angered by Stephen's attention to Germaine, and also at Bunny. Claire decides to return to Stephen and keep him just for herself. Germaine decides to leave, and Gerald decides he really wants her and so he races after her, meets her, and they decide to marry.

**REVIEWS:**

The necessity of a certain amount of planning and construction could hardly be more obviously and instructively demonstrated than by this film. It begins with a chorus in which all the modern resources of photography and sound technique are used, in a manner which obviously owes much to René Clair. The matter and texture of this chorus are not particularly attractive, but this would not be a great fault if it had some formal connection with the rest of the film. But, on the contrary, after this preliminary exhibition of a device whose whole purpose is to hold a film together, it proceeds at once to a perfectly ordinary and unformalized farce. The plot is hardly worth repeating, for it is occupied only with the ritual humours of infidelity and intoxication. Only the setting, which is in Venice, is rather more interesting than usual (though even here most of the events take place within an extremely cosmopolitan and expensive hotel), and the actors, especially Mr. Roland Young, Mr. Charlie Ruggles, and Miss Claire Dodd, are very skillful. At intervals there is an attempt to return to the stylization of the beginning of the film, but only in the most sketchy way. It is as if, in a building, some essential elements of construction were used for superficial ornament.

*The Times* (London)

The picture opens in Paris with a rich musical background, the action played in the familiar Lubitsch *montage* manner. Roland Young is playing around with Thelma Todd, the wife of Cary Grant, a big husky American javelin-thrower, who had gone to the Olympic Games at Los Angeles. As the naughty couple alight at the theatre, the chauffeur closes the door on Thelma's train, and her skirt is torn completely off. Instantly the laughing bystanders burst into song: "Madame has lost her skirt!" Then cuts all over Paris—people singing "Madame has lost her skirt!" Even the radio sends out its lightning sparks to the same rhythm. A delightful bit of business.

But best of all, that same servitor, amusingly played by Irving Bacon, is always catching Madame's skirt in something, so that "Madame has lost her skirt!" becomes one of the best running gags ever done on the screen.

Cary Grant suddenly returns from his proposed trip to Los Angeles, so that it is necessary for Roland Young to dig up a temporary wife or get a javelin in his gizzard. Lily Damita, a movie extra, needs some money and takes the job. So the whole party, including Charlie Ruggles, playboy friend of Roland Young, go off to Venice.

Here, amid the rich and gorgeous surroundings of the most romantic spot in the world, we see the bunch put through a merry series of Avery Hopwood situations, resulting in Thelma returning to her athletic husband and Roland Young becoming a romantic figure (if you can imagine it! And he does well), and at the end, "gloating in a fondla"—as Charlie Ruggles calls it, in his alcoholic moments—with Lily Damita snuggled up in his arms.

It was my introduction to Lily Damita, and I found her altogether charming. Cary Grant was also new to me, and I thought he made a splendid figure. Of course you all know Charlie Ruggles and Roland Young. It was as though they had walked right over from the *One Hour With You* sets and continued their ridiculous and amusing relationship in this picture.

The sets of *This Is the Night* are right up to the high standard of Paramount's good taste, and the photography of Victor Milner is exceptionally beautiful.

Bob Wagner, *Script*

With Charles Ruggles and Roland Young

With Thelma Todd, Roland Young and Charles Ruggles

With Charlie Ruggles

# SINNERS IN THE SUN

## 1932

With Carole Lombard

**CREDITS:**

Produced and distributed by Paramount Publix. *Director:* Alexander Hall. *Scenarists and Dialoguers:* Vincent Lawrence, Waldemar Young and Samuel Hoffenstein. From a story "Beach-Comber" by Mildred Cram. *Cinematography:* Ray June. *Release date:* May 13, 1932. *Running time:* 70 minutes.

**THE CAST:**

| | |
|---|---|
| *Doris Blake* | Carole Lombard |
| *Jimmie Martin* | Chester Morris |
| *Claire Kinkaid* | Adrienne Ames |
| *Mrs. Blake* | Alison Skipworth |
| *Eric Nelson* | Walter Byron |
| *Mr. Blake* | Reginald Barlow |
| *Mrs. Florence Nelson* | Zita Moulton |

| | |
|---|---|
| *Ridgeway* | Cary Grant |
| *Grandfather Blake* | Luke Cosgrove |
| *Grandmother Blake* | Ida Lewis |
| *Fred Blake* | Russ Clark |
| *Mrs. Fred Blake* | Frances Moffett |
| *Louis* | Pierre DeRamey |
| *Emma* | Veda Buckland |
| *Lil* | Rita LaRoy |

**SYNOPSIS:**

Doris Blake is a hardworking dress model in an exclusive shop, who is mutually in love with mechanic Jimmie Martin. She refuses to marry him until he accumulates enough money to open his own garage, and so he angrily breaks up with her. After an accidental meeting, he becomes chauffeur to Claire Kinkaid, who falls in love with him.

Doris becomes the mistress of wealthy Eric Nelson, who is about to divorce a wife he cares little about. Doris travels with Eric around the world, gambling, drinking, and watching Lil similarly traveling and gambling with Ridgeway. Lil takes poison and kills herself.

Later Doris and Jimmie meet, but again argue and go their own way. Jimmie explains the situation to Claire and leaves her. Doris, working in a dress factory, rejects Eric and finally Jimmie and Doris are brought together, for a happy ending to the story.

## REVIEW:

*Sinners in the Sun* is, in effect, a display of luxury, and the tale of a man and a girl who temporarily despise love in a cottage, but virtuously return to it at last as being of more importance than the limousines, the Long Island parties, the fashion-parades, and the underclothes that enrich their unregenerate interlude. These things have now become so much a formula that Hollywood has learned to take them not too seriously, with the result that they are less tedious then they might otherwise be. Miss Carole Lombard and Mr. Chester Morris discharge their sentimental duties with easy accomplishment, while Miss Adrienne Ames, though afflicted with dialogue of the utmost crudity, gives a genuine touch of character to the rich young woman whom our hero erroneously marries. But the film's chief merit is the slickness of its luxurious accompaniment. The dresses are good, the flow from scene to scene is smooth and glittering, and our heroine is eternally unruffled even when she has plunged into a moonlit sea, clambered upon a raft and been forcibly kissed by an amateur wrestler who applies his art to persuade her. How fortunate we are who, in this era of science, are enabled by the talkie invention to hear, as well as see, the smacks which maidenly indignation administers to the cheek of importunate millionaires!

*The Times* (London)

With Carole Lombard

With Pierre De Ramey and Carole Lombard

With Rita La Roy, Carole Lombard, Walter Byron and Paul Stanton

# MERRILY WE GO TO HELL

## 1932

With Adrienne Allen

**CREDITS:**

Produced and distributed by Paramount Publix. *Director:* Dorothy Arzner. *Scenarist and Dialoguer:* Edwin Justus Mayer. From *I, Jerry, Take Thee, Joan* by Cleo Lucas. *Cinematography:* David Abel. *Release date:* June 10, 1932. *Running time:* 88 minutes.

**THE CAST:**

| | |
|---|---|
| *Joan Prentice* | Sylvia Sidney |
| *Jerry Corbett* | Fredric March |
| *Claire Hempstead* | Adrianne Allen |
| *Buck* | Skeets Gallagher |
| *Charlice* | Florence Britton |
| *Vi* | Esther Howard |
| *Mr. Prentice* | George Irving |
| *Dick Taylor* | Kent Taylor |

| | |
|---|---|
| *Damery* | Charles Coleman |
| *Butler* | Leonard Carey |
| *Housekeeper* | Milla Davenport |
| *Baritone* | Robert Greig |
| *Minister* | Rev. Neal Todd |
| *June* | Mildred Boyd |
| *Stage leading man* | Cary Grant |

**SYNOPSIS:**

Jerry Corbett is a newspaperman who has just written a play about to be produced. However, he constantly drinks too much, and often gets into trouble. Engaged to Joan Prentice, a socialite heiress, he goes on a spree just before he is to appear at the engagement party. His friend Buck is supposed to watch Jerry but fails to do so. Later Jerry also gets drunk when his play opens. Finally Jerry and

Joan are married, although when the wedding ring is lost, it is necessary to substitute a can-opener. His continued drinking creates problems. Joan leaves her husband and returns to Chicago and her father's home. Some months later when a baby is due, Joan enters a hospital and becomes critically ill. Finally Jerry is permitted to see Joan over her father's objections and there is a promise that they will try to find a better life together.

## REVIEW:

The trouble all along with this marriage that goes to hell (almost) is that Joan loves Jerry while Jerry thinks Joan a swell girl.

Just this side of hell there is a happy ending, which presumably is what the public wants.

The trouble with the picture is, mainly, Fredric March. Jerry's role should not have been given him, and from the way he handles it he himself seems to be of the same opinion. The impression left is that he is obliging some other actor, an actor possessing the fatness of soul required of the character, with a rough idea as to how

Jerry might behave. To be sure, the March skill and grace show through. But a man made as God made March would need a disguise thicker than Mr. Hyde's to be a convincing Jerry, whose sin is obtuseness. Every lineament of March's body, not to mention his face, vibrates sensitiveness, a spirit on its toes.

Upon Sylvia Sidney falls the whole burden of injecting genuineness, and she's—swell! March's Jerry is particularly unfortunate in standing against her Joan. Sincerity and Sylvia Sidney have come to run together like the components of a stock-phrase.

Adrianne Allen enacts the role of the other woman who lures Jerry and provides on sight the best of reasons for his illusion of emotional absorption with her. She provides also, despite the artificiality of the character portrayed, a sample of star material.

Another woman functioning tellingly in the production is the director, Dorothy Arzner. Good taste seems to be the accepted trademark of the Arzner output. Unless it's her expert handling of comedy. She lives up to both trademarks here, and Edwin Justus Mayer's comedy is equal to the picture's title.

Jessie Burns, *Script*

Fredric March and Sylvia Sidney

# THE DEVIL AND THE DEEP

## 1932

With Tallulah Bankhead

**CREDITS:**

Produced and distributed by Paramount Publix. Director: Marion Gering. Original story by Harry Hervey. *Cinematography:* Charles Lang. *Release date:* August 12, 1932. *Running time:* 70 minutes.

**THE CAST:**

| | |
|---|---|
| *Pauline Sturm* | Tallulah Bankhead |
| *Lieutenant Semper* | Gary Cooper |
| *Commander Sturm* | Charles Laughton |
| *Lieutenant Jacques* | Cary Grant |
| *A Lieutenant* | Gordon Wescott |
| *Hassan* | Paul Porcasi |
| *Mrs. Planet* | Juliette Compton |
| *Mr. Planet* | Arthur Hoyt |
| *Mrs. Crimp* | Dorothy Christy |
| *Hutton* | Henry Kolker |

**SYNOPSIS:**

Commander Sturm is in charge of a submarine at a naval base in Africa. He is intensely jealous of his wife, whom he believes is continually having affairs with other men. It is evident that he is mistaken, but he treats her with insane cruelty and drives her out of the house. She meets Lieutenant Semper, but does not know that he is a naval officer; nor does he know she is the wife of his commanding officer. They spend a night on the desert. Sturm, knowing that his wife is slipping from him, is suspicious. The submarine is about to sail. Mrs. Sturm, knowing that her husband in his mad jealousy is planning something terrible, rushes to the submarine to warn Lt. Semper. Sturm traps them in his cabin; and then deliberately causes a collision, causing the submarine to sink. Lt. Semper convinces the crew that Commander Sturm has gone mad, and is able to take command, thereby saving the crew, Mrs. Sturm, and himself, but leaving Commander Sturm to perish with the submarine.

## REVIEWS:

This picture is, in my opinion, the best dramatic talkie we have yet seen. It is unabashed melodrama at times, but Charles Laughton's magnificent acting disarms criticism of the more violently sensational incidents. He appears as the jealous, half-demented commander of a submarine, stationed on the West African coast. His wife, played by Tallulah Bankhead, has endured five years of hell through his insane jealousy, but to the world at large he appears as a goodnatured fellow with an impossible wife. At length, driven from home by a maniacal outburst of rage, Tallulah meets Gary Cooper and succumbs to his manly charms, only to discover, the next morning, that he is the newly arrived second officer.

The submarine leaves port for diving maneuvers, and through an accident Tallulah is on board, with her half-mad husband and unsuspecting lover. The vessel is rammed by a liner, owing to the machinations of Laughton, and the crew are entombed at the bottom of the sea. This sequence is admirably done, in spite of the occasional use of models in the shooting. The half-mad commander orders his second officer to be arrested, but Tallulah reveals her husband's insanity, and one by one the crew make their escape by means of the emergency apparatus.

Only Laughton is left behind, and as he smashes his wife's portrait to atoms with an axe, the water rushes in and he is drowned in his cabin. Tallulah Bankhead has better opportunities than of late as the distrait wife, but she is overshadowed by Laughton's amazing performance. Gary Cooper is completely negligible as the lover.

David Fairweather, *Theatre World*

Everyone who pays a visit to the Carlton during the current run of *The Devil and the Deep* must wonder how it was that Mr. Charles Laughton was allowed to make his debut on the talking-screen in an American picture. Here is an actor not only able to create character, but a ready-made star, and it is amazing that, with the scarcity of stellar talent in British studios, he was not given an opportunity in this country.

The film has more than one incredibility of situation, and the generally thoughtful and trenchant direction of Mr. Marion Gering is marred by conventional treatment and over-staging of several scenes, and by the anti-climax of the concluding sequence, which shows Miss Tallulah Bankhead and Mr. Gary Cooper setting forth on the path of happy-ever-after in a taxicab. Artistically and dramatically, the picture ends with the death of Commander Sturm, the madman who deliberately rams his submarine in order to trap his wife and her lover, and then commits suicide by drowning in his own cabin. To say that Mr. Charles Laughton succeeds in making this frankly melodramatic premise convincing is to pay the highest possible tribute to the uncanny way in which his personality and his acting dominate the film, even when he is absent from the screen, a domination in regard to which the spontaneous comment of my neighbour at the opening perfor-

With Charles Laughton, and Tallulah Bankhead

Tallulah Bankhead, Gary Cooper and Charles Laughton

39

mance—"What's Laughton doing all this time? I know he's up to something" is significant. For this is the secret of his power—the ability to produce an atmosphere of menace, insidious, all-pervading, no less potent in the moments during which he indulges in fatuous garrulity, in maudlin self-pity, or in hearty good fellowship, as when, ravaged by jealousy, he topples from the brink of insanity to the frenzied outbursts of actual madness—a repellent study, cunning, cruel, terrible, as implacable in its acceptance of self-destruction as it is defiant of sympathy. Only a supreme master of technique would have so consistently disdained any bid for compassion. Mr. Laughton is not concerned with sentiment or popular appeal. It is his business to act. And act he does, caring only that his impersonation shall reach the standards set by his individual conception of the actor's art.

Michael Orme, *The Illustrated London News*

With Tallulah Bankhead, Arthur Hoyt, Juliette Compton, Dorothy Christy, Kent Taylor, Charles Laughton and Henry Koker

With Marlene Dietrich

# BLONDE VENUS

1932

## CREDITS:

Produced and distributed by Paramount Publix. *Director:* Josef von Sternberg. *Screenplay:* Jules Furthman and S. K. Lauren. Based on a story by Josef von Sternberg. *Cinematography:* Bert Glennon. *Songs:* "Hot Voodoo" and "You Little So and So" by Sam Coslow and Ralph Rainger; "I Couldn't Be Annoyed" by Leo Robin and Dick Whiting. *Art direction:* Wiard Ihnen. *Release date:* September 16, 1932. *Running time:* 85 minutes.

## THE CAST:

| | |
|---|---|
| *Helen Faraday* | Marlene Dietrich |
| *Ned Faraday* | Herbert Marshall |
| *Nick Townsend* | Cary Grant |
| *Johnny Faraday* | Dickie Moore |
| *Ben Smith* | Gene Morgan |
| *"Taxi Belle" Hooper* | Rita La Roy |
| *Dan O'Connor* | Robert Emmett O'Connor |
| *Detective Wilson* | Sidney Toler |

with Francis Sayles, Evelyn Preer, Clifford Dempsey, Davison Clark, Bessie Lyle, Brady Kline, Dewey Robinson, Gertrude Short, Harold Berquist, and Cecil Cunningham.

## SYNOPSIS:

Helen Faraday, wife of Ned Faraday and mother of Johnnie, uses the age-old method of extracting money from another man in order to send her husband abroad for a cure.

During all the time she sinks lower and lower in the social scale, she keeps her little boy with her. Only when it seems hopeless does she surrender him to his father. Then when suicide seems to be the only way out for her,

41

With Marlene Dietrich

the story flashes to Paris, where she is the queen of the nightclubs, there to be found by Nick Townsend, the man who caused all her trouble. Conscience-stricken, he brings her back to her husband and son.

## REVIEWS:

Marlene Dietrich's latest film, *Blonde Venus,* over which B. P. Schulberg, until recently head of Paramount's Hollywood studio, and Josef von Sternberg, the director, clashed last spring, is a muddled, unimaginative and generally hapless piece of work, relieved somewhat by the talent and charm of the German actress and Herbert Marshall's valiant work in a thankless role.

It wanders from Germany to many places in America, over to France and then back to New York, but nary a whit of drama is there in it. There is good photography, and for those who are partial to scenes in a theatre, there are some over which Mr. von Sternberg has taken no little care. But the pain of it is the dismal and suspenseless tale of a woman who sinks to selling her favors and finally ends by returning to her husband.

There is scarcely any simpathy evoked for the charac-

ters, except for a little boy. Most of the scenes are unedifying, without possessing any strength or a common sense idea of psychology. It is regrettable that Miss Dietrich, Mr. Marshall and others should have been called upon to appear in such a vehicle.

When there is any attempt at levity it is silly, and one lengthy episode might better have been left to the imagination, for it never for a moment is anything but dreary and dull.

There are good portraits of Miss Dietrich, who sings two or three songs. Mr. Marshall does as well as his lines and the situations permit. Cary Grant is worthy of a much better role than that of Townsend, and little Dickie Moore gives a suggestion of brightness to the unhealthy scenes in which he is sometimes beheld.

Mordaunt Hall, *The New York Times*

Calm realism rubs elbows with hasty improbability in *Blonde Venus,* the much-talked-of new picture directed by Josef von Sternberg and starring Marlene Dietrich, the post-Garbo darling.

The impassive, slightly cadaverous Marlene, in *Blonde Venus,* is a woman who takes life with both hands and rough-hews it to her ends. She passes from utter devotion to hopeless renunciation. She toys with defeat and despair with the maddening assurance of womankind, which realizes always that there are two weapons in life which are veritable Excaliburs—physical beauty and a sound heart.

From wife, to harlot, to popular woman of the theatre and back to wife is the gamut Miss Dietrich must pass. Her parade is a goose-step of confidence. Indeed, this is the true character of the part she plays, that of Helen Faraday, a woman who values as nothing the conventional requirements of propriety when she is faced with the grinding problems of true morality.

The theme is old as life, and almost as interesting. Helen Faraday has a sick husband but no money. She gets the money by the oldest, quickest and best method available to beautiful women. And she gets it from Nick Townsend, an attractive and gallant fellow played by Cary Grant. When Edward Faraday discovers the source of his wife's money, he repudiates her, and carries on in the fury of outraged righteousness. Helen thereupon adopts despair, becomes the sexual chattel of whoever appears, but finally recovers herself. Finally, she meets Nick again, visits Faraday in an effort to see her child, and becomes reconciled to him at the kiddie's bedside. Nick chivalrously disappears.

Marlene Dietrich and Dickie Moore

With Marlene Dietrich

Acting honors, Miss Dietrich must share with Dickie Moore, playing the youngster, Johnny Faraday. Johnny's success, on the other hand, is entirely based on the lines written for him by Jules Furthman and S. K. Lauren. The child's lines, simple, strong and completely true, are psychologically the soundest this reporter has heard on the screen. Each bit of dialogue in which Johnny takes part is a delight to the mind.

Herbert Marshall does well in the part of Edward Faraday, the injured husband. Here again, the writers saw life as it is. For Edward, after straining at one gnat of infidelity—swallows the camel of prostitution. Nothing is truer than this wage of obstinacy.

Mr. von Sternberg—or shall we say, in the face of the formidable "von," Freiherr von Sternberg?—is a director of force and instinctive cunning. His manner of handling continuity of scenes is impatient but sound, something like the prose of the De Goncourts. He wastes no time on matters which would bore the injudicious. Here is where improbability rears its horrid head.

The story, to our mind, came to one logical end when Helen staggers out of a flophouse, degraded beyond recall, with the waters of death beckoning to her. We admit that the story should not be allowed to end there. A come-back is too sweet to reject. But the interval between Helen's crushing defeat and her immense success as a cabaret singer a few months later, is covered only by a trifling dialogue *en passant*. We also admit that harlots do come

With Marlene Dietrich

With Marlene Dietrich

back and sometimes gloriously. But we submit that here is where the dramatist and the director must exercise their utmost skill and penetration. We would have cheerfully foregone many shots of trains and steamers for the sake of one sharp episode showing Helen's struggle to regain her integrity. . . .

*Blonde Venus* should be a howling box-office success. It has all the ingredients. It fills the eye, it prods at the tear-ducts, it does not tax the intelligence. To be just, it ladles out generous portions of emotional truth.

Jose Rodriguez, *Script*

This latest film of von Sternberg's has a more brilliantly polished surface than any other that America has sent us this year. For an hour, the screen is filled with a succession of lovely images—finely assembled detail and imaginatively composed settings, photographed with a camera unusually sensitive. There are three shots that I have seldom seen equalled for sheer beauty of arrangement and quality of texture: a liner entering a dock at dusk, a train flying westward through the night, and a close-up of a boy blowing a bubble. There is more pleasure for the eye in *Blonde Venus* than in a hundred of its fellows. But what does beauty ornament? A story of a wife, who becomes a kept woman for the sake of her husband, and a prostitute for the sake of her child.

As in *Shanghai Express,* Marlene Dietrich is the focus point of the film; and as in that film also, her every pose is magnificently photographed; she seems without fuss, to accept the film for what it is—a background for her personality. Von Sternberg's direction is fluent. He grows more and more expert in making hokum good-looking.

Forsyth Hardy, *Cinema Quarterly*

With Nancy Carroll

# HOT SATURDAY

1932

## CREDITS:

Produced and distributed by Paramount Publix. *Director:* William A. Seiter. *Screenplay:* Seton I. Miller. Adapted by Josephine Lovett and Joseph Moncure March. From Harvey Ferguson's novel. *Cinematography:* Arthur L. Todd. *Release date:* October 28, 1932. *Running time:* 73 minutes.

## THE CAST:

| | |
|---|---|
| *Ruth Brock* | Nancy Carroll |
| *Romer Sheffield* | Cary Grant |
| *Bill Fadden* | Randolph Scott |
| *Conny Billop* | Edward Woods |
| *Eva Randolph* | Lillian Bond |
| *Harry Brock* | William Collier, Sr. |
| *Mrs. Brock* | Jane Darwell |
| *Camille* | Rita LaRoy |
| *Annie Brock* | Rose Coughlan |
| *Ed W. Randolph* | Oscar Appel |
| *Aunt Minnie* | Jessie Arnold |
| *Archie* | Grady Sutton |

## SYNOPSIS:

Quarreling with her sweetheart, Bill Fadden, Ruth Brock spends most of an afternoon and evening with another man, Romer Sheffield. Later when she is preparing to marry Bill, and after she has lost her job due to gossip,

With Nancy Carroll

she goes to see Romer. People think the worst of Romer, but when the matter is finally explained, both he and Ruth are exonerated.

## REVIEWS:

Small-town tongues are wagging and small-town eyes are watching that Brock girl from behind drawn shades. *Hot Saturday,* which is from Harvey Ferguson's novel, describes the evolution of an idle bit of gossip in an average American community with considerable freshness and candor, and in the main manages to survive a meandering script and some uneventful writing. Nancy Carroll, as the girl caught in the net of malicious gossip, gives a lifelike portrayal; and she is acutely touching in the final episodes as she searches frantically for someone who will understand and believe her. The denouement is unintentionally ambiguous, and a rather startling conclusion at that; for the girl runs off with the notorious libertine to a marriage in New York which, if one is to believe all the things people say about Romer Sheffield, will be merely theoretical.

The title suggests the social activities of the young people on their day off, the dancing, cheap liquor and furtive amour with which they escape once a week from their routine labors. Some may raise the criticism that the behavior in *Hot Saturday* is more typical of the years the novel appeared—than of the present.

Ruth Brock, on this particular "hot Saturday," accompanies the crowd to Sheffield's place in the country. Her young man, resenting Sheffield's attentions to the girl, quarrels with her. When she is left alone in the millionaire's house for a few hours and arrives home in his car, the gossip-mongers go to work with a relish. The accumulation of outraged virtues results in Ruth's dismissal from the bank and a violent scene at home. Even her gentle, understanding sweetheart of school days turns against her.

Edward Woods, as the malicious and resentful escort, gives the most satisfactory performance in support of Miss Carroll. Cary Grant is a nonchalant young libertine as Sheffield, and Randolph Scott is solidly virtuous as the boyhood sweetheart.

Mordaunt Hall, *The New York Times*

46

Randolph Scott and Nancy Carroll

With Nancy Carroll

# MADAME BUTTERFLY

## 1932

With Sylvia Sidney

**CREDITS:**

Produced and distributed by Paramount Publix. *Director:* Marion Gering. *Screenplay:* Josephine Lovett and Joseph Moncure March. From a story by John Luther Long and the play by David Belasco. *Cinematography:* David Abel. *Composer:* Giacomo Puccini with music from his opera. Incidental music by W. Franke Harling. *Release date:* December 30, 1932. *Running time:* 86 minutes.

**THE CAST:**

| | |
|---|---|
| Cho-Cho San | Sylvia Sidney |
| Lieutenant B. F. Pinkerton | Cary Grant |
| Lieut. Barton | Charlie Ruggles |
| Goro | Sandor Kallay |
| Yomadori | Irving Pichel |
| Cho-Cho's Mother | Helen Jerome Eddy |
| Cho-Cho's Grandfather | Edmund Breese |
| Mme. Goro | Judith Vasselli |
| Suzuki | Louise Carter |
| Peach Blossom | Dorothy Libaire |
| Mrs. Pinkerton | Sheila Terry |

**SYNOPSIS:**

Lt. Pinkerton and Lt. Barton, American officers, on shore leave in Japan, meet Cho-Cho San, who is about to become a Geisha. Despite a fiancee at home, Pinkerton marries Cho-Cho San. She learns to love him in the American manner, and when Pinkerton leaves with the fleet, she continues to keep his home in Japan as he left it. She waits his return, which is delayed for three years during which time she has his child. Meanwhile not taking the Japanese marriage seriously, Pinkerton has remarried. Finally returning with his American wife, to whom he has

48

told the story of the geisha girl, Pinkerton goes to Cho-Cho San, who has been elaborately preparing for his arrival, and tells her that their affair is ended. Sending her child with a servant to her family, Madame Butterfly commits suicide.

## REVIEWS:

Another sensation of this year in relation with the problem of "Japan as seen in films" was Madame Butterfly, in which Sylvia Sidney played Cho-Cho San and Cary Grant, Pinkerton, a Paramount production directed by Marion Gering, who has gained some reputation in Japan by his success in 24 Hours. As far as the workmanship is concerned, *Madame Butterfly* is above the common level; all the players, especially Sylvia Sidney, give good performances, settings and decors are extravagant, beautiful and well designed; furthermore, the famous music by Puc-

cini is fascinating. However, in spite of these superior attributes, *Madame Butterfly* was a box-office flop in Japan, or at least in Tokyo, because the psychological developments expressed by Cho-Cho San were not accepted by the general Japanese audience. Her manner by falling in love with Pinkerton is very singular and what is worse, their marriage that is not bound with love, but other incomprehensible feelings, is utterly ridiculous. A few days pass and Pinkerton returns to America, leaving Cho-Cho San alone in Japan. After three years he comes to Japan again with an American wife and calls on Cho-Cho San, who has been waiting by the window with a baby in her hands all the night through. Cho-Cho San embraces Pinkerton, and then she recognizes a woman standing behind him. Cho-Cho San bows before him and goes inside, without any words intended to blame him for his insincerity and treachery, and at last she commits a suicide-sequence of the weakest and silliest of the whole

With Sylvia Sidney

With Sylvia Sidney

With Charles Ruggles and Sylvia Sidney

With Sylvia Sidney, Louise Carter, Charles Ruggles, Edmund Breese and Irving Pichel

picture. The Japanese women of this date regard Cho-Cho San·with not so much sympathy as contempt. . . .

To summarize what I have described above, Japanese films, both dramatic and cultural, exported and exhibited abroad, do not propagate Japan as she is today, but cater for the prejudices with which all the foreign nations are possessed, by exposing her relic of feudal days that seems even to us, Japanese, to be odd and nonsensical. Not only so, but also foreign-made films treating Japan, needless to say, convey a false Japan.

These aspects have brought about a tendency favorable for the movement of national control over films to be exported, regardless of whether their producers are Japanese or not, and also of negative or positive. It is reported by the recent newspaper article that the Japanese Department of Home Affairs has commenced to investigate the present circumstances of film control in the principal countries of the world in order to establish in Japan a national policy.

Yasushi Ogino, *Yokohama Close Up*

The plot of this film is taken from the Puccini opera and the incidental music is by the composer, but it does not attempt to be a reproduction of the opera. The story is not very suitable for this new medium, and though the long-drawn tragedy might be bearable if it were expressed in music or poetry, without any such embellishment it is apt to be painfully pathetic. Nevertheless, Miss Sylvia Sidney, who plays the part of the Japanese girl, acts with a grace and delicacy which are a great relief from this prolonged assault upon our emotions. And the Japanese settings are almost always pretty; an admirable use is made of what Swinburne called "the fortuitous frippery of Fusi-yama." Moreover, Miss Sidney fits so well into the setting that all the purely Japanese parts of the film have a certain style and consistency. But the intrusion of the American lieutenant (Mr. Cary Grant) has as disturbing an effect on the film as he had on the unfortunate Madame Butterfly. In fact, the inarticulate sentimentality of all the American characters seems to have been nicely calculated to sound a jarring note in this carefully constructed world of oriental conversion, and nothing is done to accommodate these two modes of feeling.

*The Times* (London)

With Mae West

# SHE DONE HIM WRONG

1933

## CREDITS:

Produced and distributed by Paramount Publix. *Director:* Lowell Sherman. *Screenplay:* Harvey Theu and John Bright. *Cinematography:* Charles Lang. *Release date:* January 27, 1933. *Running time:* 66 minutes.

## THE CAST:

| | |
|---|---|
| *Lady Lou* | Mae West |
| *Capt. Cummings* | Cary Grant |
| *Serge Stanieff* | Gilbert Roland |
| *Gus Jordon* | Noah Beery, Sr. |
| *Russian Rosie* | Rafaela Ottiano |
| *Dan Flynn* | David Landau |
| *Sally* | Rochelle Hudson |
| *Chick Clark* | Owen Moore |
| *Rag-time Kelly* | Fuzzy Knight |
| *Chuck Connors* | Tammany Young |
| *Spider Kane* | Dewey Robinson |
| *Frances* | Grace LaRue |
| *Steak McGarry* | Harry Wallace |
| *Pete* | James C. Eagle |
| *Doheny* | Robert E. Homans |
| *Big Bill* | Tom Kennedy |
| *Bar Fly* | Arthur Housman |
| *Pal* | Wade Boteler |
| *Mrs. Flaherty* | Aggie Herring |
| *Pearl* | Louise Beavers |
| *Jacobson* | Lee Kohlmar |
| *Mike* | Tom McGuire |

## SYNOPSIS:

Lady Lou, a beautiful and witty woman runs a Bowery saloon owned by Gus Jordon. Captain Cummings, from the nearby church mission, visits Lou regularly, hoping

With Mae West

With Mae West

to save her. She finds herself falling in love with him.

It is Lou's sentimental nature that gets her into trouble. She helps a would-be suicide, only to discover that the girl is being sold into white slavery. Finally Lou kills a nasty criminal. Captain Cummings now drops his disguise and turns out to be a police agent. He arrests Lou, but she seems not too disappointed to be taken away by Captain Cummings.

## REVIEWS:

*She Done Him Wrong* is something lustier, the overtly and successful predatory female against a colorful Bowery background. It is as frank as an old Police Gazette, and much livelier and more picturesque. It is an odd companion to be bracketed with *Little Woman* and *State Fair* and *Mama Loves Papa,* but it belongs with them as a faithful bit of Americana. Incidentally the overpowering Mae West personality shouldn't hide the fact that Lowell Sherman's direction figured pretty largely in the picture's effectiveness.

*National Board of Review Magazine*

Only one previous picture part—a small one in *Night After Night*—and now Mae West is starring! It looks as though Paramount brought Miss West along too fast. In New York she rates the billing but elsewhere, where they may not know Mae from Joan of Arc, the name over the title of this picture probably won't attract much attention the first time. Besides, there's not a box office monicker in the rest of the cast.

The only alternative to a strong drawing cast nowadays if a picture wants business, is strong entertainment. This one has neither. Many may not know it, but they'll be seeing Mae in 'Diamond Lil'. Nothing much changed except the title, but don't tell that to Will Hays.

Atmospherically, *She Done Him Wrong* is interesting since it takes the customers back to the '90s and inside a Bowery free-and-easy, but mostly following a few highlights in the career of Diamond Lou, née Lil. Its story is pretty feeble and stories are pretty important in pictures because personality is less of a factor on celluloid than in person in the talkers it seems.

With the material Lowell Sherman, the director this time instead of actor, turned in a commendable job. He tackled the script with a tongue-in-cheek attitude that takes nothing too seriously, and he restrained Miss West from going too far, something Mae has never been able to do on her own. . . .

Deletions in the script from its original 1928 legit form were few, with only the roughest of the rough stuff out. White slavery angle is thinly disguised, with the girls instead shipped to Frisco to pick pockets. Character titles are changed only slightly, such as from Lil to Lou, etc. The swan bed is in, but for a flash only, with Mae doing her stuff on the chaise lounge in this version. The closing boy friend, a Salvation Army fellow in the play, is just

52

With Mae West

Gilbert Roland and Mae West

Johnnie." All somewhat cleaned up lyrically, but Mae couldn't sing a lullaby without making it sexy. . . .

Mae West in pictures should stand out just as she did in legit—as a distinct personality. There's no one just like her and she can be built up to mean something for film box offices.

Joe Bigelow, Variety

Mae West, heretofore the stage's chief exponent of the dramatization of sex machinations, comes to the screen in her first starring vehicle, a picturization of none other than the "Diamond Lil" of recent stage memory. That Miss West is here highly effective cannot be doubted, but of the adaptability of her vehicle, her material for the common denominator of the motion picture public, there is considerable doubt.

"Diamond Lil" of the boisterous "Nineties," leaves very little undone, very little unsaid to make clear her unmistakable meaning in innumerable dialogue instances and in bits of stage business. Miss West, as the mistress (at the moment) of Noah Beery, noisy and crude saloon proprietor, is festooned with enough "rocks," often known as diamonds, to stock a store. Lady Lou, as she is known, is the toast of the saloon's crowds, from the gutter rat to the socialite.

The picture has been extremely well mounted, the atmosphere of the period and the surroundings appearing definitely authentic, and, in common with reproductions of that period, always appealing. The elder adults will be mightily drawn toward the atmosphere, at least those who are not too straight-laced.

The matter of laces becomes a most important part of the exhibitor's selling problem as far as this picture is concerned. The film is lively, contrives to be amusing, has an element of melodrama, but is rather several degrees south of the lower limit of propriety. Miss West sings several numbers which cannot be conscientiously recommended to any common or garden variety of choral society. The individual exhibitor will have to decide for himself whether he can afford to run this film, realizing that it is hard-boiled, spares the feelings of no Ladies' Aid Society.

Playing it, the exhibitor must necessarily indicate what it is, and he has the selling angles of Miss West in a well-known role, and the personal attractiveness of Cary Grant.

C. Aaronson, Motion Picture Herald

a Bowery missionary as rewritten. When Lou bumps off the villainous Rita (it's Rosie now) she still says, "I'm doing a job that I never did before."

Caster delivered some excellent types for the colorful support parts and the troupe is first rate as a whole. Numerous ex-vaudevillians besides Miss West in the cast, including Cary Grant, Fuzzy Knight, and Grace LaRue. The latter, who headlined when Miss West was chasing acrobats in the No. 2 spot, has a bit. Rafaella Ottiano is a carry-over from the original cast.

With this strong line-up and others, including Gilbert Roland, Noah Beery, David Landau and Owen Moore as background, they're never permitted to be anything more than just background. Miss West gets all the lens gravy and full figure most of the time. When not flashing the ice and steaming up the boys, she sings "Easy Rider," "I Like a Man who Takes His Time," or "Frankie and

With Nancy Carroll

# WOMAN ACCUSED

1933

## CREDITS:

Produced and distributed by Paramount Publix. *Director:* Paul Sloane. *Screenplay:* Bayard Veiller. Based on a story by Polen Banks. From a Liberty Magazine serial multi-authored by Rupert Hughes, Vicki Baum, Zane Grey, Vina Delmar, Irvin S. Cobb, Gertrude Atherton, J. P. McEvoy, Ursula Parrott, Polen Banks and Sophie Kerr. *Cinematography:* Karl Struss. *Release date:* February 17, 1933. *Running time:* 73 minutes.

## THE CAST:

| | |
|---|---|
| *Glenda O'Brien* | Nancy Carroll |
| *Jeffrey Baxter* | Cary Grant |
| *Stephen Bessemer* | John Halliday |
| *District Attorney Clarke* | Irving Pichel |
| *Leo Young* | Louis Calhern |
| *Martha* | Norma Mitchell |
| *Little Maxie* | Jack La Rue |
| *Inspector Swope* | Frank Sheridan |
| *Dr. Simpson* | John Lodge |
| *Captain of Boat* | William J. Kelly |
| *Judge Osgood* | Harry Holman |
| *Tony Graham* | Jay Belasco |
| *Evelyn Craig* | Gertrude Messinger |
| *Cora Matthews* | Lora Andre |
| *The Steward* | Donald Stuart |
| *The Band Leader* | Gregory Golubeff |
| *Cheer Leader* | Robert Quirk |
| *Third Girl* | Amo Ingraham |
| *Second Boy* | Dennis Beaufort |
| *Third Boy* | Gaylord Pendleton |

## SYNOPSIS:

Glenda O'Brien's romance with Jeffrey Baxter is endangered by the return of her old lover, Leo Young. She kills Young when he threatens to have Jeffrey murdered. She

With John Halliday and Nancy Carroll

and Jeffrey and a party of friends leave for an ocean cruise. Stephen Bessemer, Leo's partner, believes Glenda guilty, but can't convince the district attorney of a case and so joins the cruise in an attempt to obtain evidence. During the voyage a mock trial is held and Bessemer tries to get Glenda to confess, but without success. A later second attempt also fails.

## REVIEWS:

We used to play a game wherein one person wrote the first sentence or paragraph of a story, the next one the second, and so on. The result was often amusing, but not great literature.

*Liberty* commissioned ten famous authors—Rupert Hughes, Vicki Baum, Zane Grey, Vina Delmar, Irvin S. Cobb, Gertrude Atherton, J. P. McEvoy, Ursula Parrott, Polan Banks, and Sophie Kerr—to write a murder story, each doing a separate chapter. With their tongues in their cheeks (and no doubt fat checks in their purses) they accomplished the murder, which has just run serially in that popular magazine.

Paramount has made it into a picture which opens with close-ups of the shameless authors looking their prettiest—which is some job for Irvin Cobb. Then on with the tale, the fun being to guess who did what.

Nancy Carroll and Cary Grant love. Both have lived in sin, but they agree to forget it. Comes Louis Calhern out of Nancy's past, and tries to get her back. No can do, so he locks the door and all but swallows the key (who do you suppose wrote that?). Nancy refuses to come across, so Louis calls up Jack La Rue, gunman, and tells him to bump off Cary! Just in time, Nancy bashes out his brains with a bronze Academy statuette.

Nancy and Cary go on one of these "Three-day Cruises to Nowhere." Grand fun and Big Production stuff with lots of "leg-art" in the swimming pool. Cary is honorable, but Nancy can't wait for marriage and suggests—! (Who thought of *that*? One guess!)

With Nancy Carroll

With Nancy Carroll and John Halliday

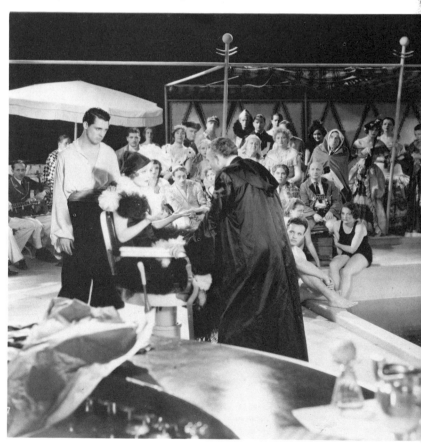

John Halliday suspects Nancy of murdering his friend, and follows out on a police boat. At a big masquerade (more Production Stuff) he frames a mock trial and though Nancy knows what he is up to (she tells it out loud in a strange interlude), she accommodatingly spills the beans of guilt.

The poor gal is arrested and brought before Irving Pichel, the kindliest and least suspicious district attorney in the world (the author of this sequence was evidently with a D.A. whom he or she wished to propitiate). Jack La Rue testifies against Nancy, so Cary Grant takes him out, horsewhips him, and brings him back to reverse his testimony. This is satisfactory to Irving Pichel, who is looking into Nancy's big blue eyes, and realizing that the story must end happily, if illegally, refuses to hold her. But Cary doesn't refuse to hold her and he crushes her to his bosom in a glorious clinch.

Baynard Veiller reduced the murder by the ten authors to manslaughter by his clever screen play. Paul Sloane directed better than one might expect, and Karl Struss shot the stuff with cinematic splendor. Jack La Rue does about the best acting, but Cary Grant is pretty fine. In fact, they all do their stuff well. But what stuff?

Rob Wagner, *Script*

Despite two of the silliest exhibitions of melodramatics, the exploitation campaign and *Liberty* mag tieup behind *Woman Accused* should aid materially in putting it across to average returns. To counterbalance the pair of moronic scenes is a wow finish that had the audience cheering.

Billed as the picture written by ten of the world's greatest authors, it is not conceivable that the literary names concerned could have permitted, let alone have written, the aforementioned offending sequences.

First sequence that went smello was the deep-dyed villainy of Louis Calhern in an effort to build up a logical reason for the girl, Nancy Carroll, to kill him. Second was the mock-trial during a "cruise to nowhere" which was carried to silly extremes. Both can be touched up by judicious cutting.

Unfortunate that Calhern and John Halliday have been handed such parts, that no amount of good trouping can surmount the ham written into each line.

For the finish, the hero, as done capably by Cary Grant, wields a blacksnake whip on the gangster, key witness against the girl, giving film fans probably their first real satisfaction at the manner in which a mobster should be handled. After a perfect buildup as a menace, Jack La Rue brings audience applause when he turns into jelly after the larruping administered by Grant.

Some novel directorial angles in the "Strange Interlude" treatment of the accused woman's fear and terror, and the atmosphere of the pleasure cruise. Nancy Carroll's work is well-done and sincere and Norma Mitchell, as her maid, gives a sweet performance. Latter's work here is of the quality that should win her a good play from the casting directors. Such people as Irving Pichel, Frank Sheridan, Harry Holman and Donald Stuart are in for short, but capably done, bits.

*Daily Variety*

With Lona Andre, Nancy Carroll, John Lodge and Norma Mitchell

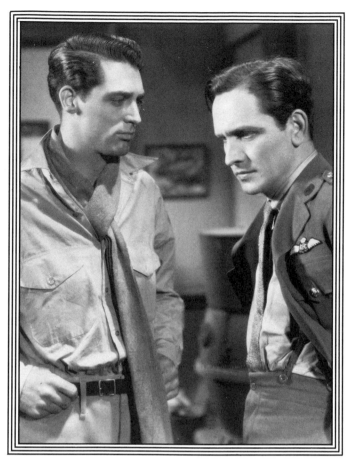

With Fredric March

# THE EAGLE AND THE HAWK

1933

## CREDITS:

Produced and distributed by Paramount Publix. *Director:* Stuart Walker. *Associate Director:* Mitchell Leisen. *Screenplay:* Bogart Rogers and Seton I. Miller. Based on a story by John Monk Saunders. *Cinematography:* Harry Fischbeck. *Release date:* May 19, 1933. *Running time:* 72 minutes.

## THE CAST:

| | |
|---|---|
| *Jeremiah Young* | Fredric March |
| *Henry Crocker* | Cary Grant |
| *Mike Richards* | Jack Oakie |
| *The Beautiful Lady* | Carole Lombard |
| *Major Dunham* | Sir Guy Standing |
| *Hogan* | Forrester Harvey |
| *John Stevens* | Kenneth Howell |
| *Kingsford* | Layland Hodgson |
| *Lady Erskine* | Virginia Hammond |
| *General* | Crawford Kent |
| *Tommy* | Douglas Scott |
| *Major Kruppman* | Robert Manning |
| *Fanny* | Adrienne D'Ambricourt |
| *French General's Aide* | Jacques Jou-Jerville |
| *Flight Sergeant* | Russell Scott |
| *French General* | Paul Cremonesi |
| *Taxi Driver* | Yorke Sherwood |

## SYNOPSIS:

Lieutenant Young is the shining light for young men who are sent to the front. Major Dunham tells Young that he is an example to the young recruits. But losing half a dozen observers in a short time gets on Young's nerves. Although he and Henry Crocker fly several successful missions together, they strongly dislike each other.

59

With Douglas Scott and Leyland Hodgson

With Leyland Hodgson and Fredric March

When the Major realizes that Young's nerves are on edge, he orders him to go on a ten day leave. During the leave many civilians chatter about the war Young would like to forget for a moment. Luckily he meets a beautiful lady who spends a pleasant evening with him.

Returning to the front, Young finds that another observer has been killed as the result of Crocker's needless escapades to win more honors. Young goes on a binge and delivers a scathing denunciation of war. He goes to his quarters and commits suicide. To cover up Young's act, Crocker takes the body up in his plane, shooting several rounds into his plane, which he lands, saying that Young was killed on a mission. Young is buried a hero.

## REVIEWS:

In *The Eagle and the Hawk,* John Monk Saunders has written a vivid and impressive account of the effect of battles in the clouds upon an American ace. It is, fortunately, devoid of the stereotyped ideas which have weakened most of such narratives. Here is a drama told with a praiseworthy sense of realism, and the leading role is portrayed very efficiently by Fredric March.

Stuart Walker's direction of this picture is thoroughly capable. Nothing appears to be overdone and no episode is too prolonged. Aside from the good work by Mr. March and Mr. Oakie, there are noteworthy impersonations by Cary Grant, Sir Guy Standing, and Miss Lombard.

Mordaunt Hall, *The New York Times*

This is an unusual and interesting picture portraying a war pilot's reactions to the business of murder on an international scale, and for ideals that almost invariably prove illusory the moment the war has ended. The pilot (Fredric March) cannot resign himself to the death of five observers who have been killed, one after another, in his plane; nor can he rest content after killing a young German ace. Decorated for his services, and held up as a shining example for young pilots, he finally commits suicide. There the picture should have ended. Unfortunately, his sixth observer, a ruthless killer who shoots defenseless enemies descending from kite balloons in parachutes, suddenly and too surprisingly becomes noble and arranges matters so the pilot will appear to have died in aerial combat. This is the prominent false note in an otherwise effectively ironical comment on the heroics of war in the air; the picture lacked the courage to carry out its convictions to the bitter end. Many of the details are realistically handled, while others will give our English cousins and others who served in the Royal Flying Corps a hearty laugh. Despite Hollywood's apparent belief, R. F. C. officers did not take baths in the densely populated back yard of a farm house, nor were squadron commanders such dear old softies as the kindly imitation in this picture; nor, out of a squadron of thirty-six flying officers, did commanders have only two heroes on whom they could depend. And five dead observers, with the pilot sitting right ahead of them yet with never a bullet in him, is hard to take seriously. Despite these defects the picture is thrilling entertainment for those who like nature in the raw.

Cy Caldwell, *New Outlook*

With Jack Oakie and Fredric March

# GAMBLING SHIP

1933

With Benita Hume

**CREDITS:**

Produced and distributed by Paramount Publix. *Director:* Louis Gasnier and Max Marcin. *Screenplay:* Max Marcin and Seton I. Miller. Adapted by Claude Binyon. From stories by Peter Ruric. *Cinematography:* Charles Lang. *Release date:* June 23, 1933. *Running time:* 72 minutes.

**THE CAST:**

| | |
|---|---|
| *Ace Corbin* | Cary Grant |
| *Eleanor La Velle* | Benita Hume |
| *Blooey* | Roscoe Karns |
| *Jeanne Sands* | Glenda Farrell |
| *Pete Manning* | Jack La Rue |
| *Joe Burke* | Arthur Vinton |
| *Baby Face* | Charles Williams |
| *District Attorney* | Edwin Maxwell |
| *First Gunman* | Harry Shutan |
| *Second Gunman* | Frank Moran |
| *First Detective* | Spencer Chartes |
| *Second Detective* | Otho Wright |
| *Indian Woman* | Evelyn Silvie |
| *Woman Detective* | Kate Campbell |
| *First Deputy* | Edward Gargan |
| *Second Deputy* | Jack Grey |
| *Conductor* | William Welsh |
| *The Sailor* | Sid Saylor |
| *Doctor* | Hooper Atchley |
| *Telephone Operator* | Larry Alexander |
| *Croupier* | Louis Natheaux |
| *Cook* | Gum Chung |

**SYNOPSIS:**

On a transcontinental train trip Ace Corbin poses as a wealthy businessman and Eleanor La Velle poses as someone from the Social Register. In reality Ace is a famous big-time gambler vacationing after the heat of a recent murder trial, and Eleanor is a moll looking for a sucker. She also happens to be the girlfriend of Joe Burke, who owns a gambling ship and is much in debt. Burke tries to interest Corbin in buying the boat without much success, until Corbin discovers that Manning, an old enemy owns the chief competition. Corbin takes over the boat, and takes all the gambling trade away from Manning. Manning takes revenge, bombs Corbin's boat. During this time Eleanor and Corbin discover the truth about each other. Manning and his gang come aboard to take over the ship, Burke is killed, but a storm comes up and Manning and his gang are washed overboard. The ship crashes on the rocks, but Corbin and Eleanor make it to shore.

## REVIEWS:

American films have for so long taught us to expect the gangster to be a thoroughly bad man that it is now too late in the day for them to try to show us a reformed gangster striving not to make use of the weapons of his trade. And that is exactly what *Gambling Ship* tries to do. Even had it been done well it would not have been worth doing. When there are bombs and machine-guns on the set, we want to see them used. Mr. Max Marcin, the producer of the film, merely treats them as scenery. If Ace Corbin must fight his old enemy for the good of his new character he might at least be allowed to use effectively the weapon with which he is familiar and not to be asked to rely on the virtues of a new idealism (born of a narrow escape in the Courts) and of the inspiration of love evoked by the lovely lady, who saves the film from complete banality by turning out to be a member of a gang herself. Even this discovery of her true status fails to give us a clash of machine-guns and armored motor-cars, though the scene is several times set for a fight. Throughout the film there is little action and practically no excitement, except for one pursuit by a speed-boat and the casting of a bomb at the gambling ship, which does not half enough damage. Nor is there enough romantic interest to redeem these shortcomings. In brief, it may be said that the film has all the makings of the familiar gangster story without actually making it. What acting the film allows is done competently by Mr. Cary Grant, Miss Benita Hume, and Mr. Roscoe Karns.

*The Times* (London)

A fair flicker. Of the gangster meller genera with a new slant in the gambling ship locale off the coast of Long Beach, California. Another new angle is in the finale where the ship's anchor is cast loose and the waves are permitted to sweep the anti-element off into the briny while the sympathetic faction of the lawless lot fights its way to safety and a suggestion of regeneration for the happy ending.

Cary Grant is the big shot gambler who thinks he's found the real thing in Benita Hume, a gambler's moll, during their cross-country trek from Chicago to Los Angeles. The

With Benita Hume and Roscoe Karns

With Roscoe Karns, Benita Hume and Hooper Atchley

fact that it's an open-and-shut 'make' on the part of both principals establishes a dubious premise from which to evolve the highly romantic aura which has been essayed. Grant thinks Miss Hume is the McCoy on the swank stuff.

Film doesn't drag, save in negligible moments, but in toto it's a familiar formula of mob vs. mob with the sympathetic Grant commandeering one bunch to hijack La Rue's more sinister hoodlums. Speaking of sinisterness, La Rue should never go Raftish and try to act up as a hero; he's the most repellent villyun in major film league and he'll stay on top of the batting order if he doesn't get the Rover Boy complex.

Grant proves his potentialities for femme box office with this inept assignment; ditto Miss Hume, who makes a difficult, chameleon characterization sound almost convincing.

Abel Green, *Variety*

With Glenda Farrell and Benita Hume

With Mae West

# I'M NO ANGEL
1933

## CREDITS:

Produced and distributed by Paramount Publix. *Director:* Wesley Ruggles. Original screenplay and dialogue by Mae West. Continuity by Harlan Thompson, with suggestions by Lowell Brentano. *Cinematography:* Leo Tover. *Composer:* Harvey Brooks. Lyrics by Gladys du Bois and Ben Ellison. *Art direction:* Hans Dreier and Bernard Herzbrun. *Sound:* Phil G. Wisdom. *Release date:* October 6, 1933. *Running time:* 87 minutes.

## THE CAST:

| | |
|---|---|
| *Tira* | Mae West |
| *Jack Clayton* | Cary Grant |
| *Bill Barton* | Edward Arnold |
| *Slick* | Rolf Harolds |
| *Barker* | Russell Hopton |
| *Alicia Hatton* | Gertrude Michael |
| *Kirk Lawrence* | Kent Taylor |
| *Thelma* | Dorothy Peterson |
| *Benny Pinkowitz* | Gregory Ratoff |
| *Beulah* | Gertrude Howard |
| *The Chump* | William Davidson |
| *Rajah* | Nigel deBrulier |
| *Bob, the Attorney* | Irving Pichel |
| *Omnes* | George Bruggeman |
| *Harry* | Nat Pendleton |
| *Chauffeur* | Morrie Cohen |
| *Judge* | Walter Walker |

## SYNOPSIS:

Big Bill Barton manages a small-time circus in which Tira appears as a sideshow vamp. She lives with a pickpocket, Slick. But Tira also keeps a hotel room in town where she has visitors up in order to shake them down.

65

Russell Hopton and Mae West

One visitor, "The Chump" is knocked out by jealous Slick, who thinking the man dead, steals his diamond ring and runs. When "The Chump" comes to, he goes to the police and has Slick arrested. Tira, needing money, agrees with Big Bill Barton to perform a dangerous lion act. The act, placing her beautiful head in the lion's mouth, is very successful. Socialite Kirk Lawrence comes backstage after the performance, with his eye on Tira. His cousin, Jack Clayton also meets her. However Kirk's romance with Tira is soon ended when he becomes engaged to a society girl. Tira is pleased since this opens the way for Jack Clayton, who she likes and who will give her a new social status. Their courtship progresses. Then she sues him for breach of promise. Jack, in self-defense, calls into court several of the men in Tira's life; but convinced she really loves him, lets her win the case in her theatrical fashion. Although their affair may not last forever, they will be happy for the time being.

## REVIEWS:

Ingenious casting had much to do with the success of *I'm No Angel*. Although her control over her vehicles at Paramount was almost absolute, unlike Chaplin in a similarly favored position, Mae West did not depend on a weak supporting cast to magnify her own personality or call attention to her humor. A strong cast, each one capable and playing his or her role with uncommon passion, lent a credibility to the film, a quality of balance and proportion which only the finest motion pictures attain.

The casting of Cary Grant in the role of the man who finally wins Tira's love was again another brilliant piece of dramatic awareness. Cary as Jack Clayton has none of the characteristics about him that had previously attracted Tira to men. When she meets Nat Pendleton (playing the trapeze artist) on her way to the hotel at the very start of the picture, she feels his muscles, and comments on them. She makes a similar overt gesture with Davidson (playing the Chump) while the two are dancing in her hotel room. But with Clayton all such pretension is dropped. Supposedly not interested just in his money, as she had been with Kirk Lawrence, seemingly in love, she feels his muscles at the end of the picture just before the fade. But in 1933 Cary Grant was narrow of line and thin of physique, not at all the Nat Pendleton image. Tira, a lion tamer, is unaccountably drawn to him, but there is something slightly incredible about their union, incredible enough for the viewer to have the same impression as one has at the conclusion of *She Done Him Wrong,* Tira cannot stay with him forever; she is insatiable and immortal. From this very subtle and almost unconscious, impression, the viewer comes away with that same sense of awe before magnitude, talent, and vibrance, which Chaplin managed only by using weak casting as a crutch.

No scene in *I'm No Angel* is extraneous. It is interesting, compelling, and enjoyable throughout. Some scenes are played with rare distinction, as that of Cary Grant's initial visit to Tira's apartment, when she decides to let Kent Taylor go, but wants Cary instead. The camera takes a

66

three-quarters shot as the conversation straggles to its conclusion, with both their minds on something other than what's being said. Cary has placed a small photograph of Mae in his coat pocket, and with his hands plunged nervously into his trouser pockets, the suit coat jutting out towards Mae, their bodies swaying closer together as they talk, Mae mumbling, "You'll hear from me," much more is implied than could ever be shown.

Jon Tuska, *Views and Reviews*

Mae West's awaited second starring picture is a runner up to *She Done Him Wrong*. Picture fails to fulfill the promise of Miss West's first picture for several reasons. First, Miss West is decidedly a character of the '90s. Minus the bustle and corsets, there's something missing from her personality. Picture will make money. The star's fans will flock to it, but it will not make her any new friends. Story and dialogue are hackneyed and outmoded, leaving the burden of entertainment on the star herself which is a hard job for anyone.

While Miss West has written some good lines for herself, she has been unable to throw plot distribution to the others.

Dialogue is crammed with double entendre, will get many a laugh from the stags, but in most cases means nothing to the average fan. Miss West has some pip lines, but nothing that will sock as did "Come up and see me some time." She sings the chorus of three numbers, but never gets vocally hot.

Cary Grant does nice work as the sweetheart but is at all times overshadowed by Miss West. Edward Arnold is oke as the grift show owner. Kent Taylor is satisfactory as the rich sucker with William Davidson good as an out of town chump.

Gertrude Michael in a small part is satisfactory. Gregory Ratoff and Irving Pichel as the opposing attorneys are excellent in the courtroom sequence, the highlight of the picture. Gertrude Howard, Miss West's maid, accounts for several good laughs.

Wesley Ruggles' direction is in keeping with Miss West's various moods, but seems to be more of a supervisory nature in most sequences. Photography is very good.

*Variety*

With Mae West

With Mae West

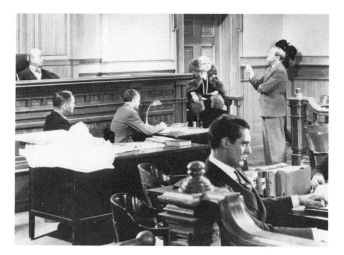

With Walter Walker, Mae West and Gregory Ratoff

With Mae West

67

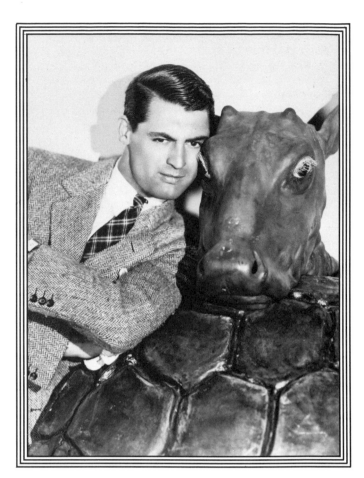

## ALICE IN WONDERLAND

1933

With Mock Turtle costume

**CREDITS:**

Produced and distributed by Paramount Publix. *Director:* Norman McLeod. *Screenplay:* Joseph L. Mankiewicz and William Cameron Menzies. From original material by Lewis Carroll. *Cinematography:* Henry Sharp and Bert Glennon. *Editor:* Edward Hoagland. *Composer:* Dmitri Tiomkin. *Musical Director:* Nathaniel Finsten. *Art direction:* Robert Odell. *Costumes and masks:* Wally Westmore and Newt Jones. *Sound:* Eugene Merritt. Technical effects by Gordon Jennings and Farciot Edouart. *Release date:* December 22, 1933. *Running time:* 90 minutes.

**THE CAST:**

| | |
|---|---|
| *Alice* | Charlotte Henry |
| *Cheshire Cat* | Richard Arlen |
| *Fish* | Roscoe Ates |
| *Gryphon* | William Austin |
| *White Knight* | Gary Cooper |
| *Leg of Mutton* | Jack Duffy |
| *Uncle Gilbert* | Leon Errol |
| *White Queen* | Louise Fazenda |
| *Humpty Dumpty* | W. C. Fields |
| *King of Hearts* | Alec B. Francis |
| *White Rabbit* | Skeets Gallagher |
| *Mock Turtle* | Cary Grant |
| *Cook* | Lillian Harmer |
| *Mouse* | Raymond Hatton |
| *Frog* | Sterling Holloway |
| *Mad Hatter* | Edward Everett Horton |
| *Tweedledee* | Roscoe Karns |
| *Joker* | Baby LeRoy |
| *Father William's Son* | Lucien Littlefield |
| *Sheep* | Mae Marsh |
| *Dodo Bird* | Polly Moran |
| *Tweedledum* | Jack Oakie |

68

| | |
|---|---|
| *Red Queen* | Edna May Oliver |
| *Plum Pudding* | George Ovey |
| *Queen of Hearts* | May Robson |
| *March Hare* | Charlie Ruggles |
| *Dormouse* | Jackie Searle |
| *Duchess* | Alison Skipworth |
| *Caterpillar* | Ned Sparks |

With Ford Sterling, Jacqueline Wells, Billy Barty, Billy Bevan, Colin Campbell, Harvey Clark, Henry Ekezian, Meyer Grace, Ethel Griffies, Colin Kenny, Charles McNaughton, Patsy O'Bryne, Will Stanton, and Joe Torillo.

## SYNOPSIS:

Alice, while reading on a summer afternoon, sees the White Rabbit run across the lawn and disappear into a hole. She follows the Rabbit, falls into the hole and finds herself in a beautiful garden. She goes through many strange experiences such as growing larger, growing smaller, swimming in a pool of her tears, and talking to strange animals. She tries to save a baby which turns into a pig and runs away. She meets the Cheshire Cat who disappears and reappears. She attends the Mad Hatter's Tea Party, but escapes it as soon as she can. After more adventures she arrives at a trial with the dreadful Queen, who, when Alice says she cannot testify, threatens to cut Alice's head off. Alice calls the Queen and her court a pack of cards and as the cards rush at her, she awakens from her dream.

## REVIEWS:

Why mince matters? *Alice in Wonderland* is, to my sober (despite repeal) judgment, one of the worst flops of the cinema. Paramount's first mistake was in attempting it. The only person in Movieland to have done it is Walt Disney. Mary Pickford, who once contemplated doing it, was right when she said that "Alice" should be made only in cartoons.

So—with a fine script (Joe Mankiewicz and William Cameron Menzies), delightful music (Dmitri Tiomkin), a splendid director (Norman McLeod), and about fifty of our best actors and actresses, the picture, when it isn't dull, is still utterly uninspired.

English children who still read *Alice in Wonderland* may get a mild kick out of it. I doubt if our young sophisticates will. It's a cinch that all the grown-ups will get is the mild fun of trying to identify the Big Names hidden behind turtle shells and teddy-bear skins. Even when they do occasionally recognize a voice they will still wonder why all these high salaries were hidden beneath bushels of props. Extras, or even children, would have been adequate to most of the parts. No acting was required. Indeed production costs could have been cut tremendously by letting cheap actors play the parts and then hiring Big Names to register five minutes of dialogue easily dubbed in.

The second mistake was in choosing a young lady to play the five or six-year-old part of Alice. Charlotte Henry is a comely youngster with an intelligent face, who looks as though she would be more interested in Vance Hoyt's nature studies in *Script* than in Fairyland. She tries hard to look wonder-eyed but can't quite make it. And with all our wonderful kid actors!

Even so there was still a chance to make a picture of fairylike charm. In all the arts there is no medium that lends itself to fantasy like the movie camera. By soft focus, shooting through silk, and other technical tricks, scenes can be given an elusive dreamlike quality that eloquently visualizes the subjective mind. Alice goes to sleep and dreams her trip to Wonderland, but we see both her and her dream in hard reality, with the flat lighting and sharp focus of the objective world. Never for a moment are we in dreamland; we are on Stage Four, witnessing the technical staff and prop boys doing their stuff. Even much of this is bad. When Alice flies through the air, she is obviously hanging by a wire (remember how well that was done in *Peter Pan*—also by Paramount?) and when she is falling down the well, she is still hanging by a wire. Nor are her skirts blown while falling. It's hard to write a review like this, for practically everybody who had anything to do with the picture is a Scripter, but when a picture is a flop, it's a flop, and it's silly to alibi. The big mistake was in undertaking it at all.

Bob Wagner, *Script*

With William Austin and Charlotte Henry

# THIRTY-DAY PRINCESS

1934

With Sylvia Sidney

## CREDITS:

*Distributing company:* Paramount Publix. *Producing company:* A B. P. Schulberg Production. *Director:* Marion Gering. *Screenplay:* Preston Sturges and Frank Partos. Adaptation by Sam Hellman and Edwin Justus Mayer from original story by Clarence Buddington Kelland. *Cinematography:* Leon Shamroy. *Release date:* May 18, 1934. *Running time:* 73 minutes.

## THE CAST:

| | |
|---|---|
| *Princess Catterina* | Sylvia Sidney |
| *Nancy Lane* | Sylvia Sidney |
| *Porter Madison* | Cary Grant |
| *Richard Gresham* | Edward Arnold |
| *King Anatole* | Henry Stephenson |
| *Count Nicholaus* | Vince Barnett |
| *The Baron* | Edgar Norton |
| *Mr. Kirk* | Ray Walker |
| *Parker* | Lucien Littlefield |
| *Managing Editor* | Robert McWade |
| *Spottswood* | George Baxter |
| *Lady in Waiting* | Marguerite Namara |

## SYNOPSIS:

Princess Catterina of Taronia gets the mumps upon her arrival in the United States, ostensibly on a good-will mission but actually to create favorable public opinion for a proposed bond issue. A substitute necessary, banker Richard Gresham has hordes of detectives search New York until Nancy Lane, a third-rate actress and perfect double for the stricken princess, is found. Nancy is unleashed to take Porter Madison, publisher of the town's most influential paper and A-1 foreigner-baiter for a sleigh ride. Over the fervid patriotic protests of the managing editor, Madison softens his rabid editorial policy. In love with the girl, but awed by the fact that she's a princess, and the girl in love with him awed by the fact that he's a big publisher—far beyond any showgirl's dreams—prevents the truth from being told. The jealous protestations of Count Nicholaus, suitor to the real princess cause complications. However the real princess recovers. Madison is chagrined to think that he had been so successfully duped, but pleased to discover that he can marry Nancy Lane.

## REVIEWS:

Sylvia Sidney would be very close to Joan Crawford in the ranking of artists on the screen. Unfortunately, Sidney's new picture, *Thirty-Day Princess,* is a complete dud to me. it's one of those effortful things in which a lot of heavy personalities try to trip it lightly. The story, again, is right out of ancient Sanskrit. The poor little girl who impersonates a princess, and, under false front, falls in love with a big shot. A double, even a triple role for Sylvia Sidney, in which she demonstrates her virtuoso technique by doing everything correctly, effectively, deftly. But I suspect that director Marion Gering is no man for comedy; he throws in everything from slapstick to drawing-room wit in the laugh-chase, but doesn't often hit.

Meyer Levin, *Esquire*

*Thirty-Day Princess* is a jolly and amusing romantic comedy about a princess from Taronia who comes to the United States to create favorable publicity for a bond issue, but unfortunately gets the mumps. In real life, of course, it is the investor in foreign bonds who gets the mumps and the megrims, while Mr. Morgan gets the commission. Deciding that a substitute Princess must be shown to the public, banker Gresham has detectives search New York for an actress who resembles the Princess. They find Nancy Lane (Sylvia Sidney) and set her on the trail of the city's most influential newspaper publisher, whose delight it has been to bait big bad bankers. This publisher hasn't any more chance of escaping Nancy than a little tailor has of escaping General Johnson and the NRA. Well, there are a lot of complications and funny situations which add up to a pretty good time if you enjoy light comedy. Miss Sidney is fine in a dual role, and Cary Grant, Edward Arnold, Vince Barnett, Henry Stephenson and others render good support. J. P. Morgan should see this picture: its comedy ideas may help him to sell some more Peruvian bonds.

Cy Caldwell, *New Outlook*

With Sylvia Sidney

With Sylvia Sidney

# BORN TO BE BAD

1934

With Loretta Young

**CREDITS:**

*Distributing company:* United Artists. *Producing company:* Twentieth Century. *Director:* Lowell Sherman. *Screenplay:* Story, dialogue and adaptation by Ralph Graves. Continuity by Harrison Jacobs. *Cinematography:* Barney McGill. *Editor:* Maurice Wright. *Musical director:* Alfred Newman. *Art direction:* Richard Day and Joseph Wright. *Release date:* May 18, 1934. *Running time:* 61 minutes.

**THE CAST:**

| | |
|---|---|
| *Letty Strong* | Loretta Young |
| *Mickey* | Jackie Kelk |
| *Malcolm Trevor* | Cary Grant |
| *Fuzzy* | Henry Travers |
| *Steve Karns* | Russell Hopton |
| *Max Lieber* | Andrew Tombes |
| *Doctor Dropsy* | Howard Lang |
| *Adolph* | Harry Green |
| *Alice Trevor* | Marion Burns |
| *Lawyer* | Paul Harvey |
| *Butler* | Charles Coleman |
| *Truant Officer* | Matt Briggs |
| *Miss Crawford* | Geneva Mitchell |

**SYNOPSIS:**

Letty Strong, a dress model, is found engaged in the rapid accumulation of money and an effort to impart to her unmannered youngster the precept that he must always be on his guard to fight back, never to let any one get away with anything. This despite the attempt of Fuzzy, an elderly bookshop owner, who had taken her in years before, to show her the error of her ways. Trouble with truant officers is apparently an everyday occurrence. When the boy is hurt by a truck driven by Malcolm Trevor, president of a large company, the mother, with the aid of a shady lawyer and equally unscrupulous doctor, tries to obtain damages. They are shown up, and the court causes her to lose her son to an institution. Interested, Malcolm Trevor assumes responsibility for the child, who is taken to his estate, and his wife, Alice Trevor, mothers the boy.

Letty gains entrance to Malcolm's home, tries to entice the boy away, fails, and then plans a compromising plot, whereby, in return for her silence, Malcolm will release the boy to her. She compels Malcolm to fall in love with her, makes a phonograph record of his pleas, but reckons without the honorable manner in which he and his wife conduct themselves. Malcolm tells his wife the truth, which revelation spikes Letty's guns. Meanwhile the boy, under the tutelage of Malcolm, has learned something of the difference between right and wrong. Letty, after Alice has saved the boy from drowning in the swimming pool, refuses to acknowledge to Malcolm that she really loves him, and walks out of the lives of her son and the Trevors, back to Fuzzy, from whom she asks a job. A reformation, we are left to infer, has been brought about in both mother and wayward son.

## REVIEWS:

This story is so bad in completed picture form, it's hard to see how it was thought to contain enough merit to warrant production in the first place. From the director, Lowell Sherman, to one of the co-stars, Loretta Young, and including the producers, a lot of first rate effort went into the making; but all wasted.

Loretta Young looks better than ever, but the story gave her too much of a handicap to do anything but look well. Her performance might be called satisfactory under the circumstances, but the same doesn't apply to Cary Grant. He gives a colorless, meaningless performance. Jackie Kelk, seemingly about seven or eight years old, must be a clever kid to be able to become so dislikeable before the picture is five minutes old, as he does here. Balance of cast, as well as the production and Lowell Sherman's deft but wasted directing, all much too good for this script.

Joe Bigelow, *Variety*

Ralph Graves, who has given several fairly interesting performances, is responsible for the narrative of *Born To Be Bad*. If this opus is any criterion of Mr. Graves's literary skill, he is scarcely to be congratulated on having temporarily abandoned his acting. It is a hopelessly unintelligent hodgepodge, wherein Loretta Young and Cary Grant have the misfortune to be cast in the leading roles.

Mordaunt Hall, *The New York Times*

With Etienne Giradol, Henry Travers, Loretta Young and Howard Lang

With Loretta Young

# KISS AND MAKE UP

1934

With Helen Mack

## CREDITS:

Distributing company: Paramount Publix. Producer: B. P. Schulberg. Director: Harlan Thompson. Associate: Jean Negulesco. Screenplay: Harlan Thompson and George Marion, Jr. Original by Stephen Bekeffi. Adaptation: Jane Hinton. Cinematography: Leon Shamroy. Composer: Ralph Rainger. Lyrics by Leo Robin. Art Direction: Hans Dreier and Ernst Fege. Sound: Jack Goodrich. Release date: July 13, 1934. Running time: 80 minutes.

## THE CAST:

| | |
|---|---|
| Dr. Maurice Lamar | Cary Grant |
| Anne | Helen Mack |
| Eve Caron | Genevieve Tobin |
| Marcel Caron | Edward Everett Horton |
| Max Pascal | Lucien Littlefield |
| Countess Rita | Mona Maris |
| Vilma | Katherine Williams |
| Magda | Lucille Lund |
| Rolando | Rafael Storm |
| Mme. Severac | Mme. Bonita |
| Mme. Durand | Doris Lloyd |
| Maharajah of Baroona | Milton Wallace |
| Plumber | Sam Ashe |
| Landlady | Helena Phillips |
| Consuelo of Claghorne | Toby Wing |
| Chairman of banquet | Henry Armetta |
| Jean (valet) | George Andre Beranger |
| Beauty clinic nurses | Judith Arlen, Jean Gale, Hazel Hayes, Lee Ann Meredith |
| Radio announcer | Helene Cohan |
| Maharajah's wife | Jean Carmen |
| Radio listener | GiGi Parrish |
| Lady Rummond-Dray | Ann Hovey |
| Beauty clinic patients | Betty Bryson and Jacqueline Wells and the Wampas Baby Stars of 1934 |

74

## SYNOPSIS:

Dr. Lamar's modernistic beauty salon, operated with all the fanfare of high-pressure business techniques, is the haven of ladies, old and young, who want to be beautiful. Loved by his plain little secretary, Anne, the Doctor creates a beautiful Frankenstein of Eve, Marcel Caron's ex-wife, who would have loved her forever the way she was. Colored by atmospheric and glamorous situations, marriage is no bed of roses for Lamar, as Eve's new beauty is the incentive to further amorous conquests, which convince the doctor that he married a lot of cosmetics. Only when Anne threatens to elope with Caron does Lamar wake up to the real love that has been right at his elbow all along.

## REVIEWS:

The picture entitled, with such knowing and antic humor, *Kiss and Make-Up* is a first-class lingerie bazaar and a third-class entertainment. It represents a triumphant attempt to achieve pictorial allure without disturbing its pious editorial point of view on the impersonal worship of feminine beauty. It crowds the screen so thickly with silk, satin and nymphs that it is with some difficulty that such agreeable players as Edward Everett Horton, Cary Grant and Genevieve Tobin succeed in projecting themselves at all.

There is a theme in the new film which, in more skillful hands, might form the basis for a good comedy. Carrying the principles of beauty culture to their logical conclusion, Dr. Lamar finally produces a masterpiece of liveliness, who is, unfortunately, so bound to the harrowing ritual of lotion, massage, diet and rest that she becomes entirely useless. Thereupon her husband (Mr. Horton) casts her off and she becomes the wife of her doctor. After a honeymoon, during which his wife devotes herself chiefly to the preservation of her face and figure, the doctor in desperation returns to Paris and wrecks his temple of beauty.

The picture occasionally achieves a briefly comic episode, like that in which an Oriental potentate leads his wives into the salon, displays a sketch showing a Western conception of the delights of the harem and angrily announces that he has been bamboozled. But *Kiss and Make Up* succeeds to a remarkable degree in being dull.

Andre Sennwald, The New York Times

Either a gag comedy with a romantic thread or a light romance with gag comedy, but more gags than romance. A nice picture lacking sufficient strength to wow but should do all right. Plot is thin, though sufficient.

Cary Grant does well as the doctor but both he and E. E. Horton play too strongly for laughs. Genevieve Tobin fills the specifications as the beauty, but acting honors go to Helen Mack as the secretary. A delightful sincere performance. Plenty of sight stuff and plenty of laughs in spots.

Winthrop Sargent, Variety

With Edward Everett Horton

With Helen Mack

With Edward Everett Horton, Helen Mack and Genevieve Tobin

# LADIES SHOULD LISTEN

1934

With Frances Drake

## CREDITS:

*Distributing company:* Paramount Publix. *Producer:* Douglas MacLean. *Director:* Frank Tuttle. *Screenplay:* Claude Binyon and Frank Butler. *Original:* Alfred Savoir and Guy Bolton. *Adaptation:* Guy Bolton. *Cinematography:* Harry Sharp. *Art Direction:* Hans Dreier and Ernst Fegte. *Sound:* Earl Hayman. *Release date:* August 10, 1934. *Running time:* 62 minutes.

## THE CAST:

| | |
|---|---|
| *Julian de Lussac* | Cary Grant |
| *Anna Mirelle* | Frances Drake |
| *Paul Vernet* | Edward Everett Horton |
| *Marguerite Cintos* | Rosita Moreno |
| *Joseph Flamberg* | George Barlier |
| *Susie Flamberg* | Nydia Westman |
| *Henri (Porter)* | Charles Ray |
| *Albert (Manservant)* | Charles Arnt |
| *Ramon Cintos* | Rafael Corio |
| *Blanche (Operator)* | Clara Lou Sheridan |
| *Operator* | Henrietta Burnside |
| *Butler* | Joe North |

## SYNOPSIS:

In Paris, Julian de Lussac, a South American nitrate concession option peddler, through no fault of his own suddenly has three women and a pair of male menaces on his neck. Susie Flamberg, an exotic old maid, throws herself at him. De Lussac is her ideal of a regular lover. Her antics first result in bringing telephone operator Anna Mirelle into the plot, as a self-constituted protector of de Lussac, and later arouse complications between Julian and her enduring fiance, Paul Vernet. Bedazzled by all the attention, but not entirely adverse to accepting it, Julian's life becomes more hectic as vampish Marguerite Cintos makes her appearance. His apartment is the rendezvous for all three; Susie and Marguerite arduously affectionate and Anna striving her utmost to keep Julian unscathed. In the climax, it's revealed that Marguerite and the villainous Ramon Cintos are just a pair of would-be blackmailers, interested solely in the nitrate potentialities; that Paul is never going to let Susie get away from him, and that in Anna, Julian has an efficient protector.

## REVIEWS:

Scenes of arriving and departing trains, automobile driving and street encounters, key a picture to realism. That's why I couldn't get into the fun of this story until I realized that it was a farce in which people were not *supposed* to act logically. When I did, I purred with delight.

The story—Alfred Savoir and Guy Bolton, scripted by Frank Butler and Claude Binyon—is a melange of bedroom-blunder stuff and smart lines. It ripples along merrily, with credit to all. Especially Frank Tuttle, director, and Earl Hyman—sound engineer! Yes, the phony thunderstorm is one of the best things in the show.

I was particularly pleased with Cary Grant. Like Clark Gable in *It Happened One Night,* he surprises everyone with his delightful flair for light comedy.

Edward Everett Horton of course clicks in every scene. (Did you ever stop to think that Eddie Horton is one of the few actors who is exactly the same in both private life and on the screen—amusing and charming?)

Nydia Westman pulls her usual darb, only better. Here is a comely young lady who does her darndest to un-sex herself. In this story her spectacles were her usual symbol of chastity. So when Eddie, her fiance, puts on the heat, instead of tearing her bodice he grabs off her glasses, with the result that she is ready for *anything*. It's one of the funniest scenes yet, and if Joe Breen sees dirt in it, rather'n fun, I'll never speak to him again. . . .

Hans Dreier and Ernst Fegte have provided beautiful and authentic sets.

Credit Douglas MacLean, producer, with having kept many daring lines and situations within the bounds of good taste.

Rob Wagner, *Script*

Basically there may have been enough comedy and farce possibility in this story, but as handled, it emerges a much too highly strained attempt at farce. A good deal of it is actually unfunny, and all of it is too synthetic.

Cary Grant is brutally miscast as a philandering young Parisian. He plays the part for comedy, miscuing several times. On the other hand, Frances Drake as his vis-à-vis, a nosey telephone girl, who listens in on conversations and has a habit of trying to straighten things out for other people, turns in her best performance yet and does much to establish herself.

With Frances Drake

With Charles Ray and Frances Drake

Picture allows Charles Ray to make a film comeback in a very minor role. Handles a comedy bit very effectively and ought to be able to go places again.

Claude Binyon and Frank Butler overworked hoke and puns in their adaptation, and these were all overstrained in the direction.

Wolfe Kaufman, *Variety*

With Frances Drake

With Edward Everett Horton and Nydia Westman

With Elissa Landi

# ENTER MADAM

1935

## CREDITS:

Produced and distributed by Paramount Publix. *Producer:* A. Benjamin Glaser. *Director:* Elliott Nugent. *Screenplay:* Charles Brackett and Gladys Lehman. Based on original play by Gilda Varesi Archibald and Dorothea Donn-Byrne. *Cinematography:* Theodor Sparkuhl and William Mellor. *Art Direction:* Hans Dreier and Ernst Fegte. *Costumes:* Trovis Banton. *Sound:* M. M. Paggi. *Release date:* January 4, 1935. *Running time:* 83 minutes.

## THE CAST:

| | |
|---|---|
| *Lisa Della Robbia* | Elissa Landi |
| *Gerald Fitzgerald* | Cary Grant |
| *Mr. Farnum* | Lynne Overman |
| *Flora Preston* | Sharon Lynne |
| *Bice* | Michelette Burani |
| *Archimede* | Paul Forcasi |
| *The Doctor* | Adrian Rosley |
| *Aline Chalmers* | Cecelia Parker |
| *John Fitzgerald* | Frank Albertson |
| *Tamamoto* | Wilfred Hari |
| *Carlson* | Torben Meyer |
| *Bjorgenson* | Harold Berquist |
| *Operator* | Diana Lewis |
| *Scorpia (on stage)* | Richard Bonelli |

## SYNOPSIS:

Gerald Fitzgerald falls in love with the temperamental opera star, Lisa Della Robbia. Married life—traipsing all over Europe, enduring his wife's tantrums at the interference of her coterie of press agents, maids, cooks and half-brother—proving not the glorious thing he had dreamed, reduction to the status of a dog-walker is the

With Elissa Landi, Sharon Lynne and Frank Albertson

last straw. As Lisa embarks on a Scandinavian concert tour, Gerald returns to the States.

A cable informing her of Gerald's divorce intentions brings her to New York along with her entire harum-scarum melange. Although Gerald and Flora Preston think they have everything nicely fixed up, Lisa is too much in love to surrender easily. She invites the pair to her performance of "Cavalleria Rusticana" and the beauties of the fine music work queer magic on Gerald. Later, at supper, Lisa, a combination of imp and angel, with the assistance of the Doctor, Archimede, Bice and Farnum, again hypnotizes Gerald and eradicates Flora.

## REVIEWS:

Music's "in" for celluloid since the smash of *Night of Love,* so prepare for a deluge of temperamental opera singers on the screen as well as on Stage 2.

Elissa Landi is about the most beautiful warbler you've seen (Mary Garden, *please* forgive me), and she sings magnificently, thanks to the smart dubbing of the Nina Koshetz voice. Lovely 'Lissa is improving as an actress by leaps, and if sometimes she lands out-of-bounds in vivaciousness, I don't mind much.

Gilda Varesi, author, starred in the play and though Miss Varesi collabed on the screen play, the yarn's tempo has been shifted from comedy drama to farce. There's

With Elissa Landi, Lynn Overman and Frank Albertson

(*Opposite page*) With Elissa Landi

With Michelette Burani

music, music everywhere, plus plenty of entertainment if you happen to be tone-deaf.

Della Robbia at twenty-five is a diva of world rep. She surrounds herself with a mad, Sangercircus world which is shared by an entourage including a chef, maid and physician, all with ariaistic tendencies. During a performance of "Tosca" in Italy, the soprano's train contacts a candle flame and tall-darknhandsome Cary Grant saves the lady from being scorched, though he himself is pretty well hotchacharred by love.

Elissa and Cary marry and soon the guy finds himself spinning on a roundabout of concerts and tantrums. Hubby wants to go to America, wifie promises to accompany him but signs for a tour at the last sec, so Cary goes home alone. Elissa signs contract after contract, for she finds fame headier than marriage. Cary threatens divorce, the songbird flies to America. You guess the finale.

Richard Bonelli sings Scarpia authoritatively. Lynne Overman as the weary, pungent manager again proves his deft comedy talents. He should draw longer assignments, for in a certain groove he's unsurpassed.

Fast direction by Elliot Nugent is marred at times by overemphasis. Camera work by Theodor Sparkuhl and William Mellor is distinguished.

Herb Sterne, *Script*

With Elissa Landi

With Myrna Loy

# WINGS IN THE DARK

1935

## CREDITS:

Produced and distributed by Paramount Pictures. *Producer:* Arthur Hornblow, Jr. *Director:* James Flood. *Screenplay:* Jack Kirkland and Frank Partos. Adaptation by Dale Van Every and E. H. Robinson. *Original:* Nell Shipman and Philip D. Hurn. *Cinematography:* William C. Mellor. *Special effects:* Aerial photography by Dewey Wrigley. *Art direction:* Hans Dreier and Earl Hendrick. *Sound:* Earl S. Hayman. *Chief of aeronautics:* Capt. Earl H. Robinson. *Release date:* February 1, 1935. *Running time:* 75 minutes.

## THE CAST:

| | |
|---|---|
| *Sheila Mason* | Myrna Loy |
| *Ken Gordon* | Cary Grant |
| *Nick Williams* | Roscoe Karns |
| *Mac* | Hobart Cavanaugh |
| *Tops Harmon* | Dean Jagger |
| *Yipp Morgan* | Bert Hanlon |
| *Joy Burns* | James Burtis |
| *Jake Brashear* | Russell Hopton |
| *Kennel Club Sec'y.* | Samuel S. Hinds |
| *The Doctor* | Arnold Korff |
| *Sheila's first mechanic* | Matt McHugh |
| *Radio announcer* | Graham McNamee |
| *Cameraman* | Alfred Delcambre |

## SYNOPSIS:

Ken Gordon is a flier attempting to perfect instruments for safe flying in the dark or fog. Sheila Mason, barnstorming sky-writing stunter, managed by Nick Williams, falls in love with him. Her affection is coldly received. At the moment when triumph for his devices seems just ahead, Gordon is blinded by a gas explosion.

Gordon, who has retired to the country accompanied only by his faithful mechanic, Mac, gets a seeing-eye dog to lead him around. Trying to be a writer, but only getting rejection slips, he never knows that the checks he cashes are the result of Sheila's taking any kind of a breakneck job that manager Williams can conceive.

As Sheila's plane is confiscated by the manufacturers in default of payment, Sheila, succumbing to Williams' continued pleas, agrees to try to hop from Moscow to New York. Making the flight, she gets safely across the Newfoundland; there fog menaces her. As she in turn calls Halifax, Portland, Boston, via radio, Graham MacNamee's voice details her dangerous progress to the world. Over Roosevelt Field the fog is thickest. Gordon, listening, suddenly discovers how much he loves her. With Mac, he crashes the hangar and goes up through the fog, gets in touch with the girl via radio. Above the clouds the fliers pour forth their love story. Then he leads her to safety by means of the instruments he perfected.

With Myrna Loy

With Myrna Loy

## REVIEWS:

After a flying start, literally and figuratively, this film sags in the middle, and then closes on another high note, the net result being a nice little picture for the family trade that, with the Grant-Loy drawing power, will do better than average at the box-office.

Cary Grant gives a splendid performance as the tragic young flyer, and Myrna Loy does well with a role not entirely her sort.

Roscoe Karns has a fat part as the girl flier's manager and gets all the laughs possible from it. A delightful surprise is an outstanding bit of work by Hobart Cavanaugh, playing, with a comic Scotch burr, the mechanic pal of Grant.

Dean Jagger, Russell Hopton and Matt McHugh stand out in bits, and the cast has been well handled by director James Flood. Earl Robinson's handling of the air stuff rates special attention and the photography, both aerial and studio is first rate.

*The Hollywood Reporter*

The keynote of *Wings in the Dark* is its persuasive living conviction, supported in every act, line and scene by the magnificently simple, unaffected and heart gripping performances of Myrna Loy, Cary Grant, Roscoe Karns, Hobart Cavanaugh and hand-picked cast, skillfully guided at every turn by the flawless pilotage of James Flood.

Myrna Loy, by many considered the most gracious lady of the screen here fulfills every demand of her admirers and will continue, by virtue of her extraordinary performance, to add to her queue of fans. Her love scenes with the blind flier, which Grant is through most of the picture, are superb, with never a slough or slopover in the emotional high spots. The characterization never misses in its delicate shadings of tender humor, compassion, restraint. She is enchanting.

Cary Grant tops all his past work. The part gave him dimension to play with and he took it headlong. He never flaws in the moving, pathetic, but inspiring behavior of a man whose career seems ruined by an accident but who comes back through a mental hell, by virtue of love and the saving ruses of friendship. His acting here lifts him definitely above his prior standing.

James Flood does find a job of timing, modulation and unerring and deftly economical pursuit of his dramatic thread, as well as the handling of his detail for novelty, surprise and above all sustained humanness, which compares with the best in ace direction. Fulfilling the high excellence of the picture is the striking aerial photography by Dewey Wrigley and the camera work of William Mellor, the technical validity of all the plane action, and a very smart job of editing, uncredited.

*Daily Variety*

With Gertrude Michael

# THE LAST OUTPOST

1935

## CREDITS:

*Distributing company:* Paramount Pictures. *Producing company:* Paramount Pictures. *Producer:* E. Lloyd Sheldon. *Director:* Charles Barton and Louis Gasnier. *Assistant director:* Edgar Anderson. *Screenplay:* Philip MacDonald. Adaptation by Frank Partos and Charles Brackett. Story by F. Britten Austin. *Cinematography:* Theodor Sparkuhl. *Editor:* Jack Dennis. *Art direction:* Hans Dreier and Earl Hendrick. *Sound:* A. W. Singley. *Release date:* October 11, 1935. *Running time:* 75 minutes.

## THE CAST:

| | |
|---|---|
| *Michael Andrews* | Cary Grant |
| *John Stevenson* | Claude Rains |
| *Rosemary Haydon* | Gertrude Michael |
| *Ilya* | Kathleen Burke |
| *Lieut. Prescott* | Colin Tapley |
| *Mirov* | Akim Tamiroff |
| *Corporal Foster* | Billy Bevan |
| *Turkish major* | Georges Renevant |
| *Nurse Rowland* | Margaret Swope |
| *Cullen* | Jameson Thomas |
| *Haidor* | Nick Shaid |
| *Amrak* | Harry Semels |
| *Armenian patriarch* | Meyer Ouhayoun |
| *Armenian officer* | Frazier Acosta |
| *Armenian guard* | Malay Clu |
| *Head nurse* | Elspeth Dudgeon |
| *Nurse* | Beulah McDonald |
| *Sergeant in general's office* | Robert Adair |
| *Sergeant Bates* | William Brown |
| *General* | Claude King |
| *Doctor* | Olaf Hytten |
| *Colonel* | Frank Elliott |
| *Surgeon* | Frank Dawson |

## SYNOPSIS:

Michael Andrews, a British officer, is captured by the Kurds. His most cruel captor turns out to be John Stevenson, a sort of Lawrence of Arabia character who frees him. Stevenson's big job is to move an Armenian tribe, friendly to the British, from the fury of the Turks. Tough and dangerous as it is moving the tribe and its belongings across the desert, through rushing torrents and over Alpine-like mountains, Stevenson has an equally tough and dangerous job in keeping Andrews away from Ilya, alluring wife of the head chief.

The job completed, the scene shifts to a hospital in Egypt, where Andrews, injured in a scuffle with Stevenson, is recuperating. Andrews gets interested in nurse Rosemary Haydon, who is the wife of Stevenson. Stevenson gets a furlough for his accomplishments and lands in Cairo. His amazed wife who hasn't seen him since their wedding day, is cold and he finally becomes aware of the situation. Bent on revenge, he takes up the trail of Andrews, who has been assigned to mop up some enemy nomad tribes. All but Andrews and Stevenson are killed in the attack on the fort. Both set off across the desert to contact an advancing relief party. Stevenson is mortally wounded by pursuing tribesmen, and commending the welfare of his wife to Andrews, dies as they meet the advancing cavalry.

## REVIEWS:

*The Last Outpost,* which will be shown shortly at the Plaza, is a curious mixture. Half of it is remarkably good and half of it quite abysmally bad. One can even put one's finger on the joins, and it will be well worth a visit if only because it indicates what might be made of the short story form on the screen. It consists of two stories unrelated except for the coincidence of characters. The first, which lasts for about half-an-hour, is a very well-directed and well-acted War story of a British secret service agent and his success in warning a defenseless tribe against a Kurd attack and inducing them to move with their flocks over a flooded river and across a snow-bound range of mountains to safe pastures. It is one of those stories of dogged physical endeavor that the film does so well. It belongs to the order of *Grass* and *The Covered Wagon.* Mr. Claude Rains as the secret service agent in Turkish uniform and Mr. Cary Grant as the incurably light-minded and rather stupid British officer whom he rescues from the Kurds both act extremely well. Mr. Rains's low husky voice, his power of investing even commonplace dialogue with smouldering conviction, is remarkable. He never rants, but one is always aware of what a superb ranter he could be in a part which did not call for modern restraint but only for superb diction. I should like to see him as Almanzor or Aurengzebe, for he could catch, as no one else could, the bitter distrust of the world, religious in its intensity, which lies behind the heroic drama.

*The Last Outpost,* if it had stopped on the mountain pass above the pastures with the officer on the way down to hospital and the comforts of Cairo and the secret agent turning back towards the enemy, would have been a memorable short film. Mr. Charles Barton, the director, has obviously used old documentaries: the crossing of the flooded river is not a California reconstruction, and all through this first section the camera is used with fine vigor to present a subject which could not have been presented on the stage.

I cannot see why we should not have serious films of this length as well as farces, short stories as well as novels on the screen. The essential speed and concision would be an admirable discipline for most directors, who are still, after seven years of talkies, tied to stage methods, and we might be saved from seeing such a good film as this padded out to full length by the addition of a more than usually stupid triangular melodrama of jealousy and last-minute rescue in the Sahara where needless to say Mr. Rains sacrifices his life at the end, for his wife's love, so that all may end in the fixed, almost Oriental, short-hand of military melodrama, "It is better so," clasped fingers and topees off and fading bugle-calls.

Graham Greene, *The Spectator*

Aside from its paltry status as entertainment fare, *The Last Outpost* has a psychological factor that will likely militate against it. Due to the Italo-Ethiopian squabble, the general run of picturegoer may not relish watching hordes of archaically equipped blacks being mowed down by machine guns.

Out of this crazy-quilt of melodrama, travelog, history, jungle clips and whatnot the mainstreeters can expect nothing but negligible returns. Because of the several battle episodes the film might find some favor among the kids in the nabes. . . .

To Cary Grant, Claude Rains and Gertrude Michael fall the assignment of giving life and conviction to the romantic segment of the plot. They all do well by their roles. Theirs is a conflict which revolves around the predicament that two co-fighters in the Mesopotamian campaign find themselves when it develops that the nurse (Miss Michael) who had taken care of Grant in a base hospital is the wife of the British intelligence officer (Rains) who had saved the latter's life. After an absence of three years, Rains suddenly appears at the hospital to recover his wife and interrupts a love affair that had the nurse hoping she was free.

Most effective portion of the film derives from legitimate shots and stock inserts showing the flight of native tribes from threatened Kurdish attack up over the mountains and across swirling rivers. Also effectively projected is the tribal treachery and butchery that the British were forced to encounter in their effort to keep the natives from taking advantage of England's war worries on the eastern flank and yielding to the cajoleries of German provocateurs. Both the trek and the envisioning of this footnote in World War history are dealt with in the fore part of the picture, and from this point on the proceedings wane in both interest and pace.

Ben Bodec, *Variety*

With Claude Rains

With Gertrude Michael

With Claude Rains

# SYLVIA SCARLETT

1936

With Katharine Hepburn

## CREDITS:

*Distributing company:* RKO Radio. *Producing company:* RKO Radio. *Producer:* Pandro S. Berman. *Director:* George Cukor. *Screenplay:* Gladys Unger, John Collier and Mortimer Affner. From novel by Compton Mackenzie. *Cinematography:* Joseph August. *Editor:* Jane Loring. *Musical director:* Roy Webb. *Art direction:* Van Nest Polglase; *Associate:* Sturges Carne. Costumes for Miss Hepburn by Muriel King. Costumes for Miss Paley by Bernard Newman. *Sound:* George D. Ellis. Music recorded by P. J. Faulkner. *Release date:* January 3, 1936. *Running time:* 94 minutes.

## THE CAST:

| | |
|---|---|
| *Sylvia Scarlett* | Katharine Hepburn |
| *Jimmy Monkley* | Cary Grant |
| *Michael Fane* | Brian Aherne |
| *Henry Scarlett* | Edmund Gwenn |
| *Lily* | Natalie Paley |
| *Maudie Tilt* | Dennie Moore |
| *Drunk* | Lennox Pawle |

## SYNOPSIS:

When Henry Scarlett, Sylvia's father, commits larceny and is forced to flee France, Sylvia goes with him disguised as a man. They join up with Monkley, a raffish cockney, and practice a bit of swindling in London. Later they take to the road with a Pierrot show. Sylvia abandons her disguise in an attempt to win an artist's love, but he refuses to take her seriously, until her rival runs away, and so clears the way for the young girl's romance with the artist.

## REVIEWS:

Those movie goers who have exalted Katharine Hepburn into a little niche of her own will probably like this picture, for Miss Hepburn makes a personal triumph of what is rather obviously only a very average picture. The story is crammed with incidents of a rather confused and unaccented type and only Miss Hepburn's fine performance saves from actual boredom this story of a vagabond Odyssey. Indeed it is doubtful if her work has ever excelled this presentation of the awkward and tremulously frustrated heroine of the tale.

Aside from Miss Hepburn's work, Edmund Gwenn is completely satisfying as the baffled and sanctimonious father who eventually goes mad. Cary Grant in the role of the unpleasant cockney also does a fine job.

Indeed the whole cast is rather notable for the excellence of its portrayal and it is only to be regretted that so much fine craftsmanship should have been hampered with so tangled a plot. The plot and its people gave the impression of purposelessness, and even the repetition of unnecessarily dramatic incidents seems hardly to give interest. In places it comes to life surprisingly, only to lose itself again in a blurry outline of extravagant situations.

*Canadian Magazine*

A curious story (Compton MacKenzie), rather jumbled in spots but so adroitly adapted (Gladys Unger, John Collier, Mortimer Offner) and so corkingly dialogued that the jerkiness is easily overlooked.

Katharine Hepburn makes a grand boy, for she is one of the few girls who can handle her body like one. You should see her run. (Nazimova could do it, too!) And that boyish hair-cut (Katie and Amelia Earhart)! How much more beautiful than these metallic marcels and corrugated-iron finger waves!

While Katie is her usual charming self (in several sequences the preview audience *cheered* her charm!) the picture is not wholly hers. Indeed, some people will think it is more Cary Grant's. He plays a big, vulgar cockney blighter so perfectly that you are jealous of every moment he's not on the screen.

And Edmund Gwenn! I thought he was grand in *The Bishop Misbehaves,* but he can play a burglar or bishop equally well.

Dennie Moore is a newcomer, but her skivvy role ought to land her places. I know the type well. London is full of 'em, and she enacts it deliciously.

But poor Brian Aherne. He acts, of course, delightfully. But his makeup! He's an artist, the sweetest artist you ever did see. Yes, Brian goes pretty on us—pretty curly hair and the prettiest and curliest little moustache!—not the low-hung but snappy Warner Baxter eyebrow moustache, nor the jaunty fish-hooks that decorate Leo Carrillo's swart pan, but a silly little fluff that looked as though it tickled. (It's the big he-man in me that makes me resent these artist effeminacies. Velvet berets and windsor ties! Gr-r-r-!)

George Cukor's direction is, as usual, superb, handicapped only by the story's jerkiness. And Joseph August's camera work is first class throughout. Once again I call

With Edmund Gwenn and Katharine Hepburn

With Dennie Moore, Edmund Gwenn, Brian Aherne and Katharine Hepburn

attention of the lip-goers to real beauty. Take a night off and study Katharine Hepburn's make-up!

Rob Wagner, *Script*

Story construction and development are beclouded, with resultant hop-skipping in the action, labored dialogue, and overstrained performances, with the exception of that of Cary Grant. Mr. Grant's is the most convincing performance, in a role which is fresh, and at the same time contributes something toward stabilizing the action, a fact which may be of value in shaping the course of showmanship.

Rovelstad, *Motion Picture Herald*

Cary Grant, doing a petty English crook with a Soho accent, practically steals the picture. This is especially true in the earlier sequences. A scene in an English mansion to which Miss Hepburn, Grant and Gwenn have gone for purposes of robbery is dominated by Grant. Throughout this interlude Miss Hepburn is in the background and pretty silly pouring herself glass after glass of champagne while tossing off free verse about the bubbles being pearls that should be returned to the sea. In other sequences Grant also stands out. Aherne enters late and never overcomes the handicap.

Picture also offers Edmund Gwenn, English legit, and Natalie Paley, from Russia and a bona fide princess, and Dennie Moore, soubrette from Broadway. Gwenn will be very useful to casting directors in Hollywood. He brings plenty of experience and versatility. It may not be so easy for the princess. Her English isn't too good and neither is her acting here. Miss Moore will be typed for goofy dames and shows promise.

Half-whimsical, almost allegorical, and with the last half having a dream-worldish element that's hard to define, and equally hard to understand, *Sylvia Scarlett* will encounter a cross-drift of indifference to some of its basic plot situations. Transition of a group of petty crooks into a troupe of vagabond actors traveling in a two-motor-coach caravan is especially harsh upon the credibility of the story.

Robert Landry, *Variety*

With Dennie Moore, Edmund Gwenn and Katharine Hepburn

With Joan Bennett

# BIG BROWN EYES

1936

## CREDITS:

*Distributing company:* Paramount Pictures. *Producer:* A. Walter Wanger. *Director:* Raoul Walsh. *Assistant director:* David MacDonald. *Screenplay:* Raoul Walsh and Bert Hanlon. Original story by James Edward Grant. *Cinematography:* George Clemens. *Editor:* Robert Simpson. *Musical director:* Boris Morris. *Art direction:* Alexander Toluboff. Set decorations by Howard Bristol. Costumes by Helen Taylor. *Sound:* Hugo Grenzbach. *Release date:* April 3, 1936. *Running time:* 76 minutes.

## THE CAST:

| | |
|---|---|
| Danny Barr | Cary Grant |
| Eve Fallon | Joan Bennett |
| Richard Morey | Walter Pidgeon |
| Russ Cortig | Lloyd Nolan |
| Cary Butler | Alan Baxter |
| Mrs. Cole | Marjorie Gateson |
| Bessie Blair | Isabel Jewell |
| Benny Bottle | Douglas Fowley |
| Don Butler | Henry Kleinbach |
| Jack Sully | Joseph Sawyer |
| Cashier | Dolores Casey |
| Myrtle | Doris Canfield |
| Editor | Edwin Maxwell |
| Mother | Helen Brown |
| Martin | Sam Flint |
| Defense attorney | Joe Picorri |
| Prosecuting attorney | Charlie Wilson |
| Red | Charles Martin |
| Malley | Francis McDonald |
| Joe | Eddie Conrad |
| Chauffeur | Ed Jones |

Joan Bennett and Edwin Maxwell

With Joan Bennett

With Walter Pidgeon

## SYNOPSIS:

As a glib-tongued hotel barbershop manicurist, Eve Fallon meets many colorful folk—cops, crooks, and the run-of-the-mill. Pretty much in love with detective Danny Barr, she nevertheless does not hesitate to resort to satirical abuse to keep the affectionate Danny in his proper place. A gem theft takes place, and as Danny investigates, Eve becomes convinced that all his attentions to Mrs. Cole are not strictly in his line of duty.

Simultaneously with Eve's losing her manicurist job and catching on as a sob-sister reporter, there's a child murder. Questioning Bessie Blair, a frightened eyewitness, Eve gets a lead that causes her to suspect Benny Bottle and tips off Danny. Benny is in jail when Eve prints a fake story that Benny has named the killer. Fearing the gang's vengeance more than he does the cops, Benny confesses, naming Russ Cortig as the killer. There's a gang-politician controlled trial and Cortig is freed. Eve is fired for printing fake stories and Danny quits the force.

Then master crook Richard Morey conspires with jewel thieves Cary and Don Butler to put Cortig on the spot. Danny witness his killing and the murderers grab him. Then Morey makes a deal with Cary Butler to deliver the jewels to Eve. She manages to tip off the police and as Danny makes a sensational escape, Morey and Butler are nabbed in the barber shop. Danny and Eve are re-united.

## REVIEWS:

As for *Big Brown Eyes,* the most brutal thing I can say is that it is a typical production. Which, callously trans-

With Joan Bennett

lated, means that if the Head Men would let the Director earn his salary by doing his job without their interference, this mild entertainment would have been electrifying. Inherently it has all the elements of the exceptional motion picture. But like a fine pair of binoculars in the hands of a child, the story moves constantly in and out of focus.

It seems incredible, to me, and I say it with the utmost sincerity, that ostensibly mature minds can consistently force inane and irrelevant attempts at humor into the life blood of a smoothly running story. There are a couple of sequences in *Big Brown Eyes* that literally groan under the imbecilic dose of moronic piffle which block the filmic flow and destroy the dramatic validity. No wonder they say the things they do about Hollywood. . . . The one faint disappointment was the work of Cary Grant, who seemed slightly ill at ease as the two-fisted detective. Grant has turned in one capable performance after another. In this, he just somehow didn't click. Perhaps it is that his innate good breeding subconsciously rebels against the role of a good-natured plebian. But don't misunderstand. His portrayal offered no point for criticism; it simply had, with the exception of one scene, nothing to recommend it. But watch for his brief little impersonation of a girl friend on the make, a clever bit of pantomime.

Director Raoul Walsh did his best with what freedom was given him; and his best is plenty good. But the production as a whole just doesn't make the grade as a compactly, well woven unit. It has everything but that one subtle, all-important quality; cohesive forward movement. If you are interested in cinematic study, see it, or go if you aren't unduly particular, and want an innocuous evening's entertainment.

Paul Jacobs, *Hollywood Spectator*

# SUZY

## 1936

With Jean Harlow

**CREDITS:**

*Distributing company:* Metro-Goldwyn-Mayer. *Producing company:* Metro-Goldwyn-Mayer. *Producer:* Maurice Revnes. *Director:* George Fitzmaurice. *Assistant director:* Sandy Roth. *Screenplay:* Dorothy Parker, Alan Campbell, Horace Jackson and Lenore Coffee. *From novel by* Herbert Gorman. *Cinematography:* Ray June. *Editor:* George Boemler. *Composer:* Dr. William Axt. *Song:* "Did I Remember," Music by Walter Donaldson. Lyrics by Harold Adamson. *Art direction:* Cedric Gibbons. *Associates:* Gabriel Scognamillo and Edwin B. Willis. *Costumes:* Dolly Tree. *Sound:* Douglas Shearer. *Release date:* July 24, 1936. *Running time:* 95 minutes.

**THE CAST:**

| | |
|---|---|
| *Suzy* | Jean Harlow |
| *Terry* | Franchot Tone |
| *Andre* | Cary Grant |
| *Baron* | Lewis Stone |
| *Madame Eyrelle* | Benita Hume |
| *Captain Barsanges* | Reginald Mason |
| *Maisie* | Inez Courtney |
| *Mrs. Schmidt* | Greta Meyer |
| *"Knobby"* | David Clyde |
| *"Pop" Gaspard* | Christian Rub |
| *Gaston* | George Spelvin |
| *Landlady* | Una O'Connor |
| *Producer* | Charles Judels |
| *Revue producer* | Theodore Von Eltz |
| *Officer* | Stanley Morner |

**SYNOPSIS:**

Suzy is an American showgirl in London in 1914. She loves and marries Terry Moore, an Irish inventor. Believing that her husband is killed by a spy, Suzy flees to Paris. War breaks out. Suzy meets Andre Charville, a famous

French aviator, and marries him. Terry Moore, very much alive, comes to Paris to do some work for Andre, meets Suzy and calls her a gold-digger but does not expose their marriage. Andre is killed by the same spy, Madame Eyrelle; while Terry is on a flying mission. When Terry returns the plane to the ground, Suzy helps him put Andre's body into the plane so that others will think he was killed in combat. Andre is honored as a hero. Terry now believes Suzy and they can now start a new life together.

## REVIEWS:

All of Hollywood's other celebrated blondes having had a recent encounter with film stories involving 1914, war and spies, it now is Jean Harlow's turn to trifle dramatically with some of the minor tragedies of those days.

Metro-Goldwyn-Mayer bought Herbert Gorman's novel, *Suzy*, for Miss Harlow. Having purchased the book and become owner of the title, the studio tossed away most of the Gorman narrative, retained the title and engaged four No. 1 scenarists to do something about a story. They have. Alan Campbell, Hoarace Jackson, Dorothy Parker and Lenore Coffee, in story conference assembled, have chosen plot No. 64—the "neither maid, wife nor widow" theme—in which to dip Miss Harlow's talents.

The story has the now familiar backgrounds of Europe in 1914, its spy scenes are brightly contrived, it has a melodramatic punch of undeniable force. The ending is intelligently arrived at and is logical.

For all that the picture was made for Miss Harlow and all the important scenes are pointed in her favor, the honors for performance go mainly to Franchot Tone, as the inventor, and Cary Grant, as the French ace.

Direction by George Fitzmaurice is brilliant, and he has had the foresight to insist on new treatment for scenes which, otherwise, would be much like dozens of scenes in dozens of other spy and war films.

*Literary Digest*

Romance, drama, war, espionage, Jean Harlow, Franchot Tone, Cary Grant, ample production and the direction of George Fitzmaurice—such are the ingredients of *Suzy,* compounded on the Metro lot and soon to be turned loose on the world at large. It will give satisfaction. We could wish for less talking than it contains, and a greater reliance on the camera in developing the psychological phases of the story, but as we seem doomed to have such pictures until Hollywood learns how to use the microphone, we will be lucky if we get none less entertaining then this well-made Metro offering.

The chief merit of the excellently written script is the businesslike manner in which the story is told, the contrasting elements beings woven into an easily flowing narrative free from non-essentials. There are intensely dramatic moments as well as some melodramatic physical thrills. The picture, in fact, has something of everything in it, being fashioned in a manner that should

With Jean Harlow and Inez Courtney

With Jean Harlow and Lewis Stone

With Jean Harlow

make it satisfactory entertainment for any kind of audience, and as no picture can be better than its direction, we may credit Fitzmaurice with having done a most creditable job. Praise is due Ray June for photography of distinction.

Performances are excellent. Jean Harlow at all times is in complete command of her role which runs the gamut from light comedy to stark tragedy. I do wish, however, that they would do something with Jean's eyebrows. The thin, penciled lines, resembling eyebrows seen only in caricatures, caught my attention when first she appeared, and thereafter I could not keep my eyes off them.

Franchot Tone grows in stature with his every performance. Always the perfect gentleman, intelligent, personable, never in word or gesture does he suggest the actor. Cary Grant, too, is something more than just a leading man. Since his outstanding performance in *Sylvia Scarlett,* his talents for varied characterizations have been recognized, and in each new venture he makes good. Here we have him as a philandering aviation hero, a part to which he does full justice. Benita Hume is effective as a war spy.

The final scene in the picture as I saw it is the only story weakness. Grant has been killed and the scene shows us his funeral. We hear a long eulogy which robs the scene of the impressiveness it would have had if its treatment had been more intelligent. There is no reason why we should hear the words of praise accorded the dead hero. A long shot to establish the fact of the speech being made, appropriate music to make it reasonable we should not hear the speech, close shots to register the emotions of some of the mourners, and sympathetic camera treatment of the entire sequence, would have made it a great screen moment. We can expect such blundering just as long as producers are governed by their obsession that the microphone is their principal tool. Here they use it to commit a cinematic crime.

*Hollywood Spectator*

With Jean Harlow

96

With Jean Harlow and George Davis

# WEDDING PRESENT

1936

With Joan Bennett

## CREDITS:

*Distributing company:* Paramount Pictures. *Producing company:* Paramount Pictures. *Producer:* B. P. Schulberg. *Director:* Richard Wallace. *Assistant director:* Ray Lissner. Original by Paul Gallico. *Cinematography:* Leon Shamroy. *Editor:* Robert Bischoff. *Art direction:* Hans Dreier and Earl Hendrick. *Sound:* Jack Goodrich. *Release date:* October 9, 1936. *Running time:* 81 minutes.

## THE CAST:

| | |
|---|---|
| *Rusty* | Joan Bennett |
| *Charlie* | Cary Grant |
| *"Stagg"* | George Bancroft |
| *Dodacker* | Conrad Nagel |
| *Archduke* | Gene Lockhart |
| *"Smiles" Benson* | William Demarest |
| *Mary Lawson* | Inez Courtney |
| *Squinty* | Edward Brophy |
| *VanDorn* | Purnell Pratt |
| *Willett* | Douglas Wood |
| *Blaker* | George Meeker |
| *Laura Dodacker* | Lois Wilson |
| *Jonathan* | John Henry Allen |
| *Sammy Smith* | George Offerman, Jr. |
| *Haley* | Damon Ford |
| *German Band* | Heine Conklin |
| | Billy Engel |
| | Ray Hanson |
| *Six Reporters* | Jack Mulhall |
| | Cy Ring |
| | Charles Williams |
| | Marshall Ruth |
| | Eddie Phillips |
| | Allen Fox |

## SYNOPSIS:

Newspaperman Charlie, who takes everything that happens with a grain of salt and quite humorously, is thrust into a responsible editorial position. His scatterbrained antics drive all his erstwhile pals to distraction. But he carries things too far and causes his girlfriend Rusty to announce her engagement to stodgy Dodacker. This news drives Charlie to some real drinking. Not so much bothered about losing her, he becomes greatly concerned about sending her a suitable wedding present. He sends everything he can think of, including fire engines, police cars, hearses to the house where the wedding is to take place. Driving up in an ambulance himself, he kidnaps the amazed bride, and they ride off together in a wagon blazoned "Insane Asylum."

## REVIEWS:

It takes the final reel to save this one from developing into a complete void of entertainment. But, even that final reel hasn't enough wallop to put *Wedding Present* in the running for top position in a dual setup. About the only

Joan Bennett and George Bancroft

With William Demarest and Edward Brophy

With Joan Bennett

persons who give the impression that they feel they've really got something in this film are Cary Grant and Joan Bennett. They try hard, but the combination of story, direction and whatnot is pretty much against them.

Paul Gallico must have founded the yarn on the fabled antics of Ben Hecht and Charles MacArthur; only in this case he's mixed the sexes. His screwball star reporters, as played by Miss Bennett and Grant, are not only pitched in farfetched concepts of the craft but they're loaded down with so many and frequent shifts of mood that the task of following them is made no easy one for the average fan. When in the latter phase of the film the pace picks up perceptibly and the proceedings take on a bona fide air of farce there's lots of cause for chuckles.

First couple of reels are devoted to showing how dizzy but at the same time brilliant this news-hounding twosome can be. Next two reveal Grant going city editor, serious and stuffshirt, with the ensuing footage expatiating on his reformation, pursuit of the girl and concoction of a nightmarish gag which wins her back. Goofy as is the behavior of this twosome the real mitt for travesty goes to the director's idea of how the boys comport themselves around a city room.

Practical-joker Grant gets the job of city editor after he has driven his predecessor, George Bancroft, to hoarseness and resignation. Grant simonlegrees the city room crew and when he resents the attempt of the girl to deflate him she quits the job and goes to New York. He, out of loneliness, walks himself soon after and when he gets to New York Grant finds that the girl had engaged herself to a writer of inspiration books, Conrad Nagel. She spurns Grant's reconciliation approaches and the reporter, recalling the girl's weakness for fires and other like excitements, pulls out the town's various emergency vehicles and yeomen, including firemen and cops; all of which turns the trick. The fadeout scene has the twosome in a clinch on the roof of pickup-wagon for a psychopathic ward.

Ben Bodec, *Variety*

Newspaper work has taken it on the nose from the cinema on more than one occasion this season, but *Wedding Present* reaches a new high in factual distortion. We do not wish to destroy the 'movie' myth about journalism, but we suggest that the situations of this photo-play are implausible, dissociated, undramatic, preposterous and dreary. The film is not fortunate in its principals. Cary Grant plays the crazy reporter turned editor in a lackadaisical manner, mouthing most of his lines and acting more like a dramatic caricature than a character. If he is not walking through his lines in this production, we never saw that feat accomplished. Joan Bennett, for her part, does little to stay the complete demoralization of the plot.

Howard Barnes, *New York Herald Tribune*

With Joan Bennett

With Grace Moore

# WHEN YOU'RE IN LOVE

1937

## CREDITS:

*Distributing company:* Columbia. *Producing company:* Columbia. *Director:* Robert Riskin. *Associate producer:* Everett Riskin. *Assistant director:* Arthur S. Black. *Screenplay:* Robert Riskin. Story based on idea by Ethel Hill and Cedric Worth. *Cinematography:* Joseph Walker. *Editor:* Gene Milford. *Musical director:* Alfred Newman. *Art direction:* Stephen Goosson. *Costumes:* Bernard Newman. *Sound:* Lodge Cunningham. Production ensembles staged by Leon Leonidoff (courtesy Radio City Music Hall) *Musical credits:* "Our Song," music by Jerome Kern; "The Whistling Boy," lyrics by Dorothy Fields; "Minnie the Moocher," music by Cab Calloway, lyrics by Irving Mills and Clarence Glaskill, arrangement by Al Siegel. Release date: February 27, 1937. *Running time:* 110 minutes.

## THE CAST:

| | |
|---|---|
| *Louise Fuller* | Grace Moore |
| *Jimmy Hudson* | Cary Grant |
| *Marianne Woods* | Aline MacMahon |
| *Walter Mitchell* | Henry Stephenson |
| *Hank Miller* | Thomas Mitchell |
| *Jane Summers* | Catherine Doucet |
| *Luis Perugini* | Luis Alberni |
| *Gerald Meeker* | Gerald Oliver Smith |
| *Mrs. Hamilton* | Emma Dunn |
| *Mr. Hamilton* | George Pearce |
| *Carlos* | Frank Puglia |

## SYNOPSIS:

In Mexico, Louise Fuller managed by astute Marianne Woods but weighted down by a trio of scatterbrained sycophants Jane Summers, Luis Perugini and Gerald Meeker, wants to get into the United States to sing at a music festival of her old maestro, Walter Mitchell. Jimmy Hudson is a wealthy tramp artist waiting in the border town. Marianne Woods, in order to get her protege across

With Grace Moore

With William Pawley and Don Rowan

With Harry Holman and Pat West

the border, arranges a marriage and quick divorce for Louise and Jimmy. The ceremony is something new in weddings, and husband and wife immediately go their own separate ways.

Later when Jimmy invades his wife's domicile to decry the trio of leeches still hanging onto her, Louise's adamant spirit gives way to a bit of affection and she accompanies Jimmy for a nocturnal ride to his farm house, where true love is born. Louise, at first promises to go away with him, but remembering her debt to Mr. Mitchell leaves, announcing she will divorce Jimmy. At the concert, Louise is unhappy and unable to go on, until Jimmy comes backstage and drives her out onto the stage. It is then she realizes his love for her.

**REVIEWS:**

When you're in love with an itinerant brush wielder whose greatest joy in life is operatic records, beautiful sunsets, and giving away ten-thousand-dollar masterpieces, life is a trying experience, even to so lovely a person as Grace Moore. In this, her latest picture, she is an Australian singer, who overstays her permit in Mexico, and is consequently detained by the United States immigration officials. Her distress is heightened by the fact that

With George Pierce and Emma Dunn

she must return to America in time to sing at her dear Uncle Walter's song festival. She appeals for help to artist Cary Grant, an independent young man who frowns on the weak-willed diva's foibles, but decides to take pity on her. Two thousand dollars, a promise of five thousand more, and a dawning love help persuade him to solve the difficulty by marrying her. He almost succeeds in ruining the festival completely by presenting her with a divorce just before she is to appear on the stage, but all ends well, of course. The lovers are reunited, Grace brings down the house with applause, and makes her dear uncle's festival a success. The picture is a worthy successor to the long line of Grace Moore triumphs. Her rendition of "Minnie the Moocher" is alone worth the price of admission.

*Scholastic Magazine*

The picture marks the debut of Robert Riskin, long famed as the screenwriting teammate of Director Frank Capra, as a director as well as author. Following the pattern of *It Happened One Night* and *Mr. Deeds Goes to Town* in which Director Capra established Clark Gable and Gary Cooper as comedians, Director Riskin herein does the same thing for Cary Grant.

*Time Magazine*

With Gerald Oliver-Smith, Luis Alberni and Catherine Doucet

With Grace Moore

With Grace Moore and Squeezit

103

# RICHES AND ROMANCE

1937

With Mary Brian

## CREDITS:

*Distributing company:* Grand National. *Producing company:* Garrett Klement Pictures. *Producer:* Alfred Zeisler. *Director:* Alfred Zeisler. *Production manager:* Frank Mills. *Adaptation:* John L. Balderston. From a story by E. Phillips Oppenheim. *Cinematography:* Otto Heller. *Art direction:* David Rawnsley. *Recordist:* A. J. Bronker. *Dialogue director:* Charles Lincoln. *Release date:* March 6, 1937 (U.S.A.); was released in Great Britain in 1936. *Running time:* 70 minutes.

## THE CAST:

| | |
|---|---|
| *Ernest Bliss* | Cary Grant |
| *Frances* | Mary Brian |
| *Sir James Aldroyd* | Peter Gawthorne |
| *Lord Honiton* | Henry Kendall |
| *Dorrington* | Leon M. Lion |
| *Masters* | John Turnbull |
| *Crawley* | Arthur Hardy |
| *Clare* | Iris Ashley |
| *The Buyer* | Garry Marsh |
| *Giuseppe* | Andrea Malandrinos |
| *Montague* | Alfred Wellesley |
| *Mrs. Heath* | Marie Wright |
| *Mrs. Mott* | Buena Bent |
| *Scales* | Charles Farrell |
| *Bill Bronson* | Hal Gordon |
| *Clowes* | Quinton MacPherson |

## SYNOPSIS:

Ernest Bliss, who has inherited £2,000,000 consults a doctor and is told he is suffering from underwork. Stung, he wagers £50,000 that he will earn his own living for

104

a year, using none of his fortune for himself. Before he finds a job as an oven salesman he gets well over the hunger line, and is helped by a goodnatured landlady.

He puts over the oven business by a free meals stunt, but has to quit when a partnership is offered him. As porter to a woman market gardener, he runs against a returned husband. As chauffeur, he receives the unusual offer from some crooks, which ends in a big fight and the smashing of his own furniture.

Maintaining through various hardships his love affair with the secretary encountered in his first job he voluntarily breaks the terms of the wager a few days before he would win it, when he finds that she is going to marry her employer in order to provide a home for a sick sister. Prominent at the wedding are the curiously assorted friends he has made in the slums.

## REVIEWS:

It is not really as amazing as all that. All that Mr. Bliss sets out do to is what millions of people are doing all the time without considering it anything out of the ordinary—that is, living on what they can earn. Ernest Bliss, poor fellow, was one of those unfortunate young millionaires who appear to regard money with the same moroseness with which normal people regard bills. The thought of so much wealth made Ernest quite ill, and Harley Street was consulted. Harley Street, in the person of Sir James Aldroyd (Mr. Peter Gawthorne) states that there is nothing organically wrong and that the best thing Mr. Bliss can do is to disappear for a year and earn his own living. Not, Sir James adds with venom, that Mr. Bliss will take the advice, which will cost him 25 guineas. Thank you. The challenge, is of course, accepted and in a moment or two we have Ernest selling gas-ovens, helping in a green-grocer's shop—there is a splendid scene of a free-fight in Covent Garden—meeting bullying employers, soft-hearted landladies, and falling in love with Frances (Miss Mary Brian), the secretary of the "gas-oveners". It is all entertaining enough in its own simple, unpretentious way, and Mr. Cary Grant helps it along with a smooth and tactful performance. His Ernest, once he is separated from his money, is a cheerful and likable young man, and it is nice to feel that once the year is up he will look upon his current account with a kindlier eye, be able to marry Frances, and give a lovely party for the dear old landlady and all the other dear old people he comes across. Not amazing, but amusing.

*The Times* (London)

E. Phillips Oppenheim's story (filmed years ago as a silent) is a bit old-fashioned and present-day filmgoers may regard it as implausible. Coincidences are highly improbable, and the whole thing, despite excellent direction and acting, moves at a pace that demands a large measure of cutting before being offered to the general public. Implausibilities include an elderly lodging house keeper who refuses to oust a man from his room, despite arrears of rent, when she could get cash from someone else. Also encountering his former gold-digger mistress who, finding him working as a chauffeur, deliberately leaves her diamond bracelet in his car.

In the end everything comes out all right, of course, and he is enabled to provide liberally for all those who were kind to him during his self-imposed poverty.

There is a mechanical progression in the photographic sequences which lacks credence, but this may be fixed by cutting, thereby speeding up the movement towards the story's culmination.

Cary Grant looks and acts the part with deft characterization. He secures laughs easily and apparently without effort. Mary Brian plays the role of the typist with a metallic harshness which would be more in keeping with the gold-digger. One expects more feminine softness and sympathy from such a role. Most of the other actors and actresses are adequate, and production details are very good.

Joshua Lowe, *Variety*

With Mary Brian and Andrea Malandrinos

# TOPPER

## 1937

With Roland Young and Constance Bennett

## CREDITS:

*Distributing company:* Metro-Goldwyn-Mayer. *Producing company:* Hal Roach. *Director:* Norman Z. McLeod. *Associate producer:* Milton H. Bren. *Screenplay:* Jack Jerne, Eric Hatch, and Eddie Moran. From a story by Thorne Smith. *Cinematography:* Norbert Brodine. *Photographic effects:* Roy Seawright. Musical arrangements by Arthur Morton. "Old Man Moon" by Hoagy Carmichael. *Release date:* July 16, 1937. *Running time:* 98 minutes.

## THE CAST:

| | |
|---|---|
| *Marion Kerby* | Constance Bennett |
| *George Kerby* | Cary Grant |
| *Cosmo Topper* | Roland Young |
| *Mrs. Topper* | Billie Burke |
| *Wilkins* | Alan Mowbray |

| | |
|---|---|
| *Casey* | Eugene Pallette |
| *Elevator Boy* | Arthur Lake |
| *Mrs. Stuyvesant* | Hedda Hopper |
| *Miss Johnson* | Virginia Sale |
| *Hotel manager* | Theodore Von Eltz |
| *Policeman* | J. Farrell McDonald |
| *Secretary* | Elaine Shepard |
| *"Three Hits and a Miss"* | Themselves |

## SYNOPSIS:

Cosmo Topper is a wealthy, but henpecked banker whose principal stockholder and his wife are wild young sophisticates living from drink to drink. They die in a motor wreck and return, in the flesh or invisibly at will, to accomplish as their redeeming deed the domestic emancipation of Topper. Their appearances and disappearances in hotel, restaurants, streets, automobiles, elevators, with

With Constance Bennett

With Billie Burke and Alan Mowbray

With Roland Young and Constance Bennett

With Roland Young and Constance Bennett

and without the more or less consenting objective of their ministrations, creates fights, panics and general consternation. When they have accomplished their purpose they say goodbye to Mr. Topper and disappear into whatever may be presumed to be their final abode.

**REVIEWS:**

Thorne Smith fans will be delighted to learn that Culver City studio has again gone stark looney. This one is about the gay couple who wander about upsetting mortals after they've been killed in a motor accident. Though it will hardly influence cinema history, *Topper* comes off a lot better than *Night Life of the Gods,* MGM's other attempt to plant the novelist's insanity on a screen.

Ghosts are far more amenable to camera tricks, of course, than walking statues. The now-you-see-me-now-you-don't theme is paradise to a photographer. It is thoroughly disconcerting to Mr. Topper, the timid banker whom the Kerbys propose to liberate from a nagging wife and humdrum career.

The giddy rigmarole is for those who can take their death ribald and their fantasy straight. Constance Bennett and Cary Grant are suitable as Kerbys. But it is Roland Young's show. Between the capricious antics of his abstract companions and the carping of Billie Burke as his wife, his talent for being harassed finds exquisite expression.

*Literary Digest*

Devotees of the farcical, fantastic and slightly Rabelaisian novels of Thorne Smith will recognize in *Topper* the skeleton of one of his better-known works, *The Jovial Ghosts.* Like most stories adapted for the screen, it has undergone many changes. For the censor's sake, much of the dialogue and nearly all the more important incidents have been excised, and a moral—rather a perfunctory moral indeed—has been appended. The result may not be Thorne Smith, but it is certainly highly amusing, and should offend no susceptibilities in its treatment of a somewhat delicate subject.

Two Bright Young People, pleasant enough, but too wealthy and only on pleasure bent, are killed in a motor smash. They find themselves still in existence, although far less material as they have only a limited amount of ectoplasm with which to become visible. Overwhelmed with a desire to do the one good deed they failed to achieve in life, they turn their attentions to a respectable and henpecked bank-manager in order to free him from his humdrum inhibitions. This good deed involves making him drunk and getting him into various highly compromising situations, which are exploited with all the ingenuity made possible by the fact that the couple can appear or vanish at will. Their work accomplished in the bank-manager's return to a repentant and loving wife, they vanish for ever, presumably into a special paradise for fluffy-minded mischief-makers.

The possibilities for farcical episodes are of course endless, and the trick-work is brilliant throughout. Fortunately, however, the fun is by no means mechanical; Constance Bennett and Cary Grant make an attractive pair of phantoms, and Eugene Pallette, as a harassed house-detective, has his best part since *The Ghost Goes West*. But above them all is Roland Young—the half-willing victim of the ghostly experiment. His performance really makes the film. The epitome of meiosis, he undergoes the most astonishing supernatural adventures with the utmost tact and good breeding. To see him, as the champagne fumes mount steadily into his well-arranged head, perform a licentious little dance with his respectably-clad feet while his torso remains magnificently aloof in the depths of a lounge chair, is an object lesson in controlled lunacy.

It may be sensible to reiterate that the film is essentially harmless and unobjectionable. The dialogue is quietly amusing rather than brilliantly witty, and contains the finest conversation ever recorded between a butler (Alan Mowbray) and his mistress (Billie Burke). On further thought, it is difficult to discern whether there is a moral to the film after all, but it cleverly gives the impression that there is one.

Basil Wright, *The Spectator*

With Eugene Pallette and Constance Bennett

With Hoagy Carmichael, George Humbert and Constance Bennett

# TOAST OF NEW YORK

1937

With Donald Meek and Edward Arnold

## CREDITS:

*Distributing company:* RKO Radio. *Producing company:* RKO Radio. *Producer:* An Edward Small Production. *Director:* Rowland V. Lee. *Screenplay:* Dudley Nichols, John Twist, and Joel Sayre. From *Book of Daniel Drew* by Bouck White and *Robber Barons* by Matthew Josephson. *Cinematography:* Peverell Marley. *Editor:* George Hively. *Musical director:* Nathaniel Shilkret. *Release date:* July 30, 1937. *Running time:* 109 minutes.

## THE CAST:

| | |
|---|---|
| *Jim Fisk* | Edward Arnold |
| *Nick Boyd* | Cary Grant |
| *Josie Mansfield* | Frances Farmer |
| *Luke* | Jack Oakie |
| *Daniel Drew* | Donald Meek |
| *Fleurigue* | Thelma Leeds |

| | |
|---|---|
| *Vanderbilt* | Clarence Kolb |
| *Photographer* | Billy Gilbert |
| *Broker* | George Irving |
| *Lawyers* | Frank M. Thomas, Russell Hicks |
| *Wallack* | Oscar Apfel |
| *President of the Board* | Lionel Belmore |
| *Bellhop* | Robert McClung |
| *Janitor* | Robert Dudley |
| *Beef Dooley* | Dewey Robinson |
| *Top Sergeant* | Stanley Fields |
| *Major* | Gavin Gordon |
| *Mary Lou* | Joyce Compton |
| *Virginia Lee* | Virginia Carroll |

## SYNOPSIS:

Jim Fisk begins as a medicine-show impressario in the South at the outbreak of the Civil War. Sending one of his two partners North to open an office, he takes the

110

other with him into the South and for four years smuggles cotton at an immense profit, which vanishes when the northern partner invests it in Confederate bonds. Bluffing with these, he contrives to obtain a controlling interest in the Erie Railroad and dispose of it at a profit of a half million dollars. Operating in the market with this stock, he becomes famous as a financial wizard and his wealth multiplies. He falls in love with an actress, who accepts his gifts and his backing in a show, although she is in love and loved by his partner. When his depredations bring poverty to small investors, the press attacks him. At the opening of the show he is publicly denounced and determines forthwith to corner the country's gold supply and raise himself beyond the reach of criticism. His partner joins forces with Vanderbilt and opposes him in his move, but only the intervention of the federal government thwarts him. A mob marches on his house, and he is killed by an assassin's bullet.

his booming laugh rocks New York and his jewels drown his actress-mistress, Josie Mansfield, played by Frances Farmer, last seen in *Come and Get It*. She sings that new hit, "The First Time I Saw You." The scenarists have given Fisk two fictitious partners, Cary Grant for love-interest and Jack Oakie for comedy.

The Fort Taylor Episode, Pike's Opera House, and Black Friday are historically accurate, though no one today will believe it. When the Commodore can no longer absorb the watered stock Fisk kept grinding out (Fisk once said publicly, "If this printing press don't break down, I'll be damned if I won't give the old hog all he wants of Erie!") he has an injunction issued for the arrests of Drew and Fisk. They escape to New Jersey where they take over Taylor Hotel, changing its name to Fort Taylor, if you please, and guarding themselves and ten million in cash with militiamen from the regiment in which Fisk had bought himself a colonelship.

## REVIEWS:

Its boisterous charm crackles from the first sequence when Jim Fisk is only a medicine show faker indulging his embryonic financial genius in the sale of soap. Methods are questionable and sales healthy. Neither are more than a bare hint of Erie stock speculations to come.

The film is a romanticized biography of Jim Fisk, whose actual life needs editing in the interest of the Hayes Office rather than of pungent movie material. Into his meteoric and ruthless career is woven a picture of American fortunes in the making, of Wall Street in the 'Sixties' when it was as lusty as the gold towns and as glamorous as Vienna.

Such a panorama is good sport—and unusual. Uncle Dan'l Drew, Commodore Vanderbilt, Fisk, Gould and the rest have received scant attention from the purveyors of entertainment. Yet, in the words of Charles and Mary Beard, "To draw the American scene as it was unfolded between the Civil War and the end of the nineteenth Century, without these dominant figures looming in the foreground, is to make a shadow picture."

Matthew Josephson's *The Robber Barons* and Bouck White's *The Book of Daniel Drew* provided the source material for the celluloid version of Dudley Nichols, John Twist, and Joel Sayre. Bowdlerized though it is, *The Toast of New York* still looks like the year's most extravagant burlesque.

Into this slapstick era of high finance Edward Arnold walks as Jim Fisk. People who found his Jim Brady too lovable will say he was specially created for this role. Fisk's generosity and popularity are as celebrated as his deft manipulation of stock. In such a role, Arnold's talents are lavish and exact. The same goes for little Donald Meek, who must have been waiting all his life to play the penny-pinching, God-fearing hypocrite, Daniel Drew, and Clarence Kolb, who shakes a turbulent Vanderbilt fist before his fine Vanderbilt profile.

When Fisk is not outwitting Uncle Dan'l's Erie control,

With Frances Farmer and Edward Arnold

With Jack Oakie, Edward Arnold and Frances Farmer

Hollywood never invented offices more dazzling than those Fisk subsequently sets up on the second floor of Pike's Opera House, where the irrepressible Jim abandons Erie puddles to make himself bigger than the very government. His attempt to corner the gold market culminates in the famous Black Friday of 1869.

Inaccuracies of detail must be forgiven Rowland V. Lee's charming expose of old New York and the lawless vigor of its leading citizens. Movie-goers, except a few of Wall Street's dearest families, may even hope that this is the first in a film cycle dedicated to Jay Gould, the Commodore himself, the elder Morgan, the first Rockefeller and the rest of Mr. Josephson's much publicized Robber Barons.

*Literary Digest*

This film is chiefly noteworthy for the rounded characterization of an early American individualist which Edward Arnold adds to his fine gallery of screen portraits, and, more than the careful and authentic reconstruction of old New York, his performance conveys the spirit of the time in which this historical drama is laid. It is the story of Jim Fisk who drops his medicine-show business at the opening of the Civil War to prosper at cotton smuggling and go on to the higher gamble of the stock market. Attacked by the press as an Ogre feeding on small investors, he conveives the gigantic scheme of cornering the nation's gold and enters upon a financial struggle with Cornelius Vanderbilt. Balked in this dream and disappointed in love, his strange career is abruptly closed by mob violence. The direction of Rowland V. Lee is turned toward a large scale portrait which will serve for all the robber barons of our checkered post-Civil War industrialism. Frances Farmer Cary Grant and Donald Meek lend support and Jack Oakie provides more than one man's share of comedy. The production is faultless and the morality of great wealth is a timely subject of discussion, so adults will undoubtedly find this production much to their liking.

Thomas J. Fitzmorris, *America*

Cover of sheet music for song "The First Time I Saw You," sung in *The Toast of New York*

With Mitchell Harris, Paul Staton and Irene Dunne

# THE AWFUL TRUTH

1937

**CREDITS:**

*Distributing company:* Columbia Pictures. *Producing company:* Columbia Pictures. *Director:* Leo McCarey. *Associate producer:* Everett Riskin. *Assistant director:* William Mull. *Screenplay:* Vina Delmar. *Story:* Arthur Richmond. *Cinematography:* Joseph Walker. *Editor:* Al Clark. *Composer:* Ben Oakland. *Lyrics:* Milton Drake. *Interior decorations:* Babs Johnstone. *Costumes:* Kalloch. *Sound:* Ed Bernds. *Release date:* October 21, 1937. *Running time:* 89 minutes.

**THE CAST:**

| | |
|---|---|
| *Lucy Warriner* | Irene Dunne |
| *Jerry Warriner* | Cary Grant |
| *Daniel Leeson* | Ralph Bellamy |
| *Armand Duvalle* | Alexander D'Arcy |
| *Aunt Patsy* | Cecil Cunningham |
| *Barbara Vance* | Marguerite Churchill |
| *Mrs. Leeson* | Esther Dale |
| *Toots Binswanger* (Dixie Belle Lee) | Joyce Compton |
| *Frank Randall* | Robert Allen |
| *Mr. Vance* | Robert Warwick |
| *Mrs. Vance* | Mary Forbes |
| *Lord Fabian* | Claud Allister |
| *Lady Fabian* | Zita Moulton |

**SYNOPSIS:**

Jerry Warriner pretends a harmless vacation in Florida, but stays in New York City playing cards with "the boys". He goes under a sun lamp to get a fake tan to make it appear he had been south. When he returns home, his wife Lucy is out, but returns shortly accompanied by a handsome voice teacher, Armand. Since neither believes

With Irene Dunne

With Miki Morita

With Alan Bridge, Edgar Dearing and Irene Dunne

114

the other's story, they decide to get divorced. There is a dispute over the ownership of Asta, the pet dog. Although Lucy wins custody, Jerry gets visiting rights. Jerry resumes his acquaintance with night club entertainer, Dixie Belle Lee, while Lucy is befriended by a wealthy oil heir, Daniel Leeson.

Lucy asks Armand to help her straighten out her argument with Jerry. Then Jerry suddenly shows up, exercising his visiting rights. She hides Armand in her bedroom before she lets Jerry in. Then Leeson arrives, and she hides Jerry in the same bedroom. The furore that results angers Leeson and he leaves. Jerry then becomes engaged to Barbara Vance, a socialite. When Lucy hears of this, she crashes a party, pretends to be Jerry's sister and feigns a drunken display, which forces Jerry to escort her from the party. Lucy still pretending to be drunk, gets Jerry to drive her to a mountain cabin and there finally they decide to patch up things.

## REVIEWS:

The season's smartest drawing-room comedy arrives unheralded, to run faster, funnier and finer than any of the all too many widely ballyhooed farces immediately preceding. Every contributor to this film stands high in accomplishment, from the ideally executed performances of Irene Dunne, Cary Grant, Ralph Bellamy and Alexander Darcy, to Leo McCarey's direction, second to none in the rare field of good comedy, and to the screen writing of Vina Delmar, who brings Arthur Richman's play of fifteen years ago to the screen without loss of verve and with gain of freshness.

James P. Cunningham, *The Commonweal*

*The Awful Truth* is one of those mile-a-minute comedies which never makes sense but which makes you giggle outrageously. At the beginning Irene Dunne and Cary Grant are a young married couple on the verge of divorce; but they soon prove to be a couple of cut-ups who delight in bedeviling each other. A great many funny things happen, most of which are maneuvered, to some extent, by Mr. Smith. He is the biggest bone of contention. Mr. Smith is a Scottish terrier.

The dialogue is snappy, the action fast, and often furious, and Irene Dunne proves herself better as a comedienne than as the beautiful-but-dignified star she once was.

*Scholastic Magazine*

The funniest picture of the season is called *The Awful Truth*. Leo McCarey's version of one of the oldest theatrical hats—the divorced pair who come to realize that marriage was nice work after all, if you could get back—seems to be a true director's triumph. Take this story and any actors and you could so easily get something that would serve you right; take these actors (Cary Grant, Irene Dunne, Ralph Bellamy) in any story, and you could get the same results or worse. But that is only speculation, what we actually have is thorough comedy, a whole pattern that is neither actor's vehicle nor technician's holiday. It is quite grown up, and even the hotter passions are endured with consideration and suavity; at the same time it has an innocent zest for the homely that makes you think back to Capra again.

Miss Dunne is getting a divorce from Cary Grant at the beginning, she can't *stand* that man, and presently she is taking up with Ralph Bellamy, who apparently plays a perfect Good Time Charley from the long timber without realizing it much. She keeps running into Mr. Grant, who is killingly polite about everything, even Charley and his mother—much more helpful than is necessary, and perhaps a shade too apt in showing up at the wrong times. This keeps going on, and there is a nance music teacher who makes a lot of trouble for his size and talent, a sour aunt and something about some motorcycle cops. I can't remember very clearly what they did because I was laughing and everybody was laughing and it kept going on like that.

The dialogue is good, clever or uproarious; but dialogue fades so quickly in the air, and here there is the necessary visual play to complement it. For one example from the whole picture, take the closing sequence, with the weakened latched door between their private rooms, his coaxing the rising breeze through the window to blow it open, stealthily adding the weight of his fingers, finally getting down to peer under it for obstructions and (from the other side) the girl lying awake and listening, suddenly the cat getting up and walking off in her private way, letting the door open on him kneeling there in the most ludicrous flannel nightgown. All this without a word, all clear and (in its small way) exquisitely final.

It is simply that way all through, gay and ridiculous, but too serenely founded in the commonplaces of actual life, to be confused with the more irritated humorous intentions of those who rack their brains for gags, falls, punch lines and the cake-dough blackout. It is a foolishness that doesn't go wrong or strained, and for this the script men must be partly responsible. In the general taste, motion and final pictorial result, above all in a sense of timing that is as delicate and steady as a metronome, you can see the hands of a man who is sufficiently an artist in movies so that he can make one out of almost anything, with almost anybody.

Otis Ferguson, *The New Republic*

With Irene Dunne

With Irene Dunne

With Katharine Hepburn and Asta

# BRINGING UP BABY

1938

## CREDITS:

Produced and distributed by RKO Radio. *Producer:* Howard Hawks. *Director:* Howard Hawks. *Associate producer:* Cliff Reid. *Assistant director:* Edward Donahue. *Screenplay:* Dudley Nichols, and Hager Wilde. From a story by Hager Wilde. *Cinematography:* Russell Metty. *Special effects:* Vernon L. Walker. *Editor:* George Hively. *Musical director:* Roy Webb. *Art direction:* Van Nest Polglase; *Associate:* Perry Ferguson. *Costumes:* Howard Greer. *Release date:* February 18, 1938. *Running time:* 102 minutes.

## THE CAST:

| | |
|---|---|
| *Susan* | Katharine Hepburn |
| *David Huxley* | Cary Grant |
| *Major Horace Applegate* | Charles Ruggles |
| *Slocum* | Walter Catlett |
| *Mr. Gogarty* | Barry Fitzgerald |
| *Aunt Elizabeth* | May Robson |
| *Dr. Lehmann* | Fritz Feld |
| *Mrs. Gogarty* | Leona Roberts |
| *Mr. Peabody* | George Irving |
| *Mrs. Lehmann* | Tala Birrell |
| *Alice Swallow* | Virginia Walker |
| *Elmer* | John Kelly |

## SYNOPSIS:

David, a young scientist, is anxious to get an endowment of $1,000,000 for his museum, and to marry his assistant, who aids him in his research. However, he meets Susan, a rich young girl, who, anxious to help him, mires him further in difficulties with the attorney representing the possible donor. She forces him,

With Katharine Hepburn

With Katharine Hepburn

With Charles Ruggles, May Robson, Katharine Hepburn and Asta

With Katharine Hepburn

With Katharine Hepburn and Walter Catlett

through the stratagem of a tame leopard, into accompanying her to her aunt's farm in Connecticut where Asta, the dog, steals the fossilized bone David needed to complete the skeleton of a dinosaur. Hunting for the bone, the escape of the tame leopard, the escape of a vicious leopard from a zoo wagon, and suspicion by the local police that Susan, David and her aunt are insane, causes many complications that take time to unravel.

## REVIEWS:

When she was college girl ten years ago, red-headed, Melpomene-mouthed Katharine Hepburn, in a trailing white nightgown cross-hatched with gold ribbon, regaled Bryn Mawr as Pandora in *The Woman in the Moon*. And since then most of Actress Hepburn's public appearances have been for the catch-in-the-throat cinema, playing alternately great ladies and emotional starvelings of brittle bravado. For *Bringing Up Baby* she plumps her broad A in the midst of a frantically farcical plot involving Actor Cary Grant, a terrier, a leopard, a Brontosaurus skeleton and a crotchety collection of Connecticut quidnuncs, proves she can be as amusingly skittery a comedienne as the best of them.

Actor Grant is an earnest, bespectacled paleontologist who is more interested in an intercostal clavicle for his nearly reconstructed Brontosaurus than he is in bony, scatterbrained Miss Hepburn. Miss Hepburn has a pet leopard named Baby, and an aunt with $1,000,000 waiting for the right museum. On the trail of the million, Actor Grant crosses paths with Actress Hepburn and Baby, loses the scent in the tangled Connecticut wildwood. In the jail of a town very like arty Westport, the trails collide. Most surprising scene: Actress Hepburn, dropping her broad A for a nasal Broadway accent, knocking Town Constable Walter Catlett an Jailmate Grant completely off balance with: "Hey, flatfoot! I'm gonna unbutton my puss and shoot the woiks. An' I wouldn' be squealin' if he hadn' a give me the runaround for another twist."

Under the deft, directorial hand of Howard Hawks, *Bringing Up Baby* comes off second only to last year's whimsical high spot, *The Awful Truth,* but its gaily inconsequent situations cannot match the fuselike fatality of that extraordinary picture. *Bringing Up Baby's* slapstick is irrational, rough-and-tumble, undignified, obviously devised with the idea that the cinemaudience will enjoy (as it does) seeing stagy Actress Hepburn get a proper mussing up.

*Time*

In view of the heavy thought that has recently gone into the question Is Humor Best For Us? I am happy to report that *Bringing Up Baby* is funny from the word go, that it has no other meaning to recommend it, nor therapeutic qualities, and that I wouldn't swap it for practically any three things of the current season. For comedy to be really good, of course, there is required something more in the way of total design than any random collection of hilarities. There must be point—not *a* point to be *made,*

With Katharine Hepburn

which is the easy goal of any literary tortoise, but a point from which to start, as implicit throughout as the center of a circle. *Bringing Up Baby* has something of the sort. The actual story goes into the troubles of a paleontologist who first offends a prospective angel for his museum, then his fiancee, and then gets into the wild-goose affairs of a girl and her leopard and terrier and other family members, ending up in jail and of course in love. That could be done in two reels. What puts the dramatic spirit into it is the character of the harebrained young thing who gets him mixed up in all this.

Katharine Hepburn builds the part from the ground, breathless, sensitive, headstrong, triumphant in illogic and serene in that bounding brassy nerve possible only to the very very well bred. Without the intelligence and mercury of such a study, the callous scheming of this bit of fluff would have left all in confusion and the audience howling for her blood. As it is, we merely accept and humor her, as one would a wife. Cary Grant does a nice job of underlining the situation; there is good support from Barry Fitzgerald, Walter Catlett, May Robson (the leopard was better than any of them, but is it art?). The film holds together by virtue of constant invention and surprise in the situations; and Howard Hawks's direction, though it could have been less heavy and more supple, is essentially that of film comedy. All of which could be elaborated, techniques analyzed, points cited, etc. But why? *Bringing Up Baby* is hardly a departure; it settles nothing; it is full of an easy inviting humor. So do you want to go or don't you.

Otis Ferguson, *The New Republic*

119

# HOLIDAY

1938

With Doris Nolan

## CREDITS:

*Distributing company:* Columbia Pictures. *Producer:* Everett Riskin. *Director:* George Cukor. *Assistant director:* Clifford Broughton. Original play by Philip Barry. *Screenplay:* Donald Ogden Stewart and Sidney Buchman. *Cinematography:* Franz Planer. *Editors:* Otto Meyer and Al Clark. *Musical director:* Morris Stoloff. *Release date:* June 15, 1938. *Running time:* 94 minutes.

## THE CAST:

| | |
|---|---|
| *Linda Seton* | Katharine Hepburn |
| *Johnny Case* | Cary Grant |
| *Julia Seton* | Doris Nolan |
| *Ned Seton* | Lew Ayres |
| *Nick Potter* | Edward Everett Horton |
| *Edward Seton* | Henry Kolker |
| *Laura Cram* | Binnie Barnes |
| *Susan Potter* | Jean Dixon |
| *Seton Cram* | Henry Daniell |

## SYNOPSIS:

Johnny Case decides to take time out from working hard to see the world around him. He becomes engaged to Julia Seton, a blonde of exalted financial and social position, who attempts to make him conform. But Johnny becomes restless. He finds a kindred soul in Linda Seton, Julia's sister. Linda falls in love with him but hides her feelings for him. After some family arguments, Julia and Johnny realize they are not suited to each other and break

With Katharine Hepburn

With Doris Nolan and Katharine Hepburn

With Henry Kolker and Katharine Hepburn

With Katharine Hepburn

their engagement. Johnny leaves, but Linda now declares her love for him and goes off with him.

**REVIEWS:**

When Philip Barry's *Holiday* was produced on Broadway in 1928, Hope Williams took the comedy's outstanding role, that of Linda Seton. Her understudy was an unknown, inexperienced actress named Katharine Hepburn. For two years Miss Hepburn marked time offstage, waiting for her chance. It never came. In 1930 the play was filmed. This time Ann Harding was Linda. Now Columbia's refilming of *Holiday* gives Katharine Hepburn her first chance at the coveted role that seems made to order for her.

The first screen *Holiday* was an almost literal transcription of the play. The modern version, brilliantly adapted by Donald Ogden Stewart and Sidney Buchman, is equally faithful, forwarding its slight story almost entirely by conversation. But it is superb conversation—part of it Barry's own, the rest brought up to date with significant and satiric topical allusions.

With Edward Everett Horton, Jean Dixon, Henry Kolker, Doris Nolan and Katharine Hepburn

122

Directed by George Cukor, the story resolves the triangle with an intelligence and penetrating humor that give an excellent cast a field day. Henry Kolker, Lew Ayres, Jean Dixon, and Edward Everett Horton are outstanding in lesser roles; Cary Grant again turns in a smooth performance of the type that has made him one of Hollywood's most-sought-after leading men.

It is more to the point that Katharine Hepburn gives one of the most successful characterizations of her screen career. Several weeks ago the Independent Theatre Owners Association attacked a batch of high-salaried stars which it considered on the skids to oblivion. Miss Hepburn was one of them. At the time, Jack Cohn, vice-president of Columbia, rallied to her defense. Now he is turning the association's attack to his own ends. The advertising campaign for *Holiday* will sound one note across the country—"Is it true what they say about Hepburn?" Judging from the film, the producer knew the answer in advance.

*Newsweek*

The lack of this warmth and simple feeling is one of the reasons, just one of the reasons, why George Cukor's version of *Holiday* is so mechanical and shrill as comedy or anything else. There are probably more good things about it than I will ever report justly to you—fun and tears in the playroom, E. E. Horton playing straight for a change, some bright jibes, the good Cary Grant and Lew Ayres—simply because the more specious it appeared, the more I noticed and resented Katharine being Hepburn till it hurt, and the Stewart-Buchman writing job that encouraged her in this to points where, that flat metallic voice is driven into your head like needles. I suppose actually it is a neat and sometimes elegant job, but under its surface of too much brightness and too many words it seems so deadly bored and weary. Hell, save your money and yawn at home.

Otis Ferguson, *The New Republic*

With Jean Dixon, Katharine Hepburn, Lew Ayres and Edward Everett Horton

With Doris Nolan and Katharine Hepburn

123

With Ann Evers, Joan Fontaine
and Douglas Fairbanks, Jr.

# GUNGA DIN

1939

**CREDITS:**

Produced and distributed by RKO Radio. *Producer:* Pandro S. Berman in charge of production. *Director:* George Stevens. *Assistant director:* Edward Killy and Dewey Starkey inspired by Rudyard Kipling's poem 'Gunga Din." *Screenplay:* Joel Sayre and Fred Guiol. Story by Ben Hecht and Charles MacArthur. *Cinematography:* John H. August. *Special effects:* Vernon L. Walker. *Editors:* Henry Berman and John Lockert. *Composer:* Alfred Newman. *Art direction:* Van Nest Polglase; *Associate:* Perry Ferguson. *Set decorations:* Dorrell Silvera. *Costumes:* Edward Stevenson. *Sound:* John E. Tribly and James Stewart. *Technical advisors:* Sir Robert Erskine Holland, Captain Clive Morgan, and Sergeant-Major William Briers. *Release date:* February 17, 1939. *Running time:* 117 minutes.

**THE CAST:**

| | |
|---|---|
| *Cutter* | Cary Grant |
| *MacChesney* | Victor McLaglen |
| *Ballantine* | Douglas Fairbanks, Jr. |
| *Gunga Din* | Sam Jaffe |
| *Guru* | Eduardo Ciannelli |
| *Emmy* | Joan Fontaine |
| *Colonel Weed* | Montague Love |
| *Higginbotham* | Robert Coote |
| *Chota* | Abner Biberman |
| *Major Mitchell* | Lumsden Hare |

**SYNOPSIS:**

British troops are stationed in the mountainous area

With Montague Love, Lumsen Hare, Victor McLaglen and Douglas Fairbanks, Jr.

With Douglas Fairbanks, Jr., Victor McLaglen and Joan Fontaine

With Ann Evers and Olin Francis

125

of India. Three sergeants, Cutter, MacChesney, and Ballantine, although good soldiers, are always playing jokes on each other. An outstation is attacked by natives and everyone killed. The sergeants are sent on the mission to determine what happened when all communication is cut off. Later the three in their adventures discover a temple hidden in the mountains where a large number of natives belonging to a Thuggee cult listen to their leader and plan to destroy the British troops in the area. The three sergeants along with their water-carrier, Gunga Din are taken prisoners. They are tortured, but then escape to the dome of the temple where by holding the cult-leader prisoner, they are able to hold off his men. At that moment the British troops approach the area, not knowing they are marching into a trap. Although badly wounded, Gunga Din climbs the dome of the temple, and blows a bugle-call warning the troops and saving the army from massacre. The British troops subdue the natives, and the three sergeants are rescued. Gunga Din, having died a hero, is given full honors.

## REVIEWS:

Since Rudyard Kipling's death in 1936, three of his stories—"Captains Courageous," "Toomai of the Elephants" *(Elephant Boy)*, and "Wee Willie Winkie"—have been transferred to the screen. The English writer's contribution to RKO Radio's *Gunga Din* is a title, a character, and the concluding lines of the Barrack Room Ballad that commemorates the heroic death of an Indian water carrier. Uncredited contributors are virtually all the previous films that have romantically chronicled British heroics in India.

Ben Hecht and Charles MacArthur, who managed to pad a story around the famous tag line "You're a better man than I am, Gunga Din!", and Joel Sayre and Fred Guiol, who adapted it, have done better than might have been expected under circumstances. Once again we have Highlanders and Lancers stationed at a cantonment near a tribe of fanatic natives who revolt under the leadership of a deranged Napoleon (Eduardo Ciannelli), and another example of the screen Britishers' predilection for marching into ambush behind skirling bagpipes.

But of fresher invention is the substory of Gunga Din (Sam Jaffe), the scrawny, subservient "bhisti" who dies bravely playing a diffident D'Artagnan to the Porthos-Athos-Aramis of three hard-boiled sergeants in the Royal Engineers, and the engaging characters of this brawling trio: Cutter (Cary Grant), with his unsoldierly weakness for treasure hunts; Ballantine (Douglas Fairbanks, Jr.), who plans to quit the service and marry, and MacChesney (Victor McLaglen), who used fair means and foul to keep the three musketeers together.

Capably acted, and given the most elaborate production in RKO Radio's history, the blood-and-blundering heroics of *Gunga Din* make for sweeping, spectacular melodrama. The preposterous story, smartly directed by

George Stevens, has the further advantage of starting off with a skirmish exciting enough to serve as climax for less ambitious juvenilia and proceeds fast and spuriously to combat on a mammoth scale. And between climaxes, as the regimental Rover Boys battle with every weapon known to warfare and brawling in the '90s, romance—contributed by Joan Fontaine—scarcely rears its pretty head to interrupt the carnage.

Sam Jaffe is almost the forgotten man in the title role of Gunga Din, as Cary Grant, Douglas Fairbanks, Jr., and Victor McLaglen fight their way through Hindus, survive the cruelty of the Thuggee torture chamber and carry-on occasionally in the old Mack Sennett comedy manner when they playfully toss dynamite around and spike the punch with "elephant elixir." However, Din, whose heroics are not confined to water-carrying as in Kipling's poem, gets his big moment when the three hero-sergeants, bloody with wounds, are surrounded by Thugs, and Din, also bleeding profusely, climbs to the topmost pinnacle of the temple's gold tower and blows the alarm for the approaching Highlanders. It is incredible that any film on which $2,000,000 was reputedly spent, for which villages and a temple were built, which is authoritatively costumed, well cast and has thrilling battle scenes against beautiful mountain backgrounds, couldn't have spent some effort on an intelligent adult story. But perhaps we are asking too much of a super-spectacle like *Gunga Din*. Perhaps we should overlook the plot's inconsistencies, the glorification of war (which is to be expected in any film that is even suggested by a poem of the imperialistic Kipling), the ungentlemanly treatment of Joan Fontaine (who is forgotten because there's a fight going on somewhere), the ham acting of the villains, and the overly robust boyishness of the heroes. We are grateful for Jaffe's gentle, patient, underplayed Din, for Grant's cheery, Cockney sergeant, and for George Stevens's good direction especially in the magnificently sweeping mob scenes.

Philip T. Hartung, *The Commonweal*

If the spectacular picture *Gunga Din* had been made by a German or an Italian company and had shown Italian soldiers killing Abyssinians or Japanese invaders murdering Chinese peasants, the government-controlled fascist producers could have used the script by our versatile twins Ben Hecht and Charles MacArthur without changing one line or one action. Only the names and costumes would be different. Three Black Shirts could not indulge in an orgy of brutality with more gusto than do the three Khaki Shirts (Cary Grant, Victor McLaglen, Douglas Fairbanks, Jr.), who dash laughingly across the screen killing right and left and exhibiting themselves as practically bullet-proof by nature. The picture is ghastly and disgusting to one who knows what war really looks like. But you are expected to leave your better feelings and your brain at home. That such a picture should be produced in the greatest and freest democracy of the world and with the approval of the Hays Office and the state boards of censorship, which protect us from the sight of a baby being born but have nothing against the inspiring influence of wholesale massacres, may be only a symptom of the cultural level on which the great industry and its mentors operate. Provided it is hypocritically disguised, the appeal to the lowest instincts is still legitimate business.

There is only one plausible character in the picture—the others are inhuman dummies—Gunga Din, the dumb water-carrier whom the Hollywood merchants of death borrowed from Rudyard Kipling's poem. Sam Jaffe plays him with the touching smile of the stupid Hindu who falls for the ''regimentals'' of India's oppressors. One would like to see more of him, but Gunga Din does little more than give a name to the picture and provide an anticlimax. It is not only a bad joke to have Kipling, who saw his first battle as Boer War correspondent in Africa, appear at the end and write his poem in time for the commander to recite it over poor dead Gunga Din; it is a cynically intended, pseudo-serious trick that puts over the whole fraud.

So much for the content of *Gunga Din*. In form it is a technically perfect show (directed and produced by George Stevens), in which fist fights, cavalry charges of thousands of riders, and artillery barrages are flawlessly represented.

Franz Hoellering, *The Nation*

With Douglas Fairbanks, Jr., Victor McLaglen, Eduardo Ciannelli and Sam Jaffe

With Douglas Fairbanks, Jr., Sam Jaffe, Victor McLaglen and Eduardo Ciannelli

Sam Jaffe

*Gunga Din,* the most expensive picture in the history of RKO, which was last week on the point of emerging from a six-year bankruptcy, unfolds a jolly story about high jinks on India's frontier. Poor old Gunga Din has small part of the proceedings. In the first part of the picture he wobbles about carrying a goatskin water bag. In the last part, he inspires a scared-looking Rudyard Kipling to produce a commemorative poem. The rest of the time Gunga Din's doings are eclipsed by those of three agile young sergeants—Cary Grant, Victor McLaglen and Douglas Fairbanks, Jr. The story of Gunga Din appears to be a sort of Anglo-Indian *Three Musketeers.* Funny, spectacular, and exciting. Typical sequence: battle between a regiment of Scots Highlanders and Thug cavalry, filmed on the slopes of Mt. Whitney last summer, with a cast of 900 extras.

As an individual product of the cinema industry, there is practically nothing to be said against *Gunga Din.* First-class entertainment, it will neither corrupt the morals of minors nor affront the intelligence of their seniors. But unfortunately, *Gunga Din* is not an isolated example of the cinema industry's majestic mass product. It is a symbol of Hollywood's current trend. As such it is as deplorable as it is enlightening.

Hollywood, however, even when it was not deliberately repeating itself, repeated itself unconsciously. *Gunga Din* is an example of this unconscious repetition. Whatever there is to be said about the minor matter of barrack-room life in India has been more than sufficiently said by the cinema many times, most recently in *Lives of a Bengal Lancer, Charge of the Light Brigade* and *Drums.*

Moving pictures are a vigorous entertainment medium. There has probably never been a moment in the world's history when more exciting things were going on than in this year of 1939. That Hollywood can supply no better salute to 1939 than a $2,000,000 rehash, however expert, of Rudyard Kipling and brown Indians in bed-sheets, is a sad reflection on its state of mind.

*Time*

128

# ONLY ANGELS HAVE WINGS

1939

## CREDITS:

Produced and distributed by Columbia. *Producer:* A Howard Hawks production. *Director:* Howard Hawks. *Assistant director:* Arthur Black. From a story by Howard Hawks. *Cinematography:* Joseph Walker. *Aerial photo:* Elmer Dyer. *Special effects:* Roy Davidson, and Edwin C. Hahn. *Editor:* Viola Lawrence. *Composer:* Dmitri Tiomkin. *Musical director:* Morris W. Stoloff. *Art direction:* Lionel Banks. *Costumes:* Kalloch. *Technical adviser and chief pilot:* Paul Mantz. *Release date:* May 25, 1939. *Running time:* 121 minutes.

## THE CAST:

| | |
|---|---|
| *Jeff Carter* | Cary Grant |
| *Bonnie Lee* | Jean Arthur |
| *Bat McPherson* | Richard Barthelmess |
| *Judith* | Rita Hayworth |
| *Kid Dabb* | Thomas Mitchell |
| *Dutchman* | Sig Ruman |
| *Sparks* | Victor Kilian |
| *Gent Shelton* | John Carrol |
| *Les Peters* | Allyn Joslyn |
| *Tex Gordon* | Donald Barry |
| *Joe Souther* | Noah Beery, Jr. |
| *Lily* | Melissa Sierra |
| *Dr. Lagorio* | Lucio Villegas |
| *Hartwood* | Forbes Murray |
| *The Singer* | Maciste |
| *Mike* | Pat Flaherty |
| *Pancho* | Pedro Regas |
| *Baldy* | Pat West |

## SYNOPSIS:

This is a story of flying "crates" over the Andes and battling storms and hardships to deliver cargoes. Jeff

With Jean Arthur

With Victor Kilian

With Rita Hayworth and Jean Arthur

With Victor Kilian, Lucio Villegas, Pedro Regas, Pat Flaherty,
Jean Arthur and Thomas Mitchell

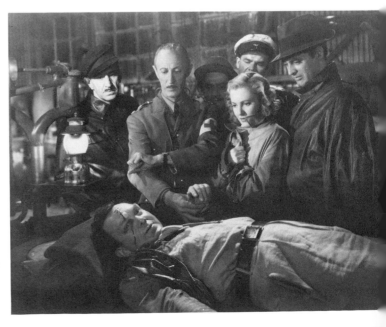

Carter is a hard-headed character, owner of an airplane firm, who drives his fliers to almost suicidal trips in decrepit planes. Bonnie Lee, a show girl, falls in love with Jeff Carter, and leaves her boat to be with him. Because of the importance of a promised subsidy from the government of the local republic, Carter spends all his efforts in keeping regular flight schedules in spite of hardships. In the meantime he ignores Bonnie. Then his former wife, Judy arrives, with her new husband, MacPherson, an ace flyer.

## REVIEWS:

The year's output of aviation films subtracts none of the vigor and little of the freshness from *Only Angels Have Wings*. More than a year in production, and coming at the tail end of an overworked screen cycle, this Columbia film easily outranks most of its plane-crashing, sky-spectacular predecessors.

Produced, directed, and written by Howard Hawks *(Ceiling Zero* and the *Dawn Patrol* of 1930), whose original story Jules Furthman has turned into a taut, economical script, this is the collective drama of a group of American aviators in the banana town of Barranca, set at the base of the mountains in the Latin-American tropics.

Worthy of script, direction, and particularly effective re-creation of its tropical setting is the film's first-rate company. Grant and Miss Arthur, perfectly cast in the leading roles, are supported by skillful and convincing characterizations, particularly by Sig Rumann as owner of the rickety plane service, Thomas Mitchell as a grounded flyer, and in lesser roles, Rita Hayworth, Allyn Joslyn, and Noah Beery, Jr. Perhaps of most interest to screen fans is the fact that Richard Barthelmess, after a three-year absence from the screen, takes to the comeback road with a splendid performance.

*Newsweek*

Howard Hawks has had an uneven if successful career, but he directed the best of all airplane pictures, *Ceiling Zero,* and so it is too bad he and an above-average cast had to be wasted on the story of *Only Angels Have Wings*. With a good story, the swift suspense so naturally brought out in movies of pilots and their job would have become a terrific thing under its own power. But this was done in the run-of-the-mill Hollywood way: get something that will wow them, gag it up, bring the girls in, bring everything else in. And so Cary Grant's troubles with a mail schedule in South America, with a girl that drops in, pilots that lose their eyesight or take chances, with the coward who is making good, etc.—this stuff soon gets out of hand because there is too much of it to fit in any line of meaning, so to keep it going the writers then throw in more stuff—the less they know the more they speak. Added to the dangers of this torturing of coincidence, there comes the slowing down necessary to fix half a dozen different things so they can work out happily for the end.

Power dives are always ripping across a theatre screen

somewhere; but in this case more could have been done. The atmosphere was right to start with, the give and take among the men, the hard-pressed finances of the outfit, the dangers known and unknown and the good likely people: Cary Grant, Jean Arthur, Thomas Mitchell, Richard Barthelmess, Allyn Joslyn, Sigfried Rumann. In the minor things, where the ridiculous or the stereotype didn't intrude, there was a swell realization of their personalities, of friendship and banter and weariness and trouble. Howard Hawks can be faultless in a sense of how to speed up a situation, or make it flexible and easy with the right emphasis, grouping, understatement. In fact, all these people did the best they could with what they were given—but look at it. The battle with mechanics and the elements, in this as in other art films, provides suspense all right; but so does hanging.

Otis Ferguson, *The New Republic*

With Melissa Sierra

# IN NAME ONLY

## 1939

With Carole Lombard

## CREDITS:

Produced and distributed by RKO Radio. *Executive producer:* Pandro S. Berman. *Director:* John Cromwell. *Regular Producer:* George Haight. *Assistant Director:* Dewey Starkey. *Screenplay:* Richard Sherman. From novel *Memory of Love* by Bessie Brewer. *Cinematography:* J. Roy Hunt. *Special effects:* Vernon L. Walker. *Editor:* William Hamilton. *Musical score:* Roy Webb. *Art direction:* Van Nest Polglase. *Associate:* Perry Ferguson. *Set decorator:* Dorrell Silvera. *Costumes:* Miss Lombard's gowns by Irene. Other gowns by Edward Stevenson. *Sound:* Hugh McDowell, Jr. *Release date:* August 18, 1939. *Running time:* 94 minutes.

## THE CAST:

| | |
|---|---|
| *Julie Eden* | Carole Lombard |
| *Alec Walker* | Cary Grant |
| *Maida Walker* | Kay Francis |
| *Mr. Walker* | Charles Coburn |
| *Suzanne* | Helen Vinson |
| *Laura* | Katharine Alexander |
| *Dr. Gateson* | Jonathan Hale |
| *Dr. Muller* | Maurice Moscovich |
| *Mrs. Walker* | Nella Walker |
| *Ellen* | Peggy Ann Garner |
| *Gardner* | Spencer Charters |

## SYNOPSIS:

Maida Walker marries Alec Walker for his wealth and position. Alec falls in love with Julie Eden, a widow who has taken a summer house near his estate. He asks Maida for a divorce, but she refuses. Maida schemes to save the marriage, not for love, but to hold onto the family money. She plays up to his parents and goes with them to Paris. She promised to get a divorce there, but has no intention of doing so. She thinks that by stalling she will weaken Julie's love for her husband. Alex falls seriously ill with pneumonia, and the doctor suggests that only someone who really loves him can pull him through. Julie is called to his bedside, gives him the strength to overcome his illness, and Maida realizes she has lost her battle.

## REVIEWS:

*In Name Only* will puzzle cinemagoers who thought they knew just what high jinks to expect when Screwball Cary Grant falls in love with Screwball Carole Lombard. Far from high jinks is the somber situation of rich young Alec Walker when he falls in love with Julie Eden, a widowed commercial artist who has taken a summer cottage near his stately county seat. For, as rarely happens in a screwball comedy but is very likely to happen in life, Alec has a tenacious wife with an undeveloped sense of humor, parents who also thought infidelity no joke. Before Lovers Grant and Lombard fight through to the clear, they have traded more punches than puns, emerged with the realization that matrimony is more than the off-screen ending to a Grant-Lombard movie.

A mature, meaty picture, based on the novel *Memory of Love*, by veteran buoolio Boooio Browor (wife of muralist Henry Varnum Poor), *In Name Only* has its many knowing touches deftly underscored by Director John Cromwell,

brought out by a smoothly functioning cast. No surprises are the easy ad-libbish styles of Stars Grant and Lombard, the enameled professional finish of oldtime Actor Charles Coburn as Alec's conventional father. Surprising to many cinemaddicts, however, will be the effectively venomous performance, as Alec's mercenary wife, of Cinemactress Kay Francis. Having worked out a long-term contract with Warner Bros. which kept her in the top money (over $5,000 a week) but buried her as the suffering woman in a string of B pictures, sleek Cinemactress Francis in her first free-lance job shows that she still belongs in the A's, that, properly encouraged, she can pronounce the letter r without wobbling.

*Time*

This is a well-made depressing little picture of unhappy marriage. It is often sentimental, but the general impression which remains is quite an authentic one—a glossy photographic likeness of gloom: fruitless discussions about Reno, polite chicanery over the long-distance 'phone, hate in the sherry glass, the rattled nerve and the despair of any day being different from today. *Dodsworth* and *Craig's Wife* come to mind: those, too, were pictures of mental distress among higher incomes, but *Dodsworth*, at any rate, had more saving humor. Humor here pops up only incidentally—with a drunk little clerk on Christmas Eve (surprisingly acted by that icy gangster, Mr. Allen Baxter),

With Carole Lombard

With Carole Lombard and Kay Francis

With Carole Lombard

With Kay Francis

134

with a scared fat youth in a restaurant-car listening to the forked war of women's tongues. I wonder sometimes where pictures like this find the money for production: the huge cinema masses surely have a shorter and sharper way of satisfying their loves and hates: are they not a little puzzled and bored by the well-groomed classy tragedy with a happy ending, the sense of sex isolated from any other kind of trouble, money or work, what Mr. Aiken has described so well as "the late night wrangles, the three-day silences, the weepings in the dark rooms face downward on dishevelled beds . . . the livid eyes of hate over the morning grapefruit"?

The picture is made quite creditably, by three people—Miss Carole Lombard, Mr. Cary Grant and Miss Kay Francis. Both actresses break new ground. Miss Lombard's wavering and melancholy voice, her bewildered eyes, which have in the past faltered so well among the rapid confused events of crazy comedy, work just as satisfactorily here—wringing out tears instead of laughs, and Miss Francis, "the best-dressed woman in Hollywood," who used to step unresiliently, with a lisp, through glamorous parts, for the first time grips our attention as the hard unscrupulous wife, who is after something more valuable than alimony, her father-in-law's money. I liked this wholeheartedly unpleasant character, who presents a cunning picture of understanding and patience to the parents, driving a wedge between them and their son, and when at last her husband's open preference for another woman forces her consent to a divorce, double-crosses relentlessly—going to Paris with the parents on the secret understanding that there she will break the truth to them and get her decree, but all the time determined to hold on, inventing delay after delay to sap the girl's trust in

her lover, until she at last returns without it. The main theme of the picture is the strain of waiting on the Paris line and listening to the time-saving lies: the atmosphere of triumphant war between a woman with complete mastery of her feelings and her tongue and an ordinary kindly man and a rather guileless girl.

But this is a classy, not a first-class picture. Shot with a refined taste for interior decoration, well-groomed, advertising only the best cars, it is oversweetened with the material for tears: Miss Lombard's young widow has a small child addicted to winsome wisecracks; the last hope of divorce crashes on Christmas Eve, with the parcels stacked beside the tree and the candles ready for lighting; the hero lies traditionally drunk before the open window of a seedy hotel. Here the film comes to life again for a few minutes with the fine study of the hotel manager—the narrow prudish face, the sly suggestion, the cigarette-case always open in the palm, the scared secretive lechery. But after that brief appearance the well-worn path of the tear-jerker has to be trodden to the bitter and the happy end. Pneumonia, the girl forbidden the bedside, the old specialist saying, "There is only one person who can give him the will to live," the white lie—"everything is all right now," and then the wife's arrival, the rash betrayal of what she's really after while the parents listen out of sight, everything cleared satisfactorily up in a few seconds, even the pneumonia—"he's sleeping now," just as though the slow dubious movements of the human intelligence could be shot by an ultra-rapid camera, happiness seeded and budded and blossomed with the knowing speed of a *Secrets of Nature* flower.

Graham Greene, *The Spectator*

With Charles Coburn, Nella Walker, Kay Francis, Jonathan Hale and Carole Lombard

# HIS GIRL FRIDAY

## 1940

With Rosalind Russell

## CREDITS:

Produced and distributed by Columbia. *Producer:* Howard Hawks. *Director:* Howard Hawks. *Screenplay:* Charles Lederer. From the play *The Front Page* by Ben Hecht and Charles MacArthur. *Cinematography:* Joseph Walker. *Editor:* Gene Havlick. *Musical director:* Morris W. Stoloff. *Release date:* January 18, 1940. *Running time:* 92 minutes.

## THE CAST:

| | |
|---|---|
| *Walter Burns* | Cary Grant |
| *Hildy Johnson* | Rosalind Russell |
| *Bruce Baldwin* | Ralph Bellamy |
| *Sheriff Hartwell* | Gene Lockhart |
| *Murphy* | Porter Hall |
| *Bensiger* | Ernest Truex |
| *Endicott* | Cliff Edwards |
| *Mayor* | Clarence Kolb |
| *McCue* | Roscoe Karns |
| *Wilson* | Frank Jenks |
| *Sanders* | Regis Toomey |
| *Diamond Louie* | Abner Biberman |
| *Duffy* | Frank Orth |
| *Earl Williams* | John Qualen |
| *Mollie Malloy* | Helen Mack |
| *Mrs. Baldwin* | Alma Kruger |
| *Silas F. Pinkus* | Billy Gilbert |
| *Warden Cooley* | Pat West |
| *Dr. Egelhoffer* | Edwin Maxwell |

## SYNOPSIS:

Hildy Johnson, recently divorced from hard-bitten man-

With Ralph Bellamy

With Abner Biberman and
Marion Martin

With Ralph Bellamy and Rosalind Russell

With Ralph Bellamy

With Frank Jenks, Gene Lockhart, Rosalind Russell, Porter Hall, Regis Toomey and Cliff Edwards

With Porter Hall, Gene Lockhart, Frank Jenks, Rosalind Russell, Pat Flaherty and Roscoe Karns

With Pat Flaherty, Rosalind Russell, Billy Gilbert, Clarence Kolb and Gene Lockhart

aging editor, Walter Burns, tells him she is leaving his newspaper to marry Bruce Baldwin, an insurance salesman and settle down to a quiet life. But she agrees to cover just one more story, in return for a $100,000 insurance policy given her fiancé. That one more story proves to her that printer's ink is inescapably in her veins, as she hides an escaped murderer and exposes political corruption.

## REVIEWS:

*His Girl Friday* "from a play by Ben Hecht and Charles MacArthur" is a remake of *The Front Page,* the movie success of 1931 and stage hit of 1928. The original has been changed this time into one of those fast-moving and idyllic comedies in which the lovers behave like villains to each other—sophisticated is the usual word for the genre. Hildy Johnson has become a woman for this purpose. She has been married to the fanatical editor and divorced from him because there was never time for love. Coming to tell him she is going to marry a simple insurance man from Albany, she soon finds herself, against her will, back on her former job as reporter. There follows the plot of *The Front Page,* with managing editor playing his tricks partly on the insurance man. By the change the accent is shifted to the lover's quarrel, and the original story loses much of its sense and punch. Yet Rosalind Russell and Cary Grant give such entertaining performances that nobody in the roaring audience seems to notice the tastelessness, to say the least, of playing hide-and-seek with a man condemned to death. The tragic elements of the original story are misused for boy-meets-girl nonsense. Charles Lederer has written the new version with great skill and Howard Hawks has directed it with liveliness but with too great a concern for the deaf.

Franz Hoellering, *The Nation*

Another film not for the squeamish is *His Girl Friday* (*Of Mice and Men* reviewed prior to this.) Directed by Howard Hawks from Charles Lederer's screenplay, it has most of the sparkle, wit and fun of *The Front Page* on which it is vaguely based. This time, however, Hildy Johnson is a girl-reporter who is tired of being a newspaper man. She wants to be a respectable woman, but her ex-husband, the managing editor, won't let her. For him, divorce isn't permanent—and neither is anything else. The Picture skims along quickly with snappy repartee and situations in which reporters are again shown as hardened skunks (but softies underneath). The editor tries all the tricks to prevent Hildy from leaving the paper and him. Rosalind Russell and Cary Grant play the piece for all that's in it, and get good support from Ralph Bellamy, John Qualen, Helen Mack, and Gene Lockhart.

Philip T. Hartung, *The Commonweal*

With Irene Dunne

# MY FAVORITE WIFE

1940

## CREDITS:

Produced and distributed by RKO Radio. *Producer:* Leo McCarey. *Director:* Garson Kanin. *Assistant directors:* Ruby Rosenberg and James H. Anderson. Story by Bella and Samuel Spewack and Leo McCarey. *Cinematography:* Rudolph Mate. *Editor:* Robert Wise. *Musical score:* Ray Webb. *Art direction:* Van Nest Polglase; *Associate:* Mark-Lee Kirk. *Set decorator:* Darrell Silvera. *Costumes:* Howard Greer. *Sound:* John E. Tribby. *Release date:* May 17, 1940. *Running time:* 88 minutes.

## THE CAST:

| | |
|---|---|
| Ellen | Irene Dunne |
| Nick | Cary Grant |
| Burkett | Randolph Scott |
| Bianca | Gail Patrick |
| Ma | Ann Schoemaker |
| Tim | Scotty Beckett |
| Chinch | Mary Lou Harrington |
| Hotel Clerk | Donald MacBride |
| Johnson | Hugh O'Connell |
| Judge | Granville Bates |
| Dr. Kohlmar | Pedro de Cordoba |

## SYNOPSIS:

Nick Arden appears in court to have his wife, Ellen, who disappeared in a shipwreck several years before, declared dead. Then Nick marries Bianca. A short time later, Ellen turns up, having finally been rescued from an island after eight years. She follows her husband and his new bride to a mountain lodge. But Nick cannot bring himself to tell Bianca, his new wife, what has happened. Later the newlywed couple return home and find Ellen

With Donald McBride

With Victor Kilian, Gail Patrick, Irene Dunne and Randolph Scott

With Irene Dunne and Randolph Scott

there, pretending to be an old friend of the family. Nick becomes jealous of his first wife when he discovers there was a man on the island with her. She hires a shoe salesman to pretend he is Mr. Burkett, the man on the island, and introduces this older man to her husband in an attempt to settle matters. But meanwhile Nick has discovered that Mr. Burkett is youthful and handsome. Nick takes Ellen to the club where Mr. Burkett lives and the three have lunch. Ellen falls into the pool, and Nick must go home to get some clothes for her. Bianca has called in a psychiatrist to help solve the matrimonial problems, but Nick walks out on her. Finally Nick realizes that he still loves his first wife and will return to her.

## REVIEWS:

Hollywood goes even more frivolous in its newest husband-and-wife comedies—what used to be called "bedroom farces." Recently there was *Too Many Husbands,* a modern travesty of the Enoch Arden story. Now *My Favorite Wife* reverses the triangle and lets bewildered Cary Grant marry Gail Patrick when who should turn up but Irene Dunne, his first wife, who has been stranded on a desert island these last seven years. The situation in any of these comedies could be cleared up in five minutes of explaining; but that wouldn't be any fun. Scriptwriters Bella and Samuel Spewack drag the thin plot, jokes and who-should-sleep-with-whom discussion on as long as possible. Garson Kanin has directed to make it all seem fresh and funny. Pretty, pert Miss Dunne could never look like anyone who's been out in the wind and sun for seven years; but she and Cary Grant with the able assistance of Randolph Scott, Granville Bates and the others, have a good time of it.

Philip T. Hartung, *The Commonweal*

There is some of the best comedy work in *My Favorite Wife,* a sort of nonsense-sequel to *The Awful Truth.* There is also some of the worst plot-making, and Irene Dunne. The story was written by Bella and Samuel Spewack and I am not going to tell it; but apart from its being quite impossible, which may be called comic license, it forces its best people to treat each other with an aimless viciousness that even Boris Karloff might hesitate to reveal to his public. And while most of the characters can manage to cover up this bankruptcy of motivation with quips and tumbles, Miss Dunne has apparently become *very* interested in acting and what may be achieved with the Human Voice. So it becomes her field day. She is not one person but seven, and if she is not all seven at once she is several in rapid succession without aid from script or meaning, running the gamut from Little Eva to Gracie Allen, from *The Women* to (by actual count) Amos and Andy. What a lark.

But this is a Garson Kanin picture and to miss it would not be sensible, for Mr. Kanin is already first-string in comedy, and comedy is no steady boarder these last few months. In addition, it shows Cary Grant developing a very pleasant style of male-animal humor, with charm and a distinct sense of where to poise or throw his weight. . . . The best indication of a director's presence is the opening scene in court, where Granville Bates as the Judge had himself a picnic. Only four people, only one room, and it went on quite a time—but so easily you would not realize till afterwards that all the heavy exposition of Act I, Scene I, had run off in it like a shout. There was another courtroom scene near the end, too, though with more people; and there were scenes here and there all the way through, covering the retreat of the story. Such flowers will not bloom unseen, but it's a pity there has to be so damn much desert air around.

Otis Ferguson, The New Republic

My Favorite Wife is the latest offering of the husband and wife script-writing team of Bella and Samuel Spewack (Boy Meets Girl), the latest comedy collaboration of Cary Grant, Irene Dunne and Producer Leo McCarey (The Awful Truth). It is also the latest variation on Too Many Husbands, though this time it is the wife who returns after she has been declared legally dead, finds that her husband has married again that morning. . . .

At times My Favorite Wife tends to get bedroomatic and limp, but it pulls itself together in scenes like those in which Cary Grant scampers between his wives' hotel rooms pursued by the distrustful but admiring clerk (Donald MacBride); or gets caught in his wife's hat and dress by a suspicious psychologist; or tears around in Gail Patrick's leopard spot dressing gown. And there is Granville Bates's first-rate bit as a dumb, irate fuddyduddy judge who, having declared Irene Dunne legally dead, declares her legally alive so he can hold her in contempt of court.

Cary Grant has made better pictures than My Favorite Wife. He has seldom collected a better fee—$100,000. For a boy who was born Archibald Leach in Bristol, England and ran away at twelve to join a tumbling act, this is not hay.

Time Magazine

With Mary Lou Harrington, Scotty Deckett, Ann Schoemaker, Irene Dunne and Gail Patrick

141

# THE HOWARDS OF VIRGINIA

1940

With Martha Scott

**CREDITS:**

Produced and distributed by Columbia. *Producer:* Frank Lloyd. *Director:* Frank Lloyd. *Associate producer:* Jack H. Skirball. *Assistant director:* William Tummel. *Screenplay:* Sidney Buchman, from the novel *The Tree of Liberty* by Elizabeth Page. *Cinematography:* Bert Glennon. *Montage effect:* Slarko Vorkapich. *Editor:* Paul Weatherwax. *Music and score:* Richard Hageman. *Art direction:* John Goodman. *Interior decorator:* Howard Bristol. *Costumes:* Miss Scott's gowns by Irene Saltern. *Sound:* William H. Wilmarth. *Technical adviser:* Waldo Twitchell. *Release date:* September 19, 1940. *Running time:* 117 minutes.

**THE CAST:**

| | |
|---|---|
| *Matt Howard* | Cary Grant |
| *Jane Peyton-Howard* | Martha Scott |
| *Fleetwood Peyton* | Sir Cedric Hardwicke |
| *Roger Peyton* | Alan Marshal |
| *Thomas Jefferson* | Richard Carlson |
| *Captain Jabez Allen* | Paul Kelly |
| *Tom Norton* | Irving Bacon |
| *Aunt Clarissa* | Elizabeth Risdon |
| *Mrs. Norton* | Ann Revere |
| *James Howard at 16* | Richard Alden |
| *Peyton Howard at 18* | Phil Taylor |
| *Mary Howard at 17* | Rita Quigley |
| *Dicey* | Libby Taylor |
| *Patrick Henry* | Richard Gaines |
| *George Washington* | George Houston |

**SYNOPSIS:**

Through the friendship of Thomas Jefferson, Matt Howard goes to work as a surveyor for the aristocratic

Fleetwood Peyton. Matt falls in love with Jane Peyton, the couple marry and return to the rough-and-ready district of Howard's earlier years.

Through the encouragement of Jefferson, Howard enters politics and when hostilities between the colonies and the mother country break out, he sides with the colonists and joins the army in spite of Jane's protestations. Eventually, he is joined by his two sons in the revolutionary movement and when his firstborn crippled son distinguishes himself by a feat of bravery, the father belatedly becomes reconciled with him. The war ends with Cornwallis' surrender at Yorktown. Matt Howard returns home to Jane.

## REVIEWS:

Elizabeth Page's best seller of last year, *The Tree of Liberty,* comes to the screen as *The Howards of Virginia.* Although using only a portion of the 985-page novel, Columbia still seems to have tackled a larger canvas than it could paint effectively, with the result that this cavalcade of Colonial and Revolutionary America, while ambitious, expensive, and generally interesting, comes to life all too infrequently.

Adapted by Sidney Buchman and directed by Frank Lloyd, the Howard saga is most effective in the sequences that recreate frontier life and manners as seen through the eyes of the woman who loves her husband while rebelling against his democratic ideas. These sequences are impressive in their homely humor and realism, though much footage otherwise wasted inevitably pulls the emotional punches in the story of Matt's relationship with his wife and children.

Obviously miscast, Cary Grant meets the exigencies of a difficult role with more gusto than persuasion. Martha Scott follows her impressive screen debut in *Our Town* with a sincere if more conventional characterization. That this history has been staged with exceptional fidelity, is due in part to the fact that its Williamsburg sequences were filmed on location in the historic city which was reconstructed by John D. Rockefeller, Jr. as a $20,000,000 project to perpetuate America's past.

*Newsweek*

When producers put their minds to it, they can make pictures that show historical events as if they were something important happening in the lives of people and not just background for another boy-meets-girl romance. *The Howards of Virginia,* based on Elizabeth Page's *The Tree of Liberty,* defies anyone not to believe in the struggles of the colonists before and during the Revolution. Frank Lloyd's excellent reproduction of a period much neglected in films should convince us that the Virginia House of Burgesses, the Resolution Against the Stamp Act, the Boston Tea Party, the suffering of that ill-clad, ill-fed Continental Army are more than a series of names and dates in a textbook. Scenes actually filmed at Williamsburg lend

With Cedric Hardwicke and Richard Carlson

With Martha Scott

authenticity to a story that is made noteworthy in a historical film through the simplicity of Sidney Buchman's screenplay. Although the story's sincerity holds one's interest, the film bogs down in its characterizations, particularly in inconsistencies that are due more to direction and script than to the actors. Grant is built up as a rough, loud, considerate, likable man who couldn't possibly be so cruel to his son; and Sir Cedric Hardwicke, as his Tory in-law, is left to flounder with a role that never becomes entirely clear. The picture also has a curious change of pace; after a slow beginning, it suddenly races to its conclusion. But in spite of these flaws never once does Mr. Lloyd's film falter in its integrity to show the earnest fight for freedom that took place in this cradle of liberty.

Philip T. Hartung, *The Commonweal*

With Paul Kelly

With Richard Alden and Phil Taylor

With Katharine Hepburn
and John Howard

# THE PHILADELPHIA STORY

1941

## CREDITS:

Produced and distributed by Metro-Goldwyn-Mayer. *Producer:* Joseph L. Mankiewicz. *Director:* George Cukor. *Screenplay:* Donald Ogden Stewart. Based on play by Philip Barry as produced by Theatre Guild, Inc. *Cinematography:* Joseph Ruttenberg. *Editor:* Frank Sullivan. *Musical score:* Franz Waxman. *Art Director:* Cedric Gibbons; *Associate:* Wade B. Rubottom. *Set decorations:* Edwin B. Willis. *Costumes:* Adrian. *Hair Styles:* Sydney Guilaroff. *Sound:* Douglas Shearer. *Release date:* January 17, 1941. *Running time:* 112 minutes.

## THE CAST:

*C. K. Dexter Haven*      Cary Grant
*Tracy Lord*      Katharine Hepburn

*Macauley Connor*      James Stewart
*Elizabeth Imbrie*      Ruth Hussey
*George Kittredge*      John Howard
*Uncle Willie*      Roland Young
*Seth Lord*      John Halliday
*Margaret Lord*      Mary Nash
*Dinah Lord*      Virginia Weidler
*Sidney Kidd*      Henry Daniell
*Edward*      Lionel Pape

## SYNOPSIS:

Newsman Macaulay Connor and his camera assistant, Liz Imbrie are given an assignment to crash the Philadelphia Main Line Lord estate on the occasion of Tracy Lord's second marriage. The pair is sponsored by Tracy's first husband, C. Dexter Haven. He is returning to save the Social Register reputation of his former in-laws

145

With Virginia Weidler, Mary Nash and Katharine Hepburn

from the threats of publisher Sidney Kidd, to give page-spread notice to the illicit love of Papa Lord for a Russian dancer unless his paper's representatives are admitted to the Lord-Kittredge nuptials.

The family reacts strongly to the trio's visitation, especially Tracy and little sister, Dinah who put on a grand show of well-bred behavior to impress the company. The domestic scene becomes more hilarious and complicated by the drafting of Uncle Willie to play the absent father's role and by recruiting the real parent for the avuncular assignment when the male head of the household suddenly appears. In the course of those position mix-ups, the real reason for the breakup of Tracy's first marriage is revealed as a personality deficiency on the part of the girl. Thanks to some alcoholic ministrations and the drinking companionship of Connor, Tracy begins to realize her frigid failings and starts to defrost. When her fiancé catches the pair returning from an early morning swim, the worst is suspected, although it was really all in good clean fun. At the moment of the marriage Tracy dismisses Kittredge and substitutes Haven for a repeat nuptial.

## REVIEWS:

To judge whether *The Philadelphia Story* is more effective on the screen than it was on Broadway would be to raise a lot of useless issues, and cloud others. I think the thing to say is that it was originally constructed for the strict tightness of a few sets, and that in remaining faithful to it, the picture's producer (Joe Mankiewicz) had

With Ruth Hussey, James Stewart and Katharine Hepburn

146

to make some of his successes the hollow victory of just overcoming obstacles. Two things have resulted from this: (1) the play has been opened out into natural shifting scenes, if not actually broadened in effect; (2) the story seems to slow up toward the end, where everything was talk anyway.

A great deal depends, for sense and meaning, on Katharine Hepburn as the central character; and there are things in the range of her personality too delicate and subtle for anything but the close, pliant observation of cameras. Here she is, as I did not find her coming through so clearly before, the high-strung but overpetted thoroughbred who must be broken to be released into the good stride of her nature; and here the breaking is a gradual and visible process at once painful, touching and funny. You know the story and Philadelphia too, and there is little new to say about the work of Miss Hepburn, whose peculiar dry radiance and intelligence, whose metallic and even mannered voice finding its special beauty, are known if not defined, easily imitated but never reproduced in their final style.

But the story is no mere vehicle; it was not written, picturized or directed as such. Donald Ogden Stewart is credited with an exceptionally bright job of screenplay writing; George Cukor seems to sit with more authority in his director's chair than he has on many another such occasion of reverential transfer; and to have Cary Grant, James Stewart, Roland Young, Ruth Hussey and John Halliday posted all about in key position was a happy thing for all. Grant is perfectly gracious to a thankless part, winning sympathy and belief. Stewart keeps to his level of near-perfection, as the impulsive, wrong-moving ordinary guy, and certainly adds another star to his honor chart for the whole sequence of moonlight and Four Roses. Young Virginia Weidler has a good part and time for herself.

Having expended so much care to such effect, they might have considered also that it is only brooks in poems which go on forever without somebody's beginning to yawn, scratch and wonder seriously whether it is the suspense or just his underwear that is climbing. They might have cut out the boob move of the writer proposing at the wedding and right before his own fiancee. They could have gone back through the last third and clipped lines of dialogue all along in the interest of general motion. They could, I suppose, have extended the very funny business at the expense of Timelife and its prose-bearing oracular baby-talk—though I wonder whether even the keen edge that is present as it is cuts any of the dull butter that must be out there haw-hawing at the performance and trundling up with a ring in its nose to the same newsstand afterwards. But there is nothing served in figuring how to do something after someone has very well proved that it's done already because he did it. Though films like *The Philadelphia Story* do little to advance the art of pictures, they may help convince some of the more discerning among cultural slugabeds that when movies want to turn their hand to anything, they can turn it.

Otis Ferguson, *The New Republic*

With Katharine Hepburn and James Stewart

The movie version of Philip Barry's *The Philadelphia Story* is years ahead of most screen dialogue. Audiences won't know what all of it means, but it's time that picture scripts got a little ahead of their public instead of ten paces behind 'em. I've noticed that audiences like a certain amount of dialogue which is over their heads. Producers ought to try it oftener.

*The Philadelphia Story* is the yarn of smart and semi-smart folks trying to cure their emotional and intellectual blindnesses and frustrations with alcohol, and it's amazing how well alcohol works in this picture. The W.C.T.U. doesn't know it, but it ought to stop this film, because it sells liquor better than any million-dollar advertising campaigns. Tracy Lord's (Miss Hepburn's) drinking in company with that poetic guy from that New York scandal sheet,

*Spy,* is what clears the atmosphere of her mis-planned love for John Howard and paves the way for her remarriage with Cary Grant. It takes a binge to cure Tracy of her gosh-awful goddessness and give her a good dose of clay feet.

Perhaps the highest honors in the picture really go to James Steward for his souse scene in Cary Grant's library. Mr. Grant is good as always, and deserves credit for playing subdued; he was a hell-raiser before the story opened, and is now the wiser and somewhat chastened ex-husband of the hard, too-exacting Tracy.

*The Philadelphia Story* is one of the few non-moronic pictures of the season.

Don Herold, *Scribner's Commentator*

With John Halliday, James Stewart, Ruth Hussey and Katharine Hepburn

With Irene Dunne

# PENNY SERENADE

1941

## CREDITS:

Produced and distributed by Columbia. *Director:* George Stevens. *Production associate:* Fred Guiol. *Assistant director:* Gene Anderson. *Screenplay:* Morrie Ryskind. From a story by Martha Cheavens. *Cinematography:* Joseph Walker. *Editor:* Otto Meyer. *Composer:* W. Franke Harling. *Musical director:* M. W. Stoloff. *Art direction:* Lionel Banks. *Sound:* John Goodrich. *Release date:* April 24, 1941. *Running time:* 120 minutes.

## THE CAST:

| | |
|---|---|
| *Julie Gardiner* | Irene Dunne |
| *Roger Adams* | Cary Grant |
| *Miss Oliver* | Beulah Bondi |
| *Applejack* | Edgar Buchanan |
| *Dotty* | Ann Doran |
| *Trina, age 6* | Eva Tee Kuneye |
| *Doctor Hartly* | Leonard Wiley |
| *Judge* | Wallis Clark |
| *Gillings* | Walter Soderling |
| *Trina, age 1* | Baby Biffle |

## SYNOPSIS:

"Penny Serenade" is the name of a recording played by Julie Gardiner as she prepares to leave her husband Roger Adams. A flashback shows the courtship of the pair, he a newspaper man and she a salesgirl in a music store. After the marriage, Julie follows Roger to Japan, where an earthquake ruins their honeymoon cottage and causes the death of Julie's unborn child. Back in America, Roger buys a country newspaper and to satisfy the maternal longings of Julie, who is unable to bear her own children, a baby is adopted. For a while it looks as if the

With Otto Han

With Irene Dunne

With Michael Morris

With Irene Dunne

With Henry Dixon, Dick Jensen, Frank Mills and Edgar Buchanan

family's precarious financial condition will prevent adoption but the child is at last adopted and raised to the age of six when death suddenly deprives the parents of their daughter. Grief almost separates Julie and Roger but the offer of another adoption brings them together again.

## REVIEWS:

George Stevens is a producer who knows what cinema audiences want, and in *Penny Serenade* he gives them what they want: two handsome stars; a warm, human, different but story-bookish plot with plenty of situations concerning love mixed with joy and unhappiness; and mainly, some cuddly babies and youngsters who do nothing but make the audience sigh "aw" in unison. Morrie Ryskind wrote this sentimental screenplay from Martha Cheavens's story. As the picture opens, Irene Dunne is walking out on a marriage-gone-sour; but before she goes she plays selections from her scrap book-record album. Flashbacks, visualized with each piece of music, bring the story up to the present. "You Were Meant For Me" recalls her first meeting with Cary Grant. "Missouri Waltz" is for the courtship. "Moonlight and Roses" for the wedding. "Poor Butterfly" for the Tokyo incidents. Ah, those ecstatic days in Japan! The bride tells her husband of the coming baby. Even his lack of enthusiasm, his selfish boyishness, his extravagance cannot quell her happiness. But comes the earthquake! And her bitter disappointment after the miscarriage when she learns she can never have more children! Back in the States life is drab indeed—until the couple adopt a baby. As Irene continues to change the records, the scenes are gay, sad, exciting, sweet, cruel, sentimental, realistic.

Stevens has directed well the episodes that hang on this trick device of a musical chronology. And his actors do not fail him. Miss Dunne is in best form as the bride, mother, the ebullient, the heart-broken wife. Cary Grant turns in a surprise performance as he fills the dramatic requirements of his serious role. These two get fine assistance from Beulah Bondi as the head of an adoption society, and Edgar Buchanan as the friend who guides the couple through their trials and estrangements. His big scene, in which he bathes the baby, will put mothers in stitches and tears of delight. But there won't be a dry eye (male or female) when Grant movingly appeals to the judge not to take away the baby. While women will swoon with compassion at the exigencies of motherhood and wifedom in *Penny Serenade,* men will bristle at the husband's lack of sympathy and under-developed character. Both will agree that the film is unusually good entertainment.

Philip T. Hartung, *The Commonweal*

*Penny Serenade* is frankly a weeper, but it is not quite like any other film I can think of. It has no preachment in the *Over the Hill* tradition; it has not the ambitious glucose of Mr. Chips; it is not revolutionary in a picture sense and I cannot imagine its material being put on in a play. It needs only three or four characters for most of the telling and its idea is simply that of a young couple who can't have a baby and so adopt one which becomes the center and the anchor of their lives, and dies at six. What now keeps them from going completely to pieces is that they are able to adopt another—and that is all of it. An errant sub-theme could have been strengthened with good effect, I think, in the steadying down of the young newspaperman-husband by marriage, tragedy and life with the kid; but this is not sufficiently worked into the texture to figure in the end. It remains a picture of the early years of marriage as they pass over so many a thousand Mr. and Mrs., so ordinary as to be terribly difficult to do.

Cary Grant is thoroughly good, in some ways to the point of surprise, for there is not only that easy swing and hint of the devil in him, but faith and passion expressed, the character held together where it might so easily have fallen into the component parts of the too good, the silly, etc. His scene with the judge is one of the rightly moving things in the picture. Edgar Buchanan is the darling boy though, and runs quietly away with every scene he is in, simply by the depth of his reality as the stumbling,

With Irene Dunne

kindly friend of the family, absurdly thick-fingered and ill-at-ease in everything but the delicate operations of the press room or washing the baby or patching troubles or cooking. It is what is known as a juicy part and usually squeezed like an orange, till it means nothing; here it is done with the right balance of humor, loyalty and love, and you will not forget Edgar Buchanan.

This is a picture not spectacular for any one thing, and yet the fact of its unassuming humanity, of its direct appeal without other aids, is something in the way of pictures growing up after all; for to make something out of very little, and that so near at hand, is one of the tests of artistry.

Otis Ferguson, *The New Republic*

With Irene Dunne and Baby Fleetwood

With Joan Fontaine

# SUSPICION

1941

## CREDITS:

Produced and distributed by RKO Radio. *Director:* Alfred Hitchcock. *Assistant director:* Dewey Starkey. *Screenplay:* Samson Raphaelson, Joan Harrison, and Alma Reville. From *Before the Fact* by Francis Iles. *Cinematography:* Harry Stradling. *Special effects:* Vernon L. Walker. *Editor:* William Hamilton. *Composer:* Franz Waxman. *Art direction:* Van Nest Polglase; *Associate:* Carroll Clark. *Set decorations:* Darrell Silvera. *Costumes:* Edward Stevenson. *Sound:* John E. Tribby. *Release date:* November 14, 1941. *Running time:* 99 minutes.

## THE CAST:

| | |
|---|---|
| *Johnnie* | Cary Grant |
| *Lina McLaidlaw* | Joan Fontaine |
| *General McLaidlaw* | Sir Cedric Hardwicke |
| *Beaky* | Nigel Bruce |
| *Mrs. McLaidlaw* | Dame May Whitty |
| *Mrs. Newsham* | Isabel Jeans |
| *Ethel (the Maid)* | Heather Angel |
| *Isobel Sedbusk* | Auriol Lee |
| *Reggie Wetherby* | Reginald Sheffield |
| *Captain Melbeck* | Leo G. Carroll |

## SYNOPSIS:

Johnnie Aysgarth, although considered a charming young man, has been cheating, lying, and stealing since school days. He is sincere for the first time in his life when he falls in love and elopes with Lina McLaidlaw. Johnny becomes involved in an embezzling scheme, and then Beaky, a foolish friend, suddenly dies. Lina begins to believe he is a murderer and that she is the next victim.

With Joan Fontaine and Billy Bevan

With Nigel Bruce

With Joan Fontaine

Every action on his part, she interprets as an attempt on her life; but when she finally confronts him, she discovers that he has no intention of killing her, that she had let her imagination run away with itself.

**REVIEWS:**

*Suspicion* may just mean Joan Fontaine and Cary Grant to a big majority, but the select should be advised at once that it is also a screen version of Francis Iles' *Before the Fact*. This electric minority may seethe at the treatment accorded one of the beautiful murder stories of the day. There is, I agree with the purists, no way to overlook the ending the movie people have given their script, for it completely undermines every spark of logic the sketch has had and must drive the mysterious Mr. Iles (a pseudonym) to brood on studio strategies and maybe even send out a series of squawks to Alfred Hitchcock for letting him down. As Mr. Hitchcock didn't rewrite the story, I suppose, but only directed what material was given him, he wouldn't seem much to be blamed.

Though there has been an insistent effort to make this novel of embezzlement and murder a cozy screen tale of domestic life in prewar England, with all the trouble really a notion in the wife's meandering mind and marital love a pretty boon abloom at the end, Mr. Hitchcock again and again manages to suggest the true Iles spirit and make of his smiling Cary Grant a plausible poisoner, a wavy-haired killer. For my part, I can't see that the wife who is so ready to believe the worst of her mate is such a lovely spirit. Just because her husband turns out to be bad about money, it doesn't mean he's a murderer, as any heiress knows.

The polish of the piece is a pleasure. Miss Fontaine is beauteous, and Cary Grant finds a new field for himself —the field of crime, the smiling villain, without heart or conscience. Crime lends color to his amiability. A generally good cast fills out the English manorial scene, with Dame May Whitty, Sir Cedric Hardwicke, and Nigel Bruce as suitable British types. And what will interest a number is the performance of Auriol Lee as a lady mystery-story writer.

John Mosher, *The New Yorker*

With Joan Fontaine, Nigel Bruce and Heather Angel

Show people have a word that is to them a final word, "sordid." If a picture is "sordid," they say—meaning if it is about the less fortunate or less admirable types of character—the public will not care for it. In a loose and very general way the rule might hold good, but it makes an absurd yardstick to measure any one picture by and it can only too easily be turned into a club to beat producers, writers and directors over the head with. The truth is that if a picture is well and soundly made and has the indispensables of interest and action, it can be "sordid" or anything else and let all prophetic crowds be damned. *The Little Foxes* has about as much concentrated evil in main story and main characters as the films have ever tackled; and *The Little Foxes* is one of the three leading pictures in the current nationwide box office.

Now comes Alfred Hitchcock with one of the better known murder stories, a clever study in the abnormal and vicious under a cloak of charm. The book was called *Before the Fact,* but they had to change the title of the movie to the much lamer one of *Suspicion,* for the reason that there is no longer actually any fact. The book itself is too slow, talky and under-characterized for my taste, but the very capacities for speed, suspense and actual people of the films could have been used to turn it into an exciting picture. Well, they weren't. The show runs an hour and three-quarters and the suspense gets less and less. Hitchcock had planned to keep both the girl in the story and the audience guessing right up to the last minute, and get away from the "sordid" at the last minute by having everything happily explained. On paper it still looks like a good idea; on film it simply breaks down, first through the nature of things and second through the film's lapses.

With Joan Fontaine

The film is well cast all down the line. Cary Grant in particular is just right for that part; the picture's most successful figure is Nigel Bruce as Beaky, which is simply the case of a grand trouper having a grand time building up a part out of what in the original was very little. As a matter of fact, one of the reasons the original wasn't followed closely enough to achieve the original effect is that as human beings—which even actors are when they're good—it is had to achieve the grim monotony of the book, which deals with a submoral scoundrel, a tidy and vapid wife and near-cretin from the public schools.

In every way save that of speed and form the production is a glossy, and done with a very shrewd eye for bringing out the inner conflict as it was redesigned. You do not say it was poor so much as that it was a disappointment, which is praise of a sort. The thing as it should have been to make sense, with certainty and horror mounting together, and faster, was not attempted—apparently because Hitchcock let an old shaky attitude scare him into thinking more of his box office than of his story logic and picture effect. He is a wise enough man in films to know better, a big enough name in films to dare more and get away with it. Every film maker with his wits about him knows the constant demand for compromise and how to accede to it gracefully; but he should know even more what can and what can't be sacrificed if he is to make good pictures. Men with their eye on the box office soon find that they can maintain fame and income without making good pictures, and presently are not making them, and finally cannot.

Otis Ferguson, *The New Republic*

Two-thirds of Hitchcock's *Suspicion* is very good, and that is enough to make a thriller. During that time Hitchcock used all his smoothness and his sharp eye for detail to build up a situation in which a loving wife (Joan Fontaine) is in danger of being poisoned by an equally loving but less trustworthy husband (Cary Grant). A best friend (Nigel Bruce, as a chubby ass) has already, mysteriously, fallen by the way. The fact that Hitchcock throws in a happy end during the last five minutes, like a conjuror explaining his tricks, seems to me a pity; but it spoils the film only in retrospect, and we have already had our thrills. A steep cliff, a letter from an insurance company, a glass of milk at the bedside—on such details and on the equivocal looks that foreshadow murder, Hitchcock fixes a fascinated gaze. So long as the magic lasts (there's a slow beginning, by the way) the film is the equivalent of the book you can't put down.

William Whitebait, *The New Statesman and Nation*

With Joan Fontaine

# THE TALK OF THE TOWN

1942

**CREDITS:**

Produced and distributed by Columbia. *Producer:* George Stevens. *Director:* George Stevens. *Associate producer:* Fred Guiol. *Assistant director:* Norman Deming. Screenplay by Irwin Shaw and Sidney Buchman. *Adaptation:* Dale Van Every. *Original story:* Sidney Harmon. *Cinematography:* Ted Tetzlaff. *Montage effects:* Donald Starling. *Editor:* Otto Meyer. *Music:* Frederick Hollander. *Musical direction:* M. W. Stoloff. *Art direction:* Lionel Banks and Rudolph Sternad. Gowns for Miss Arthur by Irene. *Sound:* Lodge Cunningham. *Release date:* August 20, 1942. *Running time:* 118 minutes.

**THE CAST:**

| | |
|---|---|
| *Leopold Dilg* | Cary Grant |
| *Nora Shelley* | Jean Arthur |
| *Michael Lightcap* | Ronald Colman |
| *Sam Yates* | Edgar Buchanan |
| *Regina Bush* | Glenda Farrell |
| *Andrew Holmes* | Charles Dingle |
| *Mrs. Shelley* | Emma Dunn |
| *Tilney* | Rex Ingram |
| *Jan Pulaski* | Leonid Kinskey |
| *Clyde Bracken* | Tom Tyler |
| *Chief of Police* | Don Beddoe |
| *Judge Grunstadt* | George Watts |
| *Senator James Boyd* | Clyde Fillmore |
| *District Attorney* | Frank M. Thomas |
| *Forrester* | Lloyd Bridges |

with Max Wagner, Pat McVey, Ralph Peters, Eddie Laughton, Billy Benedict, Harold Kruger, Lee White, William Gould, Edward Hearn, Ferike Boros, Dewey Robinson, Mabel Todd, Dan Seymour, Gino Corrado,

Frank Sully, Lee Prather, Clarence Muse, Leslie Brooks, Alan Bridge, and Joe Cunningham.

## SYNOPSIS:

Leopold Dilg, hunted on a trumped-up murder and arson charge, persuades Nora Shelley, the prettiest girl in town, to hide him in the house she has just rented to Michael Lightcap, bearded austere law school dean, who plans to spend a quiet summer writing, in anticipation of a Supreme.Court appointment.

His summer is less than quiet. He becomes involved with Dilg, first in argument, then as his attorney. Nora makes the dean realize that justice is not always in the letter of the law and he undertakes Dilg's defense. He also shaves his beard and undertakes an offensive to capture Nora.

Both men play hard to get, but Nora gets them both. Which one she keeps is not disclosed until the final moment.

## REVIEWS:

In Columbia's *The Talk of the Town* Producer-Director George Stevens successfully manages the ticklish chore of tucking in such strange bedfellows as zany comedy and social significance, rampart melodrama and quiet humor.

With Jean Arthur cast as Nora Shelley, a small-town Massachusetts schoolteacher, it was inevitable that any profound questions raised by the authors would resolve into the more basic problem of who marries Nora. The candidates for that honor are Prof. Michael Lightcap and one Leopold Dilg. Dilg is a philosophical mill hand whose predilection for the soapbox lands him in jail on a trumped-up charge of arson and murder. Lightcap is a dean of law and leading aspirant to the Supreme Court of the United States—a bearded bachelor, old beyond his years, who has rented Nora's country home expecting to spend a quiet summer writing a book.

But you can't make a movie out of a quiet literary summer. Nora livens it up by impulsively hiding the escaped Dilg in the professor's attic, then foisting herself on Lightcap as secretary-of-all-work. What happens to Lightcap after that shouldn't happen to one of the Nine Old Men—and undoubtedly never has. From here on the film owes much to the expert playing of the three co-stars. Miss Arthur and Grant have had more rewarding roles but play these with their customary finesse. Colman, getting the best break, is completely persuasive as the pedant who learns that the legalistic approach is cold comfort when justice cries for action.

The Sidney Buchman-Irwin Shaw screen play is well turned and witty and at its best when it sticks to the middle ground between farce and melodrama. The chief fault of the script is its excessive length and the fact that a standard

With Jean Arthur

lynching-mob climax is followed by a prolonged anticlimax in which Nora decides between judicial robe and denim. As a matter of fact, Nora is hardly the captain of her soul in this matter. George Stevens (*Woman of the Year*) cautiously tagged the film with two endings, and the voting of several preview audiences picked her groom.

*Newsweek*

My gripe with *The Talk of the Town* is the same complaint that I had against similar serio-comedies: *Mr. Smith Goes to Washington, Mr. Deeds Goes to Town, Meet John Doe*. It is only by a sudden fluke in the finale and a quick action on the part of one of the characters that a dreadful miscarriage of justice in this democracy is averted. Along with our debates on the practical *vs.* the theoretical aspects of law and justice, we are served some witty repartee and some very funny situations. George Stevens has adroitly directed the three principals and the fine supporting cast, including Edgar Buchanan, Glenda Farrell, Rex Ingram. If any one performance stands out, it is that of Mr. Colman. But still, when all the humor and wit are done, there remains the fact that but for Colman's last-

With Ronald Colman and Jean Arthur

With Edgar Buchanan and Jean Arthur

With Ronald Colman

With Ronald Colman and Jean Arthur

minute rescue, Grant would have died at the hands of lynchers; and a mob, even in the cultured state of Massachusetts, is an army of bloodthirsty beasts. Just because it is an American mob makes its crime no less serious than a mob of Nazis. If Mr. Stevens could have ended his film before the lynching scene (the whole is much too long anyway), he would have had a first-rate serio-comedy. As it is we have to take the film's warm and human glow with a grain of salt while we lament our own lynching problem in a world that is crying for law and adjustment.

Philip T. Hartung, *The Commonweal*

Only sourpusses and unbending esthetes aren't thankful for screwball comedies. At their best these comedies have more actual invention in situation and character and more turbulence and energy than nine-tenths of the seriously intended, pretentious movies. The recipe was invented by director Frank Capra and writer Robert Riskin in 1934, and it fails only when it isn't followed. In screwballs, relentless common sense is imposed on a lunatic situation which has come out of and continues to operate in a realistic American atmosphere. The comedy depends on someone like Jean Arthur, who sums up in her person all the characteristics of these movies: she is both an ordinary girl with ordinary reactions and a scatterbrain who wears birds' nests on her head and at normal times is out of breath from running or screaming or hitting someone on the chin. No one less cockeyed than Jean could negotiate the situation that makes you laugh. She serves also as stooge to the smart cracks of the hero, and this is what the hero is for—smart cracks. When Gary Cooper or Henry Fonda plays the Jean Arthur role, the girl supplies the bright banter. The main thing is the gag and the laugh, and the butt is always conventional living. But the social criticism is only a foil for laughs, except in Frank Capra's worst moments, when preaching takes seriously Christmas-card sentiments. Screwballs magically please and criticize in one picture everybody, from tory to radical, the people who laugh most at prat-falls and those who laugh most at Noel Coward. They are apt to have a high level of invention in characterization and observation of contemporary life. And in any case they are a triumph of the gag-writing art.

*Talk of the Town,* the latest example, is in between the best and the worst, but follows the formula closely enough to be good. One reason is that Jean Arthur is in it, not only to talk through her nose but to hide Leopold Dilg from the police. Eventually, with the help of a Supreme Court Justice, she saves Dilg from being lynched. Unfortunately, I found it hard to believe in Cary Grant as a soap-box orator and impossible to take Colman for Felix Frankfurter.

The playing, then, in all the main cases, is more stereotyped than fitting; but the big blanks that this draws are the long waits in between laughs and action, when Dilg and Judge become involved in the interpretation of the law. Director George Stevens directs, and not for the first time, at a pace which is more thorough than funny and shows his usual predilection for sentimentality. For some reason, the regard of Colman's valet for his master and the fondness between Colman and Grant turn out to be a little morbid. And somehow I can't take my lynching so lightly, even in a screwball. Still, I am all for this kind of comedy, for reason noted earlier, and for players like Arthur and Grant, who can mug more amusingly than most script writers can write.

Manny Farber, *The New Republic*

With Jean Arthur

160

With Ginger Rogers

# ONCE UPON A HONEYMOON

1942

## CREDITS:

Produced and distributed by RKO Radio. *Producer and Director:* Leo McCarey. *Screenplay:* Sheridan Gibney. *Original Story:* Leo McCarey. *Cinematography:* George Barnes. *Editor:* Theron Warth. *Musical Score:* Robert Emmett Dolan. *Art Direction:* Albert S. d'Agostino and Al Herman. *Release date:* November 27, 1942. *Running time:* 116 minutes.

## THE CAST:

| | |
|---|---|
| *Katie* | Ginger Rogers |
| *Pat O'Toole* | Cary Grant |
| *Baron Von Luber* | Walter Slezak |
| *Le Blanc* | Albert Dekker |
| *Borelski* | Albert Bassermann |
| *Elsa* | Ferike Boros |
| *Cumberland* | Harry Shannon |
| *Anna* | Natasha Lytess |
| *Dieinock* | John Banner |

with Hans Conried, Peter Seal, John Peters, Walter Stahl, Russell Gaige, Alex Melesh, George Irving, William Vaughn, Otto Reichow, Bob O'Connor, Hans Schumm, Bob Stevenson, Walter Bonn, Gordon Clark, Jack Martin, George Sorel, Albert Petit, Henry Victor, Bill Martin, Dell Henderson, Frank Alten, Arno Frey, Fred Niblo, Bert Roach, Johnny Dime and Henry Guttman.

## SYNOPSIS:

Pat, an American radio correspondent, is covering Europe in 1938 when he meets Kate. She is an American burlesque queen posing as a society woman and married to Baron Von Luber, an Austrian baron who is also a secret agent for the Nazis, and who helps the fifth column penetrate into Central Europe. While following Baron Von

With Ginger Rogers

With Ginger Rogers and Alex Melesh

With Ginger Rogers and George Irving

162

Luber, in an effort to obtain information about him and to finally expose him as an agent, Pat falls in love with Kate, whom he finally marries when the Baron is exposed.

**REVIEWS:**

*Once Upon a Honeymoon* is another of these modern comedies about our woeful times.

Leo McCarey who is responsible for this film's good production is also responsible for its uneven direction. The comedy is hilarious at times, but the tragedy is harrowing (as full well it might be in a film that uses Hitler's calendar after *Der Tag* as its locales). The mixture is not always happy, and too often McCarey allows Sheridan Gibney's screenplay to stand still and just talk. The film's two hours seem endless when this movie forgets to move. Not that the acting is dull. Ginger Rogers turns in a delightful performance as Katie O'Hara affecting a Philadelphia accent. Cary Grant is quite believable as the radio news analyst who turns on his French and German dialects and Irish charm with equal facility. Walter Slezak, a past master at Austrian barons, makes this one almost likeable in spite of his treachery. McCarey has directed the supporting cast well. But in spite of the funniest scenes and in spite of some of the good argument the script presents against Hitler, it is the underlying note of tragedy that makes the lighthearted humor seem too irresponsible. For me even the final episode in which Rogers pushes Slezak into the ocean isn't really a joke. Or perhaps I'm being overly sensitive about all this. Maybe the whole should be accepted as a legend; and the hilarious laughter that follows Slezak's drowning (as he's on his way to soften the U. S. for Hitler) is symbolic.

Philip T. Hartung, The Commonweal

As the title indicates, *Once Upon A Honeymoon* has some of the elements of a fairy-tale. But its background of human misery in a world going to pieces under the Nazis is terribly realistic. The story is quite often gay and funny, but it is also quite often grim. With deft touches, director-producer McCarey splashes laughter, suspense, romance, and tragedy onto his canvas.

Scholastic Magazine

Although it has been more than two years since McCarey worked at his job, his current *Once Upon a Honeymoon* demonstrates that he is still one of Hollywood's great comedy directors. Evidently he thought it necessary to make a film that reflected current events; at the same time, he felt that the events could use a little comedy relief. The result is probably a screen hit, but the attempt to play for both laughs and significance against a terrifying background of Nazi aggression is, on the whole, a little disappointing.

For a story that follows Hitler's brutal swath through Europe, this one has less action than you'd expect and more chit-chat than is good for the dramatic theme. Even so, McCarey does remarkably well with the uninspired story at hand, particularly when calling on Grant's and Miss Rogers's acknowledged gift for deft comedy. The supporting cast is excellent.

Newsweek

With Ginger Rogers

# MR. LUCKY

## 1943

With J. M. Kerrigan

**CREDITS:**

Produced and distributed by RKO Radio. *Producer:* David Hempstead. *Director:* H. C. Potter. *Screenplay:* Milton Holmes and Adrian Scott. *Original story: Bundles for Freedom* by Milton Holmes. *Cinematography:* George Barnes. *Special effects:* Vernon L. Walker. *Editor:* Theron Warth. *Music:* Roy Webb. *Musical director:* C. Bakaleinikoff. *Art direction:* Albert S. d'Agostino and Mark-Lee Kirk. *Release date:* 1943. *Running time:* 100 minutes.

**THE CAST**

| | |
|---|---|
| *Joe Adams* | Cary Grant |
| *Dorothy Bryant* | Laraine Day |
| *Hard Swede* | Charles Bickford |
| *Captain Steadman* | Gladys Cooper |
| *Crunk* | Alan Carney |
| *Mr. Bryant* | Henry Stephenson |
| *Zepp* | Paul Stewart |
| *Mrs. Ostrander* | Kay Johnson |
| *Greek Priest* | Vladimir Sokoloff |
| *Commissioner Hargraves* | Walter Kingsford |
| *Gaffer* | Erford Gage |
| *McDougal* | J. M. Kerrigan |
| *Foster* | Edward Fielding |
| *Siga* | John Bleifer |
| *Joe Bascopolus* | Juan Varro |
| *Dealer* | Don Brodie |

with Frank Mills, Mary Forbes, Mary Stuart, Rita Corday, Ariel Heath, Joseph Crehan, Kernan Cripps, Hal K. Dawson, Robert Strange, Frank Henry, Charles Cane, Budd

164

Fine, Hilda Plowright, Lloyd Ingraham, Emory Parnell, Major Sam Harris, and Florence Bates.

## SYNOPSIS:

Joe, a handsome gambler, is owner of the big gambling ship, Fortuna. He and his smooth, tough group are seeking money to bankroll operations in the South Atlantic when the draft board nails three of them. Joe assumes the identity of a dead crony to escape the draft and pursue his profession, and wheedles his way into a war relief outfit that is in need of money. With considerable difficulty he persuades them to let him run a gambling concession at a ball, but learns that his dead friend was an ex-convict needing but one more conviction for a life term. When an heiress falls for him the real complications begin and suspense increases until the various problems are solved by the end of film.

## REVIEWS:

The author of RKO Radio's *Mr. Lucky* is one Milton Holmes, a former professional at the Beverly Hills Tennis Club, who wrote his first story when he was down on his luck and showed it to Cary Grant when he was feeling optimistic. What Grant saw in this, his initial solo-starring film, was a gaudy chance to play a draft-dodging gangster who loads the dice against a social war relief agency until a determined heiress gentles him in the ways of righteousness and the war effort.

From the standpoint of Grant's faithful feminine admirers, the story was undoubtedly worth the money (Holmes picked up $30,000 down and ten-week contract at $500 the week). However, while the script has its bright and original moments, the overall theme of redemption is as realistic as Hans Christian Andersen, and occasionally several times as arch. . . .

Newsweek

The interesting fact about *Mr. Lucky,* a movie worthlessly concerned with a gambler and his war problems, is that it is as creative technically as it is uncreative in all other ways—intellectually, morally and emotionally. Its unacademic approach to its disgusting story, like hitching Count Fleet to a garbage truck, does not, on the whole, lead to much. Besides the vulgarity of its story, there is a wanton trading on the talents of its star, Cary Grant, and since the technique is only grafted on to the first part of the picture, the total effect is of a bad movie. But there are some things about the technique that can be called exciting and important.

Mainly the technique takes advantage of geography—the position of a person in relation to his environment and the people occupying it with him—using distorted photography, sound and acting, and some symbolism. This produces an intrinsically cinematic form, and a three-dimensional one. For instance, when the gambler gets

entangled with the ladies and bankroll of War Relief, Inc., the entangling is a combination of architecture, pantomine and movie devices used with almost acrobatic invention, which is quite a different thing from just making speeches about entanglement.

The best and funniest things, like some business with knitting, take place inside these useful partitions, but the most interesting spots are where the action and the means

With Alan Carney, Paul Stewart and Charles Bickford

With Henry Stephenson and Laraine Day

With Vladimir Sokoloff

of showing it are distorted not only to carry on the story but at the same time to comment on it. When Grant first makes his appearance, his walk, whistling and finger-flipping are all stepped up to the tempo of exaggeration, while the scene is shot at such an angle as to show him really cutting a swath through his world; so that we have Grant getting from one place to another and a caricature of him as Joe the Greek as well.

It is possible that the awfulness of the story is what drove the producers into the rashness of using a fancy method, and at that a method which is something a movie maker can get his teeth into. In *Mr. Lucky* although H. C. Potter, the director, must have had fun, this technique fails, being wrapped around the first half of something that is very cheap, a movie which uses war and the Greeks glibly, as a socially acceptable solution to its glib story of a gambler.

There is some very nice supporting work from Florence Bates, Charles Bickford (a welcome return), Gladys Cooper and Vladimir Sokoloff, as you would expect from any of them, and a promising performance from the vaudeville mimic, Allen Carney, as Joe's henchman, wonderfully named Krunk. Also, Hollywood has a discerning ability to hunt out the best of Tin Pan Alley that has been buried under the years to use its ballroom scenes or incidental music: here it digs out "Something to Remember You By," which is a valuable service. Admirers of Cary Grant will be shocked; but after they have hardened themselves against the indecent exploitation of him, they will at least find *Mr. Lucky* interesting, like a bad salad with an intelligent dressing.

Manny Farber, *The New Republic*

*Mr. Lucky* is what is known as a vehicle picture. If it weren't for Cary Grant's persuasive personality the whole thing would melt away to nothing at all. Its story is preposterous. The leading character is a rogue, a draft dodger, an unscrupulous gambler. He carefully specifies that he is a gambler, not a gangster; but his methods tend toward the latter classification. H. C. Potter has directed all this with an understanding of cinema. Even though you don't believe the events as you see them, most of the incidents prove entertaining, especially those that show Joe in action with the War Relief ladies. As I said, *Mr. Lucky* depends on Grant's ability to hold you. Perhaps this is just wherein the picture is dangerous; the first thing you know, you like this loose-moraled chiseler because of the way he tilts his hat or kids you so delightfully before he cheats you. Films frequently get mixed up in their ethics; it is difficult to decide what this one is trying to sell us—gamblers, draft dodgers, converted gangsters, or Mr. Grant. Maybe only Mr. Grant, but it chooses a strange way to do it.

Philip T. Hartung, *The Commonweal*

With Robert Hutton

# DESTINATION TOKYO

## 1944

## CREDITS:

Produced and distributed by Warner Brothers. *Producer:* Jerry Wald. *Director:* Delmer Daves. *Screenplay:* Delmer Daves and Albert Maltz. *Original story:* Steve Fisher. *Cinematography:* Bert Glennon. *Special effects:* Lawrence Butler and Willard Van Enger. *Editor:* Chris Nyby. *Music:* Franz Waxman. *Musical director:* Leo F. Forbstein. *Art direction:* Leo K. Kuter. *Sound:* Robert Lee. *Narration:* Lou Marcelle. *Release date:* January 1, 1944. *Running time:* 135 minutes.

## THE CAST:

| | |
|---|---|
| *Captain Cassidy* | Cary Grant |
| *Wolf* | John Garfield |
| *Cookie* | Alan Hale |
| *Reserve* | John Ridgely |
| *Tin Can* | Dane Clark |
| *Exccutive* | Warner Anderson |
| *Pills* | William Prince |
| *Tommy* | Robert Hutton |
| *Dakota* | Peter Whitney |
| *Mike* | Tom Tully |
| *Mrs. Cassidy* | Faye Emerson |
| *English Officer* | Warren Douglas |
| *Sparks* | John Forsythe |
| *Sound Man* | John Alvin |
| *Torpedo Officer* | Bill Kennedy |
| *Quartermaster* | William Challee |
| *Yo Yo* | Whit Bissell |
| *Commanding Officer* | John Whitney |
| *Chief of Boat* | George Lloyd |
| *Toscanini* | Maurice Murphy |

with Pierre Watkins, Stephen Richards, Cliff Clark, Deborah Daves, Michael Daves, Jack Mower, Mary Linda, Carlyle Blackwell, Kirby Grant, Lane Chandler, Joy Bar-

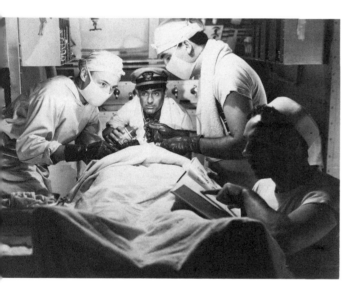

With William Prince and Dane Clark

With William (John) Hudson and Warren Douglas

With Warner Anderson, John Ridgeley, William Prince and
John Garfield

lowe, Bill Hunter, George Robotham, Dan Borzage, William Hudson, Charles Sullivan, Duke York, Harry Bartell, Jay Ward, and Paul Langton.

## SYNOPSIS:

Somewhere on the West Coast, the submarine *Copperfin* gets its orders to sail. On Christmas Eve, while the men are singing carols and exchanging gifts in the gallery, Captain Cassidy opens his sealed orders and discovers his destination is Tokyo. A prearranged meeting at Kiska with an American plane, enables the submarine to pick up Lt. Raymond, a meteorologist who continues with the *Copperfin* until it reaches the Japanese shoreline.

Lt. Raymond, Wolf, and Sparks, the submarine's radio man are put ashore to gather information vital to the navy for its planned attack on Tokyo. Aboard the submarine, submerged at the bottom of Tokyo Bay, waiting for an opportunity to get inside the nets, one of the crew becomes ill and the pharmacist's mate discovers the boy has acute appendicitis. The untutored pharmacist, aided by the captain and members of the crew, performs the operation.

The three men ashore succeed in their mission, radioing their knowledge to the airplane carrier U.S.S. *Hornet* which is then steaming toward the Islands of Japan. At the moment when United States bombers roar over the Japanese ships in Tokyo Bay, Captain Cassidy takes his chance of slipping out of the bay. When the *Copperfin* torpedoes a Japanese carrier, its presence in the harbor is discovered. After a struggle against depth charges, the captain orders the *Copperfin* surfaced, spots one lone Japanese destroyer and orders torpedoes fired. The Destroyer sinks, and the *Copperfin* escapes to the high seas.

## REVIEWS:

Even moviegoers who have developed a severe allergy for service pictures should find *Destination Tokyo*, the high among the superior films of the war. Certainly, in technical exposition and sheer, harrowing melodrama, the Warner Brothers' newest tribute to the armed forces rates very near the top of the list.

What with the film running two hours and fifteen minutes, just everything that could and does happen to an American submarine—short of an unhappy ending—occurs aboard the *Copperfin*.

As the *Copperfin's* captain, Cary Grant gives one of the soundest performances of his career; and John Garfield, William Prince, Dane Clark, and the rest of the all-male cast are always credible either as ordinary human beings or extraordinary heroes.

*Newsweek*

In *Destination Tokyo*, we live intimately with the crew of the U.S.S. *Copperfin* from Christmas Eve of 1942 until many months later, when the submarine drags its war-scarred hulk back into San Francisco Bay. It was, as its captain predicted, "a long time between beers," and the trip proves full of excitement and suspense. Director Delmer Daves spends much footage acquainting us with the men before the real action starts. There is the usual diversified cross-section: the serious, capable captain (Cary Grant); the talkative cook with the foreign accent (Alan Hale); the big, friendly Irish guy (Tom Tully); the tough lug who has been around and will talk about his conquests with women (John Garfield); the serious pharmacist's mate who got an A in chemistry and thinks he's an atheist (William Prince); the wet-behind-the-ears youngster who is intense about everything (Bob Hutton); the Greek whose patriotism is misunderstood, the executive officer, etc., etc. Once the excitement starts, things happen with a bang. The *Copperfin* goes to the Aleutians, picks up a reserve officer, is attacked by Japanese planes, has to dislodge (in a sequence that is breathless with suspense) an unexploded bomb from its aft deck, finally gets into Tokyo Harbor after eluding a series of mine fields and submarine nets, discharges three men who go ashore to make readings which are radioed to the *Hornet!* Then we see the bombardment of Tokyo. And just about as we feel we've watched as many thrills as any one film should hold, the camera takes us back to the *Copperfin* as we follow her course out of Tokyo Harbor and into her own terrific depth bombardment by Japanese destroyers. This long scene has almost enough material for a full length movie, and while it conveys successfully the strain of being in a submarine on which ash cans are falling one after the other, it is almost more than any audience can take, particularly an audience that has sat through the series of climaxes already provided by this story. For me the two most thrilling sequences were those showing the green youngster crawling forward to un-fuse the bomb, and later the appendectomy performed by the inexperienced pharmacist's mate (an operation you must have read about in one of its many accounts). *Destination Tokyo* could have been a better movie had it been shorter and had it not tried to be the last and most complete visualization of submarine warfare. As it stands, it is a praiseworthy tribute to the men who serve under the sea and are heroes without giving a thought to heroics.

Philip T. Hartung, *The Commonweal*

# ONCE UPON A TIME

## 1944

With Janet Blair

## CREDITS:

Produced and distributed by Columbia. *Producer:* Louis Edelman. *Director:* Alexander Hall. *Assistant director:* William Mull. *Screenplay:* Lewis Meltzer and Oscar Saul. *Adaptation:* Irving Fineman. Based on a radio play, "My Client Curly" by Norman Corwin and Lucille F. Herrmann. *Cinematography:* Franz F. Planer. *Editor:* Gene Havlick. *Music:* Frederick Hollander. *Musical direction:* M. W. Stoloff. *Art direction:* Lionel Banks and Edward Jewell. *Set decorations:* Robert Priestley. *Sound:* John Goodrich. *Release date:* May 11, 1944. *Running time:* 89 minutes.

## THE CAST:

| | |
|---|---|
| *Jerry Flynn* | Cary Grant |
| *Jeannie Thompson* | Janet Blair |
| *"The Moke"* | James Gleason |
| *Pinky Thompson* | Ted Donaldson |
| *McKenzie* | Howard Freeman |
| *Brandt* | William Demarest |
| *Gabriel Heatter* | Art Baker |
| *Dunhill* | Paul Stanton |
| *Fatso* | Mickey McGuire |

## SYNOPSIS:

Jerry Flynn, a glib producer, is about to have his theatre foreclosed. He tosses a nickel over his shoulder and it is picked up by Pinky. The boy offers Flynn a peek into a mysterious shoe box and the producer is captivated by Curly, the wonder worm, who dances to Pinky's music.

A famed radio commentator tells the story of the friendship between the boy and caterpillar, and how the worm learned to dance, despite natural obstacles. It is a publicity sensation and the trio becomes celebrities. But Pinky's sister and guardian, Jeannie Thompson, doesn't like all the fuss about the youngster. She clashes with Jerry Flynn in a pretty display of temper and of course romance blossoms between the producer and Miss Thompson.

But Flynn is a heel at heart and he arranges to steal the worm from the boy for a $100,000 sale to Hollywood. At the last minute he relents, realizes how low he is, and apologizes to Pinky. It is too late. The worm is missing. The boy has lost faith and Flynn is as disgusted with himself as is Jeannie. He tries in vain to win back the youngster. Then, strumming "Yes, Sir, She's My Baby," on the piano one afternoon, he stirs a beautiful butterfly out of a cocoon. It is the worm. Pinky is called, plays his harmonica and, friends again, Flynn, Pinky, and Jeannie watch the butterfly waltz around the room and then out into the world.

With John Abbott, Fred Howard, Ted Donaldson, Janet Blair, Charles Arnt, William Demaest, James Gleason, Lucille Brown, Don Barclay and Ian Wolfe

With James Gleason

With Howard Freeman

With Ted Donaldson

171

**REVIEWS:**

Just as if to prove that all their contemporary fables and romances don't have to be used as background for musical films, Hollywood presents a couple of glossy new movies that trip along their merry and escapist path without so much as a reference to war, labor or even a song of social significance. Perhaps these films were made to appeal to audiences who are "fed-up with war pictures." Or perhaps they were made for soldiers who prefer non-war entertainment films. In any case, their locale is a romantically realistic America that looks like New York and Indiana but excludes current events like invasions, strikes and coming elections. Such are the places dreamed up in these films.

Alexander Hall has directed this film well enough—though slowly. In spite of the good acting and characterizations by Cary Grant and Janet Blair, and especially by James Gleason as Flynn's assistant and Ted Donaldson as the beaming kid with great faith, there just isn't enough material here for a full-length feature. All this might have made a delightful short. (It was originally a radio sketch by Norman Corwin.) But even with its amusing satire on commercialism and uplifting message of optimism and goodness, the film runs dry and is too obviously prolonged. The climax, in which Curly walks out on bickering mankind and teaches a lesson in nature, is quite effective. All this is called, appropriately enough: *Once Upon A Time*.

Philip T. Hartung, *The Commonweal*

It would be nice to see some screen "fantasy" if it were done by anyone with half a heart, mind, and hand for it. But when the studios try to make it, duck and stay hid until the mood has passed. The story of a dancing caterpillar which became an international personality, a political and religious symbol, and a baby Armageddon for science, commercialism, and what is popularly thought of as innocence and idealism might, with great skill, imagination, and avoidance of whimsy, become wonderful. But *Once Upon A Time* is not wonderful. It is just less witty and more gently intentioned than the overrated radio hit—the Corwin "My Client Curly"—from which it was developed.

James Agee, *The Nation*

With Ted Donaldson and Janet Blair

With Barry Fitzgerald

# NONE BUT THE LONELY HEART

1944

**CREDITS:**

Produced and distributed by RKO Radio. *Producer:* David Hempstead. *Director:* Clifford Odets. *Associate producer:* Sherman Todd. *First Assistant director:* Ruby Rosenberg. *Screenplay:* Clifford Odets. From novel by Richard Llewellyn. *Cinematography:* George Barnes. *Special effects:* Vernon L. Walker. *Editor:* Roland Gross. *Musical score:* Hanns Eisler. *Musical director:* C. Bakaleinikoff. *Art direction:* Albert S. D'Agostino and Jack Okey. *Set decorations:* Darrell Silvera and Harley Miller. *Costumes:* Renie. *Production designer:* Mordecai Gorelik. *Release date:* September 22, 1944. *Running time:* 113 minutes.

**THE CAST:**

| | |
|---|---|
| *Ernie Mott* | Cary Grant |
| *His Mother (Ma Mott)* | Ethel Barrymore |
| *Aggie Hunter* | Jane Wyatt |
| *Ada* | June Duprez |
| *Twite* | Barry Fitzgerald |
| *Jim Mordinoy* | George Coulouris |
| *Did Pettyjohn* | Roman Bohnen |
| *Ike Weber (pawnbroker)* | Konstantin Shayne |
| *Lew Tate* | Dan Duryea |
| *Mrs. Tate* | Rosalind Ivan |
| *Miss Tate* | Dierdre Vale |
| *Ma Chalmers* | Eva Leonard Boyne |
| *Ma Snowden* | Queenie Vassar |
| *Millie Wilson* | Katherine Allen |
| *Cash* | Joseph Vitale |
| *Taz* | Morton Lowry |
| *Knocker* | William Challee |
| *Slush* | Skelton Knagg |
| *Ma Segiviss* | Virginia Farmer |
| *Marjoriebanks* | Art Smith |
| *Ike Lesser* | Milton Wallace |
| *Sister Nurse* | Helen Thimig |

| Flo | Renie Riano |
| Percy | Marcel Dill |

with David Clyde, Roy Thomas, Amelia Romano, Claire Verdera, Elise Prescott, Charles Thompson, Herbert Heywood, Helena Grant, Walter Soderling, Polly Bailey, Bill Wolfe, George Atkinson, Barry Regan, Ted Billings and Rosemary Blong.

## SYNOPSIS:

Just before the beginning of World War II, Ernie Matt, a young Englishman, is embittered over the loss of his father in the last war and the struggle of his mother to avert poverty by operating a second-hand store. He joins a band of thieves and is nearly caught only to return home and find his mother had become a "fence" to gain quick wealth because she knew she was soon to die of cancer. His mother dies in the prison hospital. Ernie hopes he can find a better life.

## REVIEWS:

*None But The Lonely Heart,* a story about the education of a young man in London's pre-war slums, is an unusually sincere, almost-good film and was made under unusually unexpected auspices. Its star, Cary Grant, asked that it be made, and plays its far from Cary Grantish hero so attentively and sympathetically that I all but overlooked the fact that he is not well constituted for the role. Its most notable player, Ethel Barrymore, seemed miscast too, but I was so soft as to be far more than satisfied by her beauty and authority. Its director, Clifford Odets, who also turned Richard Llewellyn's novel into the screen play, is still liable to write—or preserve from the book—excessive lines like "dreaming the better man"; he suggests his stage background as well as his talent by packaging his bits too neatly; and his feeling for light, shade, sound, perspective, and business is too luscious for my taste. But I believe that even if he doesn't get rid of such faults he will become a good director. I base my confidence in him chiefly on the genuine things about his faith in and love for people, which are as urgent and evident here as his sentimentalities; on two very pretty moments in the film, one of two drunken men playing with their echoes under an arch, the other of two little girls all but suffocated by their shy adoration of the hero; and on the curiously rich, pitiful, fascinating person, blended of Cockney and the Bronx, whom he makes of a London girl, with the sensitive help of June Duprez. I suppose I should be equally impressed by the fact that the picture all but comes right out and says that it is a bad world which can permit poor people to be poor; but I was impressed rather because Odets was more interested in filling his people with life and grace than in explaining them, arguing over them, or using them as boxing gloves.

James Agee, *The Nation*

From the RKO lot comes Clifford Odets' first writer-director chore, *None But the Lonely Heart,* with a musical score by Hanns Eisler. A perplexing mixture of good and bad, authentic and phony, the picture must certainly list on its credit side the experiments Odets and Eisler have made in the flexible interplay of music, sound effects and words. No one element dominates the soundtrack throughout. In a moment of high dramatic tension, when the hero is feeling suddenly impelled to burst the bonds of an oppressive existence, the music stands alone, rising to a virtual assault on the senses of the audience. Sound effects battle with words for supremacy in a garage scene and take over entirely in a jarring and violent automobile accident. Sometimes words, music and effects are blended for a moment of high effectiveness, as in a scene when two drunks make close harmony under a bridge that echoes with their erratic measures. Not all the results are so successful. There is a weak dependence on banal contrasts of laughter and crying, laughter and argument; a music-box is called too obviously and frequently into play; dramatic motivations of musical effects are sometimes tenuous at best. But consistently successful or not, the soundtrack is contributing a full share to the total effect.

There are more than the usual number of fine performances in *None But the Lonely Heart.* Cary Grant, as the good-for-nothing Ernie Mott, has a rare chance to burrow inside of a character and come out with something more than his usual charm and skillfully turned comic touches. Ethel Barrymore, as Ernie's mother who is too devoted to be very wise, is generally restrained and moving, and June Duprez brings a haunting quality to the strangely written part of the girl in the case. Barry Fitzgerald, Konstantin Shayne, Jane Wyatt, George Coulouris are among the other excellent players who leave their marks on the film.

Clifford Odets is still too much in the habit of theatre thought, and his script bogs down frequently in static conversational scenes that are death to the movement of the film. The natural development of the story is further disturbed by several unmotivated and unnecessary attempts to relate the case of Ernie Mott to the larger problems of a world on the verge of a second world war. These interpolations, along with the appearance of a number of unexplained characters and situations that may well have been carried over from the original novel, make for a general uncertainty and diffusion in the script. Such drawbacks are not enough, however, to prevent *None But the Lonely Heart* from taking firm hold on the audience from the first scene through to the last.

Hermine Rich Isaacs, *Theatre Arts Magazine*

*None But The Lonely Heart* is a huge mishmash that tackles the daring and important movie subject of the ugly side of modern society with just about the stalest, trashiest material I have ever seen. It is like setting out to see New York and finding yourself traversing the same old short cut from home to the grocery store.

The film's path—ostensibly pursuing Ernie Mott, a

Cockney character played by Cary Grant like Cary Grant, through London's East End slums in "his search for a free, noble and better life in the second quarter of the twentieth century"—actually tells how he comes home to be a good boy to his mother, Ethel Barrymore, when he is told she is dying of cancer. After they are reconciled he becomes so appalled by the poverty around them that he turns gangster, and his mother, in a try to get the money that will keep him from being a gangster, winds up in the penitentiary for racketeering. The picture ends with the son, evidently through as a gangster, meditating on "when the world is going to get off its knees." His wise old buddy (Barry Fitzgerald parodying his Hollywood self) tells him that the job will have to be done by the young people, but agrees with the boy that it will be done and that the bomber flying overhead is the first sign of the world's regeneration. This essential story I think is terrifying.

The film's message that the poor must scrape, thieve or kill to live and have only their own lonely hearts to tide them over, just seeps through at the end, despite the fact that dozens of people have been made sad or bad by that time. . . . The most important facts in it are still the violent, melodramatic hurdles, which are supposed to decide everything, including who is good, who is bad, how you should feel inside the theatre and how you should act outside it. The characters' motivations for turning into gangster or loving son still escape you; you have the same trouble liking the good people and hating the bad. Besides, the people are so nice, folksy, exotically talented, strong and wise that it is impossible for *them* to be inhabitants of a barren world. And things like cancer, a noble great lady—especially Ethel Barrymore—in prison for petty thievery, are so spectacular in themselves that you can't feel very grim or mournful.

I felt an essential lack of the evil, hardness, hunger, loneliness and frustration that seem to be what the film was interested in. Instead there is a great deal of lush, pretty lighting, settings, views, events, talk and people. The central material is constantly being obliterated. Either some decoration is too energetic (the halo lighting behind the heroine's head, the double image produced by placing people in front of mirrors); or the structure is clothed in gingerbread (Ernie Mott is made a genius at rifle-marksmanship, music, mechanics, prize-fighting, talking and philosophy when he really needs only a couple of these talents, and he has a ferocious-looking dog which is given about four times the attention necessary); or some element of the production is grotesque enough to step in front of the image (Cary Grant's consciousness of his own acting and posing invariably does; so does the director's interest in what funny things the camera can record). Many entertaining things in the picture, such as a funny scene of a drunk echoing his voice in a tunnel, and much of the film's gangster material still seems to be covering up for what the authors really had to say. Whether or not you agree with their idea of the modern world and people, their use of a dime-store melodrama seems the

With Ethel Barrymore and Barry Fitzgerald

With Ethel Barrymore

With Ethel Barrymore

vaguest, least convincing one to show it with, and the treatment and secondary material look as if they are trying to take your mind off both the theme and the triteness of the plot.

It is a very long film and it has some excellent things that should be mentioned. The blunt, journalistic treatment of a scene in which Ernie's gang beats up and robs the pawnshop owner seems to me as accurate as anything I have seen for catching the kind of skilled barbarism the Nazis practice—I don't think the movie calls the victim Jewish but it portrays him beautifully that way. He is played by Konstantine Shayne (whose bit as Karkov in *For Whom the Bell Tolls* was also the best performance of last year) with a very exact kind of unbowing dignity, goodness and melancholy. . . .

This is one of the biggest hodgepodges Hollywood ever constructed. I doubt that Clifford Odets, who wrote (from Richard Llewellyn's novel) and directed it, would ever have used such a plot or so artificial folk in a play of his own, but he probably wouldn't have been allowed to make this movie either if he had wanted to change the original novel's material. No doubt he would have preferred actors who looked more like slum people than Barrymore, Grant, Jane Wyatt or June Duprez, but the studio undoubtedly didn't. Nor will studios countenance the ridding of people like Grant or Fitzgerald of their stereotyped screen personalities. The movie is most firm and good when it is dealing with Jews, night clubs, penny arcades and gangsterism, which Odets knows about, and achieves with them a successful, peculiar synthesis of New York East Side and faint Englishness. Technically the film is a stew of literature, theatre, John Ford's, German and modern Hollywood movies. The whole thing, to quote one of the characters, "needs a solid base." It also, to quote the same person in this movie, "fries in its own fat."

Manny Farber, *The New Republic*

With Jane Wyatt

# ARSENIC AND OLD LACE

1944

**CREDITS:**

Produced and distributed by Warner Bros. *Producer:* Frank Capra. *Director:* Frank Capra. *Assistant director:* Russ Saunders. *Screenplay:* Julius J. Epstein and Philip G. Epstein. From the play by Joseph Kesselring as originally produced on stage by Howard Lindsay and Russell Crouse. *Cinematography:* Sol Polito. *Special effects:* Byron Haskin and Robert Burks. *Editor:* Daniel Mandell. *Music:* Max Steiner. *Musical direction:* Leo F. Forbstein. *Orchestral arrangements:* Hugo Friedhofer. *Art direction:* Max Parker. *Sound:* C. A. Riggs. *Release date:* September 23, 1944. *Running time:* 118 minutes.

**THE CAST:**

| | |
|---|---|
| *Mortimer Brewster* | Cary Grant |
| *Jonathan Brewster* | Raymond Massey |
| *Elaine Harper* | Priscilla Lane |
| *Abby Brewster* | Josephine Hull |
| *Martha Brewster* | Jean Adair |
| *O'Hara* | Jack Carson |
| *Mr. Witherspoon* | Edward Everett Horton |
| *Dr. Einstein* | Peter Lorre |
| *Lieutenant Rooney* | James Gleason |
| *Teddy "Roosevelt" Brewster* | John Alexander |
| *Reverend Harper* | Grant Mitchell |
| *Brophy* | Edward McNamara |
| *Taxi Driver* | Garry Owen |
| *Saunders* | John Ridgely |
| *Judge Cullman* | Vaughan Glaser |
| *Doctor Gilchrist* | Chester Clute |
| *Reporter* | Charles Lane |
| *Gibbs* | Edward McWade |
| *Man in Phone Booth* | Leo White |
| *Marriage License Clerk* | Spencer Charters |
| *Photographer* | Hank Mann |
| *Umpire* | Lee Phelps |

With Edward McWade, Jean Adair and Josephine Hull

Josephine Hull, Raymond Massey, Peter Lorre and John Alexander

## SYNOPSIS:

Two sweet but crazy old ladies, Abby and Martha Brewster, live in a secluded area of Brooklyn Heights. They have out of kindness poisoned a number of lonely old men. Mortimer Brewster, their nephew, has just married Elaine Harper, daughter of a minister who lives next door to the sisters. The happy couple are about to leave on their honeymoon when Mortimer becomes involved in his aunts' problems. When he finds a body in the windowseat, he discovers what they have been doing. Another mad but harmless relative thinks that he is "Teddy" Roosevelt and digs four-by-six-foot sections of the Panama Canal in the basement, sections suitable for the burial of "yellow fever victims" found by the aunts. Shortly after this discovery, another mad relative, Jonathan, a wanted criminal, and his friend, Dr. Einstein, arrive with another body. Later these two decide to kill Mortimer and Elaine, thinking they know too much. A neighborhood policeman recognizes Jonathan, and the police arrive just in time. At the same time, Mr. Witherspoon, superintendent of "Happydale," arrives to take "Teddy" away and the two aunts agree to go with him. As they are leaving, one of the aunts tells Mortimer that he was adopted. Relieved at not being one of the mad Brewsters, Mortimer rushes into Elaine's arms.

## REVIEWS:

Those lovable old Brewster sisters have had their picture "took." The Brewster sisters, just to refresh your memory, are those adorable spinsters who run a rooming house in Brooklyn, and are the very epitome of good citizenship—except for their pernicious habit of serving poisoned elderberry wine to lonely old gentlemen and burying them in the basement. Mercy killings, they call them, and don't try to tell them their motive isn't humane; you might hurt their feelings.

In this celluloid version of *Arsenic and Old Lace,* directed by Frank Capra, Warner Bros. has followed closely the basic pattern of the stage hit and it comes to the screen as a sure-fire box office hit. Completed two years ago, its release awaited the end of the stage run.

In the screen adaptation by Julius and Philip Epstein, the part of the drama critic has been expanded, and a marked departure in the plot finds him married at the start of the story instead of about to be. As played by Cary Grant in a sort of wild, tumultuous manner, the role dominates throughout.

Most of the play's clever lines have been retained, and a few good ones added—a very few. Much of the added dialogue aimed to provoke laughs fails to come off, and some of the expanded situations cause a slight drag in the otherwise rapid tempo. The film needs further editing.

Cary Grant's role as written for the screen is strongly slapstick, but despite the handicap he scores remarkably well. Miss Lane is capital as the young bride and often quite amusing.

*Citizen News*

With Raymond Massey, Jean Adair and Josephine Hull

If there are reservations about the celluloid re-working of *Arsenic and Old Lace,* they are chiefly concerned with Grant. For some reason or other, a fine actor merely mugs through the part of the sane member of the Brewster clan. Since he is a star, his part has been built up out of all proportion to the plot. That is not to his advantage.

Howard Barnes, *New York Herald Tribune*

Capra has left the play pretty well intact—in fact, more so than the previous adaptations, which he embellished with special social significance.

More is made of the Grant character than on the stage. Indeed, he carries this picture with pantomime, facial expressions and a wild sort of farcical delivery of lines. He is an expert at that.

The pruning shears could well be invoked in some of the episodes, because the pantomime is overdone. This overemphasis on silent action was doubtless purposed to allow for the laughs at the time the film was made, but audiences do not laugh that long over many of the scenes at this late date. In that particular result, this film is somewhat obviously a museum piece. Some may also object to the fact it gives such large scope to slapstick.

Raymond Massey makes his impersonation as sinister as desirable. Josephine Hall and Jean Adair are pluperfect in their parts.

Edwin Schallert, *Los Angeles Times*

My favorite scene is the one from the picture *Arsenic and Old Lace* which begins with Cary Grant making the spine-chilling discovery that his two dear old maiden aunts are poisoners who have murdered some dozen men.

The old ladies' sweetly matter-of-fact attitude toward their gruesome hobby is a superb blend of horror and comedy, and the scene develops uproariously.

I was helpless with laughter as I watched Cary change from a normal young man to a decidedly dizzy one, talking to himself, staring into the window seat from which bodies mysteriously appeared and disappeared, and making various wild attempts to cope with the situation.

Ida Lupino, *Saturday Evening Post*

With Raymond Massey and Peter Lorre

With Raymond Massey, Peter Lorre and Jack Carson

179

# NIGHT AND DAY

1946

With Donald Woods and Monty Woolley

## CREDITS:

Produced and distributed by Warner Bros., Inc. *Producer:* Arthur Schwartz. *Director:* Michael Curtiz. *Assistant directors:* Frank Heath and Robert Vreeland. *Screenplay:* Charles Hoffman, Leo Townsend, and William Bowers. Based on the career of Cole Porter. *Adaptation:* Jack Moffitt. *Cinematography:* Peverell Marley and William Skall. *Technicolor direction:* Natalie Kalmus and Leonard Doss. *Special effects:* Robert Burks. *Montages:* James Leicaster. *Editor:* David Weisbart. Music and lyrics by Cole Porter. Additional music composed and adapted by Max Steiner. *Musical director:* Leo F. Forbstein. Vocal arrangements by Dudley Chambers. Production numbers orchestrated and conducted by Ray Heindorf. *Art direction:* John Hughes. *Set decorations:* Armor Marlowe. *Costumes:* Milo Anderson. *Makeup:* Perc Westmore. *Sound:* Everett A. Brown and David Forrest. Dance numbers created and directed by LeRoy Prinz. *Dialogue direction:* Herschel Dougherty. *Dance Costumes:* Travilla. *Release date:* July 2, 1946. *Running time:* 132 minutes.

## THE CAST:

| | |
|---|---|
| Cole Porter | Cary Grant |
| Linda Lee Porter | Alexis Smith |
| Himself | Monty Woolley |
| Carole Hill | Ginny Simms |
| Gracie Harris | Jane Wyman |
| Gabrielle | Eve Arden |
| Anatole Giron | Victor Francen |
| Leon Dowling | Alan Hale |
| Nancy | Dorothy Malone |
| Bernie | Tom D'Andrea |
| Kate Porter | Selena Royle |
| Ward Blackburn | Donald Woods |
| Omar Porter | Henry Stephenson |
| Bart McClelland | Paul Cavanagh |
| Wilowsky | Sig Ruman |
| Specialty Singer | Carlos Ramirez |
| Specialty Dancer | Milada Mladova |
| Specialty Dancer | George Zoritch |
| Specialty Team | Adam and Jayne DiGatano |

| | |
|---|---|
| *Caleb* | Clarence Muse |
| *Petsy* | John Alvin |
| *O'Hallaran* | George Riley |
| *Producer* | Howard Freeman |
| *Director* | Bobby Watson |
| *First Peaches* | John Pearson |
| *Second Peaches* | Herman Bing |
| *Herself* | Mary Martin |

## SYNOPSIS:

At Yale in 1914 Cole Porter begins his career writing songs for school productions. When the war begins, Porter goes to France where he receives a leg wound that almost ends his career. However, he is determined, and after a number of failures, is able to court success with a number of his now-famous songs. Before his success his family is not enthusiastic about his choice of career but after his successes, they are happy. Later disagreements with his wife cause many problems. He almost loses his legs again as a result of a horseback riding accident, but is pulled through as another of his musicals becomes a Broadway hit.

## REVIEWS:

In Hollywood they are acclaiming the twentieth anniversary of the talkies. The Warners with a proprietary interest in the event have designated *Night and Day,* their motion-picture biography of Cole Porter, as the anniversary film. If they planned to celebrate some of the incredible inanities that have been perpetrated in the name of talk during the past two decades, they could not have chosen a better film with which to do it. But the sound track was designed to carry a load of music as well as words, and it must be admitted that the score of *Night and Day,* a radiant web woven tight of Cole Porter's melodies, makes it seem well worth having struggled through the first twenty years.

*Theatre Arts Magazine*

It is an interesting point that in a couple of new musical films, the music is the main attraction. Even in competing with elaborate casts, lush technicolor and production designed to knock your eye out, the music is what you'll remember long after you've forgotten the faint-hearted efforts of stars to enact thin stories. Perhaps this is as it should be if entertainment is the prime motive, but such films do little to forward the cause of cinema.

In *Night and Day* the music of Cole Porter comes through beautifully. It is a pleasure to hear again such numbers as "What Is This Thing Called Love?," "I've Got You Under My Skin," "Begin the Beguine," "I Get a Kick Out of You." But these good songs pop up like pegs in a story without drama. No doubt the writers thought in basing their script on Porter's "career" instead of his life, they could avoid issues that might be precarious in portraying real people who are still alive. Unfortunately the

With Monty Woolley

With Alexis Smith, Monty Woolley and Ginny Simms

181

film makes many of these real people no more real than the dummies in a department store window.

The main conflict in the latter part of *Night and Day* seems to be between Cole (Cary Grant so underplaying the role that he's always Cary Grant) and his wife (Alexis Smith in a series of handsome gowns). She, rather rightfully, resents their house (full of actors and producers) being like Grand Central Station and her husband's I-love-you-but-I'm-busy attitude. Monty Wolley plays himself, the Yale professor who became Cole's good friend and adviser as well as the man who came so definitely to dinner that his beard now belongs to the world. He puts his all into Porter's brilliant satirical song: "Miss Otis Regrets." Ginny Simms and Jane Wyman handle most of the songs and do them very well—Miss Simms specializ-

ing on those originally written for Ethel Merman. There are of course several good production numbers sung and danced by a variety of specialists. Once again Mary Martin manages to steal the show with her deft interpretation of "My Heart Belongs to Daddy." But it is difficult to single out any one of Porter's songs as best; in fact "You're the Top" could very well have been the film's title. Perhaps it should have been; then the script-writers might not have given us that ridiculous scene which shows Grant at the piano composing "Night and Day" and being inspired by the "drip, drip, drip of the rain drops" and the presence of Alexis Smith. (Porter really wrote it for Fred Astaire.)

Philip T. Hartung, *The Commonweal*

With Ginny Simms

With Ingrid Bergman

# NOTORIOUS

1946

**CREDITS:**

Distributing company: RKO Radio. Producer: Alfred Hitchcock. Director: Alfred Hitchcock. Assistant producer: Barbara Keon. 1st Assistant director: William Dorfman. Screenplay: Ben Hecht. From an original subject by Alfred Hitchcock. Cinematography: Ted Tetzlaff. Special effects: Vernon L. Walker and Paul Eagler. Editor: Theron Warth. Music score: Roy Webb. Musical director: C. Bakaleinikoff. Art direction: Albert S. D'Agostino and Carroll Clark. Set decoration: Darrell Silvera and Claude Carpenter. Costumes: Edith Head. Sound: John E. Tribby and Terry Kellum. Release date: July 22, 1946. Running time: 103 minutes.

**THE CAST:**

Devlin — Cary Grant
Alicia Huberman — Ingrid Bergman

Alexander Sebastian — Claude Rains
Paul Prescott — Louis Calhern
Mme. Sebastian — Madame Konstantin
"Dr. Anderson" — Reinhold Schunzel
Walter Beardsley — Moroni Olsen
Eric Mathis — Ivan Triesault
Joseph — Alex Minotis
Mr. Hopkins — Wally Brown
Ernest Weylin — Gavin Gordon
Commodore — Sir Charles Mendl
Dr. Barbosa — Ricardo Costa
Hupka — Eberhard Krumschmidt
Ethel — Fay Baker

with Antonio Moreno, Frederick Ledebor, Luis Serrano, William Gordon, Charles D. Brown, Ramon Nomar, Peter Von Zerneck, Fred Nurney, Herbert Wyndham, Aileen Carlyle, Harry Hayden, Dink Trout, John Vasper, Howard Negley, George Lynn, Eddie Bruce, Don Kerr, Warren Jackson, Howard Mitchell, Sandra Morgan, Tom Coleman,

With Louis Calhern

With Claude Rains and Ingrid Bergman

Lillian West, Beulah Christian, Alameda Fowler, Garry Owen, Patricia Smart, Lester Dorr, Candido Bonsato, Tina Menard, and Virginia Grett.

**SYNOPSIS:**

Alicia Huberman's German father gets twenty years on a conviction for treason. The daughter, embittered and romantically footloose, goes on a beautiful binge. While stoking it away, she meets Devlin, an American intelligence officer deliberately around for a purpose. Having had her wires tapped, he knows she opposed her father and registered her patriotism for America. This fits her for a job in Rio de Janeiro where I. G. Farben, the worldwide German chemical cartel, is up to some deviltry, nature unknown. The idea is presumed resentment over her father's imprisonment and death, plus her German antecedents, will provide her entree into the Farben circle.

Alicia accepts. She falls in love with Devlin, who also falls for her. Only he can't get the luridness of her past out of his mind. She meets Alexander Sebastian, head Farben man, who knew and admired her in Washington, D.C. Sebastian romances Alicia. She marries him because Devlin seems permanently out of her reach. Her investigation centers around an apparently innocent bottle of wine. Stealing Sebastian's key to the wine cellar, she passes it to Devlin, who discovers the bottle hides ore, later established as uranium, which means the atom bomb. But Sebastian also discovers things: the key incident, a broken wine bottle, and concludes Alicia is an American agent.

Falling back on his mother, Mme. Sebastian, for advice, Sebastian gets it; slow poisoning for Alicia, but no exposure of the incidents because this would mean death for Sebastian at the hands of his brother conspirators. When Alicia fails to keep a rendezvous with Devlin after five days he investigates, makes his way to her bedroom, learns what has happened and proceeds to carry her to safety. Sebastian fails to interfere since it would expose him and what has happened. But his clique, suspicious now, calls Sebastian to an accounting, inevitably meaning his death.

**REVIEWS:**

The unease that assaults an artist transplanted bodily out of his native soil has affected even veteran director Alfred Hitchcock who, since his arrival in Hollywood, has consistently failed to live up to the standards of *Thirty-Nine Steps* and *The Lady Vanishes*. A celebration is therefore in order for his most recent effort, *Notorious*. With a highly polished script by Ben Hecht, and with Ingrid Bergman and Cary Grant to bring glamour and sultry vitality to the leads, Mr. Hitchcock has fashioned a film in the supercharged American idiom of the sort that made *Casablanca* popular. With a minimum of tricks and an uncluttered story line, he tells of a beautiful American spy who marries an enemy leader and is rescued at Zero hour by her secret service superior when her husband tries to poison her.

Hermine Rich Isaacs, *Theatre Arts Magazine*

One thing that a slick, handsome production like Alfred Hitchcock's *Notorious* does is to make you wonder fleetingly what international intrigue is really like, and what kind of lives international agents lead, anyway. Our own national investigations seem to indicate that agents of that sort are earnest, mousy people with conveniently unmemorable faces, operating with power and money behind them, perhaps, but with quiet middle-class respectability written all over them. What, if anything, connects them with the traditional, top-hatted, morning-coated diplomatic service; why are they so sheepishly tongue-tied when "unmasked"—no shrugs, no epigrams, no brilliant last-minute juggling with documents, no sensational suicides in high places? This is the kind of query

that the earlier Hitchcock would have been delighted to work on; lately, however, he seems contented enough to ring the changes on stock plots and characters, to give us only the incredible vagaries and the flamboyant indiscretions of the wealthy international set in Miami and points south.

Not that *Notorious* is precisely a dull picture; but we have seen so many of its kind lately that even Hitchcock's superior bag of tricks does very little to retard the inevitable functioning of the law of diminishing returns. Either because the *Casablanca* cycle of movies has left us blase, glutted with the type, or because Hitchcock himself has slipped into a rut, *Notorious* seems to lack pace, and there are fewer and fewer than ever of those little clutching moments of excitement and recognition which made, say, *The Lady Vanishes* the kind of movie that is remembered and discussed years after it has disappeared from the local houses. Something seems to have happened to the

With Ingrid Bergman

185

With Ingrid Bergman, Madame Konstantin and Claude Rains

dialogue, too; no irony, no wit, and only one small laugh near the beginning—Ingrid Bergman says to Cary Grant: "My car is outside"; "Naturally," he answers. From then on they take themselves and their pleasures with a heavy seriousness which suits Bergman's talents very well, but leaves Cary Grant with very little to do but fold his arms and look ominous—a sad waste of an actor with a very pretty talent for verbal comedy and the most expressive spine in Hollywood.

Claude Rains plays what I am sure is intended to be an unsympathetic role; he is Alexander Sebastian, German representative for the I. G. Farben company in Rio de Janeiro. . . .

Unfortunately it is difficult not to find Rains' baggy-eyed, shrewd-face villainy more interesting, and therefore more sympathetic, than the virtue of Cary Grant and his large, bleak American Superiors, one of whom spends a great part of his time lying on a hotel bed eating crackers and peanut butter. Besides, any hero who lets romantic considerations prevent his being efficient at the job he is assigned is likely to look foolish and unintelligent beside the villain, whose lack of morals (contrary to observable fact) often is accompanied by a stern disregard of sentimentality. The good are often simple and stupid and the wicked complex and clever. It is, I suppose, no wonder that we have in real life such difficulty with international intrigue; and it is presumably too late to hope for a divine script-writer who will step in and adjust the balance. We can only cultivate sharper wits and a more realistic attitude—the epigram, the shrug, and the adroit juggling of documents.

D. Mosdell, *The Canadian Forum*

186

With Shirley Temple and Rudy Vallee

# THE BACHELOR AND THE BOBBY SOXER

## 1947

## CREDITS:

*Distributing company:* RKO Radio. *Producer:* A Dore Schary Production. *Director:* Irving Reis. *Assistant to producer:* Edgar Peterson. *Assistant Director:* Nate Levinson. Original story and screenplay by Sidney Sheldon. *Cinematography:* Robert de Grasse; Nicholas Musuraca. *Special effects:* Russell A. Cully. *Editor:* Frederic Knudtson. *Composer:* Leigh Harline. *Musical director:* C. Bakaleinikoff. *Art direction:* Albert S. D'Agostino and Carroll Clark. *Set decorations:* Darrell Silvera and James Altwies. *Costumes:* Edward Stevenson. *Sound:* John L. Cass and Clem Portman. *Release date:* September 1, 1947. *Running time:* 95 minutes.

## THE CAST:

| | |
|---|---|
| *Dick* | Cary Grant |
| *Margaret* | Myrna Loy |
| *Susan* | Shirley Temple |
| *Tommy* | Rudy Vallee |
| *Beemesh* | Ray Collins |
| *Thaddeus* | Harry Davenport |
| *Jerry* | Johnny Sands |
| *Tony* | Don Beddoe |
| *Bessie* | Lillian Randolph |
| *Agnes Prescott* | Veda Ann Borg |
| *Walters* | Dan Tobin |
| *Judge Treadwell* | Ransom Sherman |
| *Winters* | William Bakewell |
| *Melvin* | Irving Bacon |
| *Perry* | Ian Bernard |
| *Florence* | Carol Hughes |
| *Anthony Herman* | William Hall |
| *Maitre d'Hotel* | Gregory Gay |

## SYNOPSIS:

Dick, a practical artist, comes first to the attention of Margaret, a judge, as an arrestee, following a cafe episode,

With Shirley Temple

With Ray Collins

and although she disapproves of and scolds him, she acquits him for lack of evidence. The next day Dick lectures to an art class at the local high school. In that class is Susan, Margaret's impressionable little sister who sees Dick as a knight in shining armor. Later she crashes his apartment, while he is out, and is discovered there with him, following his return by Margaret and her friend Tommy, an assistant district attorney. By the implications of the quite innocent situation, Dick is guilty of enough things to get him twenty years, including the punching of Tommy's nose, but the judge, advised by her uncle, a psychiatrist, arranges for Dick to go unprosecuted on the promise that he will pretend to be Susan's boyfriend long enough for the latter to recover from her infatuation. So Dick escorts Susan to a basketball game, a picnic, and so forth, aping the jive talk and adolescent mannerisms of her generation, and trying to restore to her affections the nice young man her own age who has been her boy-friend up to now. Susan finally sees Dick in proper perspective, and he and Margaret find they are in love with each other.

## REVIEWS:

Without taxing or insulting your intelligence, some new comedies are providing some hearty laughs and a good excuse for timely escape into air-cooled cinema palaces. The plot of *The Bachelor and the Bobby-Soxer* won't solve any major problems about the younger generation, but its lines are amusing and the members of its handsome cast are bubbling with anxiety to entertain. Cary Grant is pleasantly coy as the artist-playboy who finds himself squiring a love-sick seventeen-year-old in order to avoid a more trying sentence. Because Shirley Temple is such an attractive young actress, the task should be consider-ably lightened for him; but high-school girls these days have extraordinary ideas about how their knights in shining armor should behave and poor Mr. Grant finds himself doing many things that hardly fit his age. He's a good sport about the whole thing (even during the obstacle race at the picnic) until he realizes how much he prefers Shir-ley's older sister, played by Myrna Loy, who looks lovely but acts like a cold tomato because she's a female judge who takes herself very seriously indeed. Rudy Vallee, in another of his clever portraits of a stuffed shirt, is more to her liking—until she too sees Cary lustrous in armor. Irving Reis has directed his cast for laughs and succeeds in getting them. Ray Collins, as a court psychiatrist, tries to inject a serious note on the behavior of adolescents who have crushes; but even he succumbs to the spirit of this playful comedy.

Philip T. Hartung, *The Commonweal*

For years we have taken for granted that it is not neces-sary, even for a critic, to see every individual film which comes out of Hollywood in order to be a competent judge

188

of the Hollywood movie; having seen one or two musical extravaganzas, for example, with or without technicolor, we have thankfully exercised what we hold to be a legitimate privilege and avoided the rest. This policy of careful selection enables us to maintain toward movies in general a childlike attitude of expectancy and potential delight, a set of what strikes the truly omnivorous fan as absurdly high standards of movie entertainment, and a perennial capacity for furious disappointment when the expectancy is betrayed and the standards flouted. This month, however, responding to pressure from a see-them-all-before-you-judge theorist, we inspected *The Road To Rio* (Bing Crosby, Bob Hope), and *The Bachelor and the Bobby-Soxer* (Cary Grant, Myrna Loy, Shirley Temple), which ordinarily we would dismiss as defying rational discussion. We emerged with an even more jaundiced view of American movie comedy than before, and a resolution to return next month to our original position of commenting only on films which are passable entertainment to begin with, and ignoring absolute tripe with a spotless conscience.

*The Bachelor and the Bobby-Soxer* is funnier than *The Road to Rio,* but not much. Cary Grant plays the part of an artist who has quite a reputation (undeserved, of course, but you know how people are), as a roué. His dismay at finding himself victimized by his own ambiguous behavior is really quite comic, and so, in a limited way, are his antics which he performs in order to escape from the absurd position of middle-aged knight-in-shining-armor to a seventeen-year-old girl. What really holds our fascinated attention, however, is the whole Hollywood conception of the normal American adolescent, to say nothing of its picture of an American court of law presided over by a female judge. It was not, however, until we had seen *The Secret Life of Walter Mitty* over again that we realized at least in part why it is that American movie comedy as a whole seems stale and flat (though by no means unprofitable, apparently). *The Secret Life of Walter Mitty* is a very funny film, even on a second seeing, because Danny Kaye is an excellent mimic, and a virtuoso in the field of artificial comedy. Mitty's life in fantasy is intended however to contrast with his life as a typical suburbanite young man dominated by his mother and hag-ridden by the active malice of inanimate objects; this comedy of contrast was clear and genuinely humorous in Thurber's original story. Unfortunately nobody in Hollywood has the slightest idea of what real life is, and Hollywood's idea of what the real is is so fantastic that what results in the movie version of Walter Mitty is a confused kind of juxtaposition of two fantasies, neither of which has any relevance whatever to normal experience (supposing there is such a thing).

D. Mosdell, *Canadian Forum*

*The Bachelor and the Bobby-Soxer* is a nice, clean, sunny old-fashioned farce. . . . The only fault I found with Reis' direction, and it's a noticeable one since it occurs twice, is an episode in which two characters chase each other around a table. The device is just a little like showing

indecision by pacing up and down in a small area—not excessively imaginative. Otherwise Reis has directed Cary Grant and Myrna Loy so that they appear as charming as they can be. With Shirley Temple very little variation is possible. She is a sweet young girl, the audiences are enchanted by her, and that's that.

The story is simple and stylized; sure-fire stuff guaranteed to do no perceivable harm. . . . Cary Grant has now developed a characterization that is constant, fool-proof, engaging, hardy and warranted to be attractive. The audience laughed so hard I missed some of the lines.

Shirley O'Hara, *The New Republic*

With Johnny Sands, Rudy Vallee and William Hall

# THE BISHOP'S WIFE

## 1947

With David Niven

## CREDITS:

Distributing company: RKO Radio. Producing company: Samuel Goldwyn Productions. Producer: Samuel Goldwyn. Director: Henry Koster. Screenplay: Robert Sherwood and Leonardo Bercorici. From a novel by Robert Nathan. Cinematography: Gregg Toland. Special photographic effects: John Fulton. Editor: Monica Collingwood. Music by Hugo Friedhofe. Orchestral arrangements: Jerome Moross. Vocal direction: Charles Henderson. Musical direction: Emil Newman. Art direction: George Jenkins and Perry Ferguson. Set direction: Julie Heron. Costumes: Irene Sharaff. Makeup: Robert Stephanoff. Hair stylist: Marie Clark. Sound: Fred Lou. Release date: November 13, 1947. Running time: 105mins.

## THE CAST

| | |
|---|---|
| Dudley | Cary Grant |
| Julia Brougham | Loretta Young |
| Henry Brougham | David Niven |
| Professor Wutheridge | Monty Woolley |
| Sylvester | James Gleason |
| Mrs. Hamilton | Gladys Cooper |
| Matilda | Elsa Lanchester |
| Mildred Cassaway | Sara Haden |
| Debby Brougham | Karolyn Grimes |
| Maggenti | Tito Vuolo |
| Mr. Miller | Regis Toomey |
| Mrs. Duffy | Sara Edwards |
| Miss Trumbull | Margaret McWade |
| Mrs. Ward | Ann O'Neal |
| Mr. Perry | Ben Erway |
| Stevens | Erville Alderson |
| Defense Captain | Bobby Anderson |
| Attack Captain | Teddy Infuhr |
| Michel | Eugene Borden |
| First Lady in Michel's | Almira Sessions |
| Second Lady | Claire DuBrey |
| Third Lady | Florence Auer |

| Hat Shop Proprietress | Margaret Wells |
| Hat Shop Customer | Kitty O'Neill |

*Hysterical Mother:* Isabel Jewell; *Blind Man:* David Leonard; *Delia:* Dorothy Vaughan; *Cop:* Edgar Dearing; *Saleslady:* Edythe Elliott; *Boy at table:* Don Garret; *Girl at table:* Shirley O'Hara; *Santa Claus:* Joseph J. Greene

## SYNOPSIS:

Dudley is an angel who could be any man with faith and a good heart. He comes to the aid of Henry Brougham, an Episcopalian bishop, in answer to the latter's prayer for help in obtaining funds for a new cathedral. The overworked bishop has begun to lose faith and also feels that his marriage is failing. He knows but is unable to tell anyone that Dudley is an angel. Dudley proceeds to make Julia, the bishop's wife, find more happiness in life, while Henry continues to spend most of his time thinking of the new cathedral. In the end the new church remains unbuilt, but Dudley has shown the bishop the right way, has brought happiness and a touch of romance back into the life of Julia, and has given renewed confidence to old Professor Wutheridge.

## REVIEWS:

After a talky start, Director Henry Koster weaves a picture that is at times quite lovely; and in the skating scene it gets as close to poetry as movies ever do. The argument bogs down occasionally and can hardly be considered orthodox. But as a sophisticated Christmas carol, *The Bishop's Wife* comes through nicely and should please adults who like their movies off the beaten track.

Philip T. Hartung, *Commonweal*

Robert Nathan's early novel (1928), *The Bishop's Wife*, has been revived by Samuel Goldwyn (with help on the script from Robert Sherwood and Leonardo Bercovici) to honor the current boom in cinema angels. Unlike the majority of his predecessors, however, Mr. Nathan's angel is not beyond descending to diabolical methods to achieve his heavenly purposes, and the gleam in his eye is scarcely seraphic.

If the angel is considerably less tedious than most, it is, first of all, because the miracles he is called upon to perform are onerous neither to him nor to his audience. A flick of the hand and a bottle of brandy refills perpetually; a smile and every woman within its range feels divinely beautiful. Certain other of his feats, conceived with a heavier hand, are retrieved from disaster by the direction of Henry Koster who wisely refrains from bearing down full weight on the script. But it is Cary Grant's playing that rescues the role of the angel named Dudley from the ultimate peril of coyness. With nothing more than a beaming countenance and an air of relaxation that is cer-

With Elsa Lanchester

With Monty Woolley and Loretta Young

191

tainly not of this world, he achieves a celestial manner without so much as a hint of wings on his dark blue suit. An expert cast is on hand to show by reflection what Cary Grant has refrained from making irksomely explicit. David Niven's prelate is a wistful and absent-minded character who is scarcely a match for Dudley. As the Bishop's wife, Loretta Young is sufficiently lovely to make even an angel fall; and in lesser roles Monty Woolley, James Gleason and Elsa Lanchester react to Dudley's miraculous passage with characteristic gaiety.

The Bishop had prayed to God for guidance in how to separate Mrs. Hamilton, a rich parishioner, from sufficient money to build a cathedral. God sent him Dudley and Dudley had soon resolved his dilemma by threatening Mrs. Hamilton with the name of her long-lost lover. Now, Dudley convinces both her and the Bishop that God could better be served by abandoning the cathedral project in favor of helping the needy. This is a refreshingly practical notion and comes with the lure of novelty from a screen which has heretofore thrown its weight—in the manner of *The Bells of St. Mary's*—in favor of building churches. For this reason alone *The Bishop's Wife* should commend itself to the public.

Hermine Rich Isaacs, Theatre Arts Magazine

This fantasy will probably entertain you and put you in gay Christmas spirits. However, if you've read Robert Nathan's book upon which the film was based, you will be disappointed.

For Mr. Nathan at his best has a hard-to-equal gift for spinning delicate fragile fantasies that often come closer to touching upon the truth of people's lives and emotions than do the most realistic novels. His *Bishop's Wife* was the story of a successful Episcopalian bishop who is determined to build a huge new cathedral in his city. He is so wrapped up in cultivating the wealthy people in his diocese that he has no time for his family or for really religious matters. As his worries over the cathedral pile up, he prays for help in solving his problems. An angel comes to his rescue—in the form of a young man named Michael.

In the film the angel's name has been changed to Dudley. This one fact should warn you that the movie version of Mr. Nathan's story is going to pursue a different path from the original.

For the name Michael suggested a naive youth—someone sweet, gentle, and innocent. And this was the nature of Mr. Nathan's angel. The name Dudley, on the other hand, is the kind of name Hollywood uses to suggest a comic character—and that's what we get in the film.

Instead of Nathan's golden-haired youth, we find Cary Grant playing angel in his best man-of-the-world manner. Grant's Dudley performs minor miracles with the sophisticated air of a magician doing sleight-of-hand tricks. Dudley is a fellow who knows what to order in the best French restaurants, and how to buy women's hats. In fact, he's one of the most worldly gentlemen we've ever seen. His "boy scout" manners hardly fit in with the rest of his characterization. And it's practically impossible to visualize Dudley in a halo.

While Dudley is very entertaining, it's hard to be sure his antics aren't in the long run a genial ribbing of religious values, rather than an affirmation of those values.

Although the story winds up with the bishop coming around to a more attentive attitude toward his wife and a less materialistic attitude toward religion, the reason for his turnabout is somewhat questionable. His change of heart is prompted chiefly by the fact that his wife has become fonder of Dudley than of himself. Then he momentarily forgets his cathedral because he is jealous of Dudley.

Since the film ends with a beautifully worded sermon about what Christmas means, it's easy to overlook much of the dubious logic by which the film arrives at its conclusion. But when a film undertakes to bring audiences a spiritual message, we wonder whether the director doesn't owe it to us to clothe such messages in less muddled characterizations and to dispense with caricature.

Scholastic Magazine

192

With James Gleason and Loretta Young

With Loretta Young

With Myrna Loy and Melvyn Douglas

# MR. BLANDINGS BUILDS HIS DREAM HOUSE

## 1948

### CREDITS:

Selznick Releasing Organization. Release of an RKO Radio production. *Producer:* Presented by Dore Schary, Norman Panama and Melvin Frank. *Director:* H. C. Potter. *1st Assistant director:* James Lane. *Screenplay:* Norman Panama and Melvin Frank. Based on a novel by Eric Hodgins. *Cinematography:* James Wong Howe. *Special effects:* Russell A. Cully. *Editor:* Harry Marker. *Music:* Leigh Harline. *Musical director:* C. Bakaleinikoff. *Art direction:* Albert S. D'Agostino and Carroll Clark. *Set decorators:* Darrell Silvera and Harley Miller. *Costumes:* Robert Kalloch. *Makeup:* Gordon Bau. *Sound:* Francis M. Sarrer and Clem Portman. *Technical Advisor:* John Swope. *Release date:* March 25, 1948. *Running time:* 94 minutes.

### THE CAST:

| | |
|---|---|
| *Jim Blandings* | Cary Grant |
| *Muriel Blandings* | Myrna Loy |
| *Bill Cole* | Melvyn Douglas |
| *Simms* | Reginald Denny |
| *Joan Blandings* | Sharyn Moffett |
| *Betsy Blandings* | Connie Marshall |
| *Gussie* | Louise Beavers |
| *Smith* | Ian Wolfe |
| *Tesander* | Harry Shannon |
| *Mr. Zucca* | Tito Vuolo |
| *Joe Appollonio* | Nestor Paiva |
| *John Retch* | Jason Robards |
| *Mary* | Lurene Tuttle |
| *Carpenter Foreman* | Lex Barker |
| *Mr. P. Delford* | Emory Parnell |

with Will Wright, Frank Darien, Stanley Andrews, Cliff Clark, Franklin Parker, Charles Middleton, Cy Slocum, Jack Jahries, Robert Bray, Frederick Ledebur, Don Brodie, Hal K. Dawson, Kernan Cripps, Ralph Stein, Gene Leslie, Mike Lally and Bud Wiser.

### SYNOPSIS:

A typical Manhattan family faced with the housing shortage and the necessity of vacating their apartment, give

194

in to the desire to have their own place in the sun and start looking for a "dream house" in suburban Connecticut. The Blandings contact a realtor, who knows he has a couple of fish when they come to see him, and without consulting their lawyer they buy a 170-year-old house for five times the amount it is worth. That is when the trouble starts; the house begins to show its age problem by problem; Mr. Blandings' job suffers; they tear down the old house, and after a series of trying and comical events they build their "dream house."

## REVIEWS:

*Mr. Blandings Builds His Dream House* is cut from the same piece of goods as *George Washington Slept Here* and is just as amiable. It deals once again with city folk going to the country and getting into all kinds of rural housing difficulties. This time, the joke is more elaborate than it was in *George Washington Slept Here,* since it describes not only the perils of living in the country but also those of living in town, and I think the additional material is all to the good. The pictures, based on Eric Hodgins' account of the problem of getting along with architects and builders, many of whom are just as eccentric as he makes them out to be, includes all the standard ingredients, from the closet in the hall that disgorges everything in it when the door is opened to the springs in the cellar that rise like the Mississippi without warning. The film has been quite ingeniously put together, and it is fortunate in having Cary Grant, Myrna Loy, and Melvyn Douglas as its principals.

*The New Yorker*

The causes for laughter being fairly scarce in the world just now, moviegoers cannot but be the more grateful for two such films as *Sitting Pretty* and *Mr. Blandings Builds His Dream House.* Both of these are light comedies. Both are dexterously written, played, and directed. Both deal with subjects that Professor Toynbee would unquestionably consider trivial. Yet there is more truth in these smiling films than can be found in most of Hollywood's serious efforts.

Who can say where the frivolous stops and the serious begins? Often they are no more than ends of the same stick. A frown maintained too long becomes ridiculous, precisely as a smile which never gives way to gravity can be dangerous.

No doubt Horace Walpole congratulated himself upon the distinction he made when he pointed out, "Life is a comedy to the man who thinks and tragedy to the man who feels." But Walpole's aphorism satisfied us less than it pleased him. Most of us are not as compartmented as he seemed to believe. We cannot say with any exactness when we have ceased to feel and begun to think. We tend to think our feelings even as we feel our thoughts. On the subject of comedy, a subject which is apt to lose its laughter the very moment it is analyzed, we are certain of one thing. To enjoy a joke we must understand its point. Let a child overhear adults laughing at a story which is beyond either his vocabulary or his experience and he will say, "What's funny? I don't get it." Getting it is an essential part of the fun.

That is one reason why *Sitting Pretty* and *Mr. Blandings* prove irresistible. There is no avoiding recognition of what they are about. You need never have depended upon a sitter to win an evening's freedom or dreamed of buying a house in the country, to be included in their gaiety. They speak as directly to the childless or the nurse-equipped as they do to the most contented of city-dwellers.

Time and again these columns have complained about Hollywood's habit of divorcing its films from life and creating, in the name of specious glamour, an overrich, overdressed dream world—a sort of Celluloidia—in which reality plays no part. It is a world of escape; a world where characters seldom cease to be characters and become people. Its doors are apt to be barred on rent, school, and wash-day worries. It is a land where the make-up man is careful to paint humanity out and mannikins in. Its women are not women but magazine covers. They have the contours of volcanoes; their mouths are crimson banners; their eyelashes long as awnings. The men of this lush and chromiumed universe drive only the newest and shiniest cars. Regardless of the professions they follow, they work on schedules as free as Casanova's in which to pursue or be pursued. The homes they live in are as swollen as their owner's budgets. In them kitchens are the size of amphitheatres, hall-bedrooms take on the dimensions of terminals, and suburban boudoirs belong less to housewives than to Du Barrys. Inevitably such a world excludes rather than includes practically all moviegoers. It may invite them to realize their dreams, but it does not often permit them to recognize their lives. . . .

The truth is that *Mr. Blandings Builds His Dream House* is precisely the comedy George S. Kaufman and Moss Hart hoped to write in *George Washington Slept Here.* It, too, deals with that perilous buttercup urge which in the spring will overtake and seduce sane mortals who, until then, have lived their lives in comfortable metropolises. It, too, narrates the misadventures invited by those sufficiently unwise to forswear the pleasures of the city for the costly risks of building in the country. But unlike *George Washington Slept Here,* which was funny mainly as an idea, *Mr. Blandings* is funny both as an idea and in its execution.

No doubt the reason for this is that *Mr. Blandings* stays closer to personal experience. Its ordeals seem less invented than survived. Moreover, they have been shared by so many home-builders that most moviegoers cannot help but know that what they are laughing at is the truth.

John Mason Brown, *Saturday Review*

Next to an exciting mystery or horror film there's nothing so relaxing as a good comedy. But what makes one man laugh makes the next guy scowl. I have listed below a

With Myrna Loy

With Myrna Loy and Melvyn Douglas

few notes on recent pictures that may tickle your funny bone. *Blandings* is the only one that had me rolling in the aisles (what a silly figure of speech!), however the others may roll you. Every man to his own aisle.

No doubt the secret of *Mr. Blandings Builds His Dream House* is that you see yourself, as this city dweller and his family endure the confinements of a small New York apartment, dream of a home in the country, buy one, get fleeced right and left as they rebuild, but finally survive everything and live to enjoy the place in spite of all the plotting of man and nature against them. Director H. C. Potter knows people and has given us a series of funny episodes that range from documentary-like shots of New York and its crowded millions to bucolic scenes of the hinterlands complete with the vicissitudes of the open spaces and commuter trains. Of course Eric Hodgins's original story deserves much of the credit for the fun; scriptwriters Norman Panama and Melvin Frank have broadened the themes, but they have retained the warm humor and clever satire of the Hodgins book. The cast is excellent: Cary Grant giving one of his best portrayals as the frustrated advertising man, Myrna Loy looking and acting like the ideal wife, Melvyn Douglas responding as this couple's best friend and lawyer, and a large group of supporting players, not forgetting the real estate agent who knows a sucker when he sees one and he sees one. The Grant-Loy-Douglas triangle is a little forced, and the film is rather long for its single home-building theme. But the laughs continue to the end; and while you may agree with Grant that anyone who builds these days is crazy, you are more likely to agree with Douglas that the result is worth it.

Philip T. Hartung, *Commonweal*

With Myrna Loy, Sharyn Moffett and Connie Marshall

With Betsy Drake

# EVERY GIRL SHOULD BE MARRIED

1948

## CREDITS:

*Distributing company:* RKO Radio. *Producer:* Don Hartman. *Director:* Don Hartman. *Associate producer:* A Dore Schary Production. *Assistant Director:* Sam Ruman. *Screenplay:* Stephen Morehouse, Avery and Don Hartman. From short story by Eleanor Harris. *Cinematography:* George E. Diskant. Special effects by Russell A. Cully. *Editor:* Harry Marker. *Music by* Leigh Harline. *Musical director:* C. Bakaleinikoff. *Art direction:* Albert S. D'Agostino and Carroll Clark. *Set decorations:* Darrell Silvera, and William Stevens. *Costumes:* designed by Irene Sharaff. *Makeup:* supervised by Gordon Bau. *Sound:* Francis Sarver and Clem Portman. *Release date:* December 25, 1948. *Running time:* 84 minutes.

## THE CAST:

| | |
|---|---|
| *Dr. Madison Brown* | Cary Grant |
| *Roger Sanford* | Franchot Tone |
| *Julie Hudson* | Diana Lynn |
| *Anabel Sims* | Betsy Drake |
| *Mr. Spitzer* | Alan Mowbray |
| *Mary Nolan* | Elizabeth Risdon |
| *San McNutt* | Richard Gaines |
| *Gogarty* | Harry Hayden |
| *Soda Clerk* | Chick Chandler |
| *Violinist* | Leon Belasco |
| *Pierre* | Fred Essler |
| *Saleslady* | Anna Q. Nilsson |

## SYNOPSIS:

Anabel Sims, a saleswoman in children's wear in Roger Sanford's department store, sees Dr. Madison Brown, a baby doctor, and decides he's for her. She checks on his collegiate days, his bachelor habits, his eating inclinations, his favorite clothes down the line to his shorts (he prefers blue), and welds the information into the weapons of her formidable arsenal. Dr. Brown is wise to it all and

With Dan Foster and Betsy Drake

resists until it's too late despite deception, fabrication and a lot of other practices in which well-bred young ladies are not supposed to indulge.

## REVIEWS:

According to RKO's bubbly and light-headed little comedy *Every Girl Should Be Married,* eligible bachelors are unsocial creatures who like to shut themselves up in fusty rooms full of stuffed fish and moose antlers. A girl who wants to marry one of them has to take matters in her own hands and launch her assault with the ingenuity of a process server.

This may sometimes be true in fact, but it isn't necessarily funny in the movies. Mostly responsible for making it so in this case is a gangling, effervescent lass named Betsy Drake whose previous film experience amounts to a Hollywood screen test.

Grant, Tone, and Diana Lynn all contribute their share of humor to the better moments of this contrived and over-cute business. But they have deliberately kept off the cen-

With Betsy Drake

ter of the stage in favor of Miss Drake, whose frenetic charm and wind-blown naturalness are sometimes nerve-racking but more often thoroughly appealing.

*Newsweek*

Your enjoyment will be determined by how you feel about exasperatingly aggressive females. Some men may be only annoyed; others may like seeing one of their sex hoodwinked—but women undoubtedly will be delighted. A probing into the mores of courtship, made *spontaneously funny* at *times* by a cast expert at subtly timed comedy.

Jane Lockhart, *The Rotarian*

Newcomer Betsy Drake seems to have studied, but not learned, the tricks and inflections of the early Hepburn. Her exaggerated grimaces supply only one solid laugh—when Hero Grant mimics them cruelly and accurately. In the past, Cary Grant has shown a talent for quietly underplaying comedy. In this picture, he has trouble finding comedy to play.

*Time Magazine*

With Franchot Tone

With Betsy Drake and Franchot Tone

199

# I WAS A MALE WAR BRIDE

## 1949

With Ann Sheridan

**CREDITS:**

*Distributing company:* 20th Century-Fox. *Producers:* Sol C. Siegel. *Director:* Howard Hawks. *Assistant director:* Arthur Jacobson. *Screenplay:* Charles Lederer, Leonard Spigelgass and Hagar Wilde. From a novel by Henri Rochard. *Cinematography:* Norbert Brodine and O. H. Borradaile. *Special photographic effects:* Fred Sersen. *Editor:* James B. Clark. *Composer:* Cyril Mockridge. *Orchestration:* Herbert Spencer. *Musical direction:* Lionel Newman. *Art Direction:* Lyle Wheeler, and Albert Hogsett. *Set decorations:* Thomas Little and Walter M. Scott. *Sound:* George Leverett, and Roger Heman. *Release date:* September 2, 1949. *Running time:* 105 minutes.

**THE CAST:**

| | |
|---|---|
| *Captain Henri Rochard* | Cary Grant |
| *Lt. Catherine Gates* | Ann Sheridan |
| *Captain Jack Rumsey* | William Neff |
| *Tony Jowitt* | Eugene Gericke |
| *WACS* | Marion Marshall |
| | Randy Stuart |
| *Innkeeper's Assistant* | Ruben Wendorf |
| *Waiter* | Lester Sharpe |
| *Seaman* | Ken Tobey |
| *Lieutenant* | Robert Stevenson |
| *Bartender* | Alfred Linder |
| *Chaplain* | David McMahon |
| *Shore Patrol* | Joe Haworth |
| *Trumble* | John Whitney |
| *Sergeants:* | William Pullen |
| | William Self |
| *Shore Patrol* | John Zilly |
| *Sergeant* | Bill Murhy |

with Otto Reichou, William Yetter, Barbara Perry, Andre Charlot, Alex Gerry, Gil Herman, Ben Pollock, William McLean, Russ Conway, Harry Lauter, Mike Mahoney, Kay

200

Young, Lillie Kann, Carl Jaffe, Martin Miller, Paul Hardmuth, John Serrett and Patricia Curts.

## SYNOPSIS:

Captain Henri Rochard is a polished, suave French captain, and Lt. Catherine Gates, an American WAC officer, is his assistant. With their vibrant, but conflicting personalities they find each other obnoxious, presumptuous and dangerous, but their hatred turns to love and marriage. Once married, Catherine decides to return to America, but her husband Henri will not be permitted immediate entry to the United States unless he comes as a "war bride." Their problem is how to live as husband and wife, since Army regulations prohibit men in WAC billets; women in the bachelor quarters, or army personnel in civilian hotels. Not until they see New York City are their problems solved.

## REVIEWS:

Although some of the proceedings may try the Legion of Decency's patience, they are handled too delightfully by both Grant and Miss Sheridan to offend any but the most squeamish. And under Howard Hawks's direction, the end product is one of the most sparklingly original comedies of the year.

*Newsweek*

A temperamental French army captain and a strong-minded WAC lieutenant stationed in Occupied Germany spend the first half of this comedy hating each other and the second half trying to find a way for the captain to emigrate to the United States. There is a short intermission between halves in which the two sparring partners get married.

The film is poorly paced. By the time Captain Rochard and Lieutenant Gates get to the altar, it seems as if we've had our money's worth. But, no—complications are barely beginning. It appears that the only provision under which Rochard may accompany his wife back to the States is the law regulating the immigration of war brides. It is with this embarrassing predicament that the film finally gets down to the business announced in the title.

The comedy has its share of bright and breezy moments. Cary Grant is a past master at playing the handsome he-man thrown for a loss by a difficult dame or an undignified situation. But none of the boy-girl situations in this opus is original enough to stand being spun out for two hours.

*Scholastic Magazine*

Moviegoers who just want to laugh without having to consider the reality of what they see should get plenty of chuckles out of *I Was a Male War Bride*. The humor

With William Self and Ann Sheridan

gets a bit bawdy at times, but Cary Grant, as the French captain, and Ann Sheridan, as the WAC who married him, put their all into the fun and manage to keep things moving at a fast pace.

Philip T. Hartung, *The Commonweal*

An entirely nonsensical story, but *good for many laughs*. Much of the footage, being of the "bedroom farce" variety, is not for children, or for that matter for squeamish adults. One real asset is the setting—the film actually was shot in German towns and countryside and in "occupation" offices.

Jane Lockhart, *The Rotarian*

With Ann Sheridan, Robert Stevenson and Kenneth Tobey

With Ann Sheridan

With Paula Raymond

# CRISIS

1950

## CREDITS:

*Distributing company:* Metro-Goldwyn-Mayer, Loew's Incorporated. *Producing company:* Loew's Incorporated. *Producer:* Arthur Freed. *Director:* Richard Brooks. *Assistant director:* Howard Koch. *Screenplay:* Richard Brooks. *Short story:* "The Doubters" by George Tabori. *Cinematography:* Ray June. *Special effects:* A. Arnold Gillespie and Warren Newcombe. Guitar solo by Vincente Gomez. *Editor:* Robert J. Kern. Music by Miklos Rozsa. *Art direction:* Cedric Gibbons and Preston Ames. *Set decorations:* Edwin B. Willis. *Associate:* Hugh Hurd. *Makeup:* Jack Dawn. *Sound:* Douglas Shearer. *Hair styles:* Sydney Guilaroff. *Release date:* July 4, 1950. *Running time:* 95 minutes.

## THE CAST:

*Dr. Eugene Ferguson*       Cary Grant

| | |
|---|---|
| *Raoul Farrago* | Jose Ferrer |
| *Helen Ferguson* | Paula Raymond |
| *Senora Isabel Farrago* | Signe Hasso |
| *Col. Adragon* | Ramon Novarro |
| *Gonzales* | Gilbert Roland |
| *Sam Proctor* | Leon Ames |
| *Dr. Emilio Nierra* | Antonio Moreno |
| *Rosa Aldana* | Teresa Celli |
| *General Valdini* | Mario Siletti |
| *Cariago* | Vincente Gomez |
| *Senor Magano* | Martin Garralaga |
| *Father Del Puento* | Pedro de Cordoba |
| *Senora Farrago* | Soledad Jimenez |
| *Rubio* | Jose Dominguez |
| *Marco Aldana* | Robert Tafur |
| *Luis* | Maurice Jara |

with Rodolfo Hoyos, Jr., Rita Conde, Roque Ybarra, Felipe Turich, Charles Rivero, Mickey Contreras, Captain Garcia, Carlos Condi, George Lewis, Carlo Tricoli, Ken-

With Paula Raymond and Ramon Novarro

With Leon Ames and Paula Raymond

neth Garcia, Harry Vejor, Trina Varela, Bridget Carr, Audrey Betz, Robert Lugo, Myron Marks, Alex Montoya, Margaret Martin, Juan Duval, Al Haskell, Rafael Gomez, Z. Yacconelli, Fernando Del Valle, A. Carrillo, Robert Polo, Jerry Riggio, Melba Meredith, Lillian Israel, Carlotta Monti, Connie Montoya, George Norarro, Orlando Beltran, Eddie Gomez.

## SYNOPSIS:

While in a Latin American country, Dr. Eugene Ferguson, a famous brain surgeon, and his wife Helen are kidnapped. They are brought to the governmental palace where he is told to operate on the sick dictator, Raoul Farrago. Dr. Ferguson is told that he must kill Farrago on the operating table. Ferguson goes through with the operation and saves Farrago's life. However, the dictator dies when the palace is stormed by the revolutionists.

## REVIEWS:

*Crisis* is a bold piece of movie adventuring. Under Dore Schary's progressive administration at MGM, we are now considered adult enough to enjoy an unbuttoned screenplay on the violent temperature that erupts in Latin-American civil war and dictatorship.

Cary Grant is more brittle and diamond-brilliant than before as the enlightened doctor. His sincerity in the story's guts is its premise for being believed. Jose Ferrer is cunning to the point of evil genius.

Reed Porter, *The Mirror* (Los Angeles)

Richard Brooks' first effort as a two-way creator (writer-director) is *Crisis*.

A curious thing has happened in his transferral of the George Tabori original story to the screen. The writer in him has neglected to make his story move.

There is an old rule of thumb that motion pictures can and should move. Motion is essence. Through motion—through the limitless motion possible in the cinema—you can tell a story perhaps more effectively than in any other medium.

In *Crisis* Brooks has not done this. The scenes he has written are static and talky.

Yet there is no doubt that Brooks' direction is masterful. Within the framework of a pedestrian script, he has made his actors convincing and exciting.

It is true that Brooks has a superlative cast headed by Jose Ferrer and Cary Grant—but even these seasoned performers take on new dimensions with Brooks telling them how to do it.

Darr Smith, *Los Angeles Daily News*

With Leon Ames, Paula Raymond
and Signe Hasso

With Paula Raymond

With Jose Ferrer

# PEOPLE WILL TALK

1951

**CREDITS:**

*Distributing company:* 20th Century-Fox. *Producer:* Darryl F. Zanuck. *Director:* Joseph L. Mankiewicz. *Assistant director:* Hal Klein. *Screenplay:* Joseph L. Mankiewicz. Based on the play *Dr. Praetorius* by Curt Goetz. *Cinematography:* Milton Krasner. *Special effects:* Fred Sersen. *Editor:* Barbara McLean. *Composers:* Brahms and Wagner. *Orchestration:* Edward Powell. Conducted by Alfred Newman. *Art direction:* Lyle Wheeler and George W. Davis. *Set decoration:* Thomas Little and Walter M. Scott. *Costumes:* Charles LeMaire. *Makeup:* Ben Nye. *Sound:* W. D. Flick, and Roger Heman. *Release date:* September 2, 1951. *Running time:* 109 minutes.

**THE CAST:**

| | |
|---|---|
| *Dr. Noah Praetorius* | Cary Grant |
| *Annabel Higgins* | Jeanne Crain |
| *Shunderson* | Findlay Currie |
| *Prof. Elwell* | Hume Cronyn |
| *Prof. Barker* | Walter Slezak |
| *Arthur Higgins* | Sidney Blackmer |
| *Dean Lyman Brockwell* | Basil Ruysdael |
| *Miss James* | Katherine Locke |
| *John Higgins* | Will Wright |
| *Miss Pickett* | Margaret Hamilton |
| *Mrs. Pegwhistle* | Esther Somers |
| *Technician* | Carleton Young |
| *Business Manager* | Larry Dobkin |
| *Nurse* | Jo Gilbert |
| *Dietician* | Ann Morrison |
| *Old Lady* | Julia Dean |
| *Secretary* | Gail Bonney |
| *Student Manager* | William Klein |
| *Haskins* | George Offerman |
| *Mabel* | Adele Longmire |
| *Coonan* | Billy House |
| *Photographer* | Al Murphy |

| | |
|---|---|
| *Toy Salesman* | Parley Baer |
| *Cook* | Irene Seidner |
| *Gussie* | Joyce MacKenzie |
| *Night Matron* | Maude Wallack |
| *Bella* | Kay Lavelle |
| *Doctor* | Ray Montgomery |

Students: Paul Lees
Wm. Mauch
Leon Taylor

With Jeanne Crain

## SYNOPSIS:

Because of his mysterious background, Dr. Noah Praetorius, who teaches at the university, is under investigation by Professor Elwell. In the hospital where Dr. Praetorius works, he meets and treats Annabel Higgins, who has tried to commit suicide because she is unmarried and about to have a baby. He decides to marry her. She begins to think he married her out of pity rather than love. But he convinces her that this is not so. The investigation is finally concluded in his favor.

## REVIEWS:

This cinematic oddity—a disjointed but strangely intriguing combination of comedy, satire, drama, farce and fantasy—was written for the screen and directed by Joseph L. Mankiewicz. You may recall Mr. Mankiewicz as the gentleman who won two Oscars last year for his *All About Eve* and two more the year before for *A Letter To Three Wives*. For each of these distinguished pictures Mankiewicz reshaped another writer's serious work into a comic-dramatic smash hit. In *People Will Talk* he repeats the trick—not with such extraordinary success perhaps, but with enough humor, wit and directorial ingenuity to make it one of the more entertaining pieces of the year.

For *People Will Talk* his source was a German play by Curt Goetz called *Dr. Praetorius*—a medical school drama about a crusading professor who fights professional prejudices, academic reaction, hidebound tradition and sundry medical myopias—and is as a result subjected to public ridicule, professional persecution and collegiate condemnation.

A strange theme for comedy, perhaps, but Mankiewicz has rewritten and recharged it into a lively, wise and witty piece about men of medicine—their fads and foibles—and has touched it all with a gentle hilarity, a neat dose of waiting-room and hospital-ward humors, patient-vs.-physician ironies, and an amusing if unconventional love story.

The film veers frequently and sometimes disconcertingly from comedy to drama, from farce to scalpel-sharp satire; but it remains at all times good entertainment.

In cast, dialogue, situation and approach the picture is grown-up—which is to say, in the medical school setting where much of the action takes place, students, physicians

With Julia Dean and Katherine Locke

With Sidney Blackmer and Jeanne Crain

With Jeanne Crain

With Walter Slezak and Sidney Blackmer

and patients discuss medical matters in plain English and not in politely elliptical gobbledegook. The film's heroine is an unmarried and unexpectedly expectant mother, our medico-hero is a frank and easygoing healer who treats the girl for what she doesn't suspect ails her, and later, in a quite unprofessional fashion, he comes to pity, love and finally marry her.

Others in the unorthodox cast are similarly, and shockingly unconformist. The doctor's best friend and body servant is a gaunt, twice-convicted murderer with a rare sense of humor, while his second-best friend is a roly-poly Einsteinian physicist-chemist with a special fondness for miniature trains, bull fiddles and knockwurst. The doctor's prospective father-in-law is a genial failure, an ingratiating moocher and alcoholic; and his bitterest enemy is a glum professor of anatomy, a psychopathic misanthrope, a sadistic dissector of corpses, people and emotions.

These unusual ingredients for comedy have, as noted, been mixed with skill, and are spiced with some caustic comments on the pomposities of certain latter-day disciples of Aesculapius, several gentle hints that physicians ought never forget that patients are people, not pill receptacles—that a psychosomatic bellyache hurts just as much as one caused by green apples—that it is shameful to try to fit invalids' eating and sleeping habits into the ironbound hospital mechanization programs that begin with a pre-dawn awakening of the sick—that ill people are minds surrounded by bodies, and that both deserve consideration if the patient is to get well. The human spirit, this rare physician feels, has dignity; and sick people need that dignity far more than the healthy. . . .

*Cue Magazine*

We've no space to go into particulars—to discuss the inventiveness and skill of Mr. Mankiewicz' story telling, the cleverness of his people's talk (of which, we might state, there is plenty) or the arch humor of his exposé. Neither can we do more than mention the delightfulness and the good sense of the performance of Cary Grant as the professor, of Jeanne Crain as the troubled girl, of Finlay Currie as the mysterious companion and of Hume Cronyn, Walter Slezak, and many more.

All we can say is that a picture so mature and refreshingly frank as to hold that an erring young woman might be rewarded with a wise and loving mate is most certainly a significant milestone in the moral emancipation of American films, not to mention an unexpected portent to greet an eager reviewer on his return.

*People Will Talk* should foment chatter, but that should be all to the good.

*The New York Times*

And once again, Hollywood's ranking "genius"—the only man to win four Academy Awards in two years—has something to say and says it frankly and funnily.

The film, which has a three-way plot, concentrates on one of the strangest and most adult love affairs ever to emerge from Hollywood. The wedding between Dr. Praetorius and Deborah Higgins takes place when the doctor knows she is more than a month pregnant, although he is not responsible—a situation handled in perfect taste, and resulting in an exceptionally happy union.

These heterogeneous plot strands are welded together by Grant, who turns in one of the most intelligent performances of his nineteen-year Hollywood career. And Miss Crain proves, as she did in *Pinky,* that she is ready to graduate from her usual pigtail roles. Much of the credit for an impressive film goes to the very adult and literate writing of Mankiewicz.

*Newsweek*

Cary Grant is excellent as Praetorius, making this strange, supremely noble but unpompous individual a warm, believable human being. Jeanne Crain is more skillful than usual as the girl, and supporting actors Hume Cronyn, Sidney Blackmer, and Finlay Currie, are uncommonly good, proving not only that they are capable actors but that Mankiewicz the director, is as outstanding as Mankiewicz, the writer.

Ann Helming, *Hollywood Citizen-News*

With Walter Slezak

With Jeanne Crain

209

# ROOM FOR ONE MORE

1952

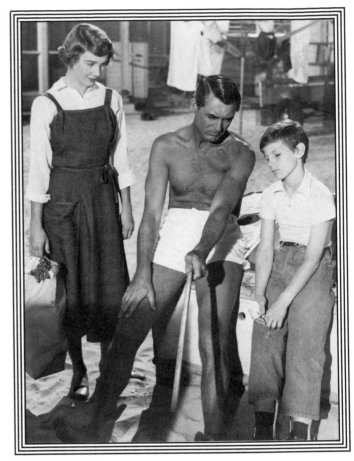

With Betsy Drake and Clifford Tatum, Jr.

## CREDITS:

*Distributing company:* Warner Bros. Pictures. *Executive Producer:* Jack L. Warner. *Producer:* Henry Blanke. *Director:* Norman Taurog. *Assistant director:* Sherry Shourds. *Screenplay:* Jack Rose and Melville Shavelson. From book by Anna Perrott Rose. *Cinematography:* Robert Burks. *Editor:* Alan Crosland, Jr. Music by Max Steiner. Orchestrations by Murray Cutter. *Art direction:* Douglas Bacon. *Set decoration:* William L. Kuehl. *Costumes:* Leah Rhodes and Marjorie Best. *Makeup:* Gordon Bau. *Sound:* Charles Lang. *Release date:* January 26, 1952. *Running time:* 97 minutes.

## THE CAST:

| | |
|---|---|
| *"Poppy" Rose* | Cary Grant |
| *Anna Rose* | Betsy Drake |
| *Miss Kenyon* | Lurene Tuttle |
| *Mrs. Foreman* | Randy Stuart |
| *Harry Foreman* | John Ridgely |
| *The Mayor* | Irving Bacon |
| *Mrs. Roberts* | Mary Lou Treen |
| *The Doctor* | Hayden Rorke |
| *AND THE CHILDREN* | |
| *Jane* | Iris Mann |
| *Teensie* | George Winslow |
| *Jimmy-John* | Clifford Tatum, Jr. |
| *Trot* | Gay Gordon |
| *Tim* | Malcolm Cassell |
| *Ben* | Larry Olson |

## SYNOPSIS:

The Rose home is a happy, uninhibited place where "Poppy" Rose, a city engineer, tries hard to make ends meet. Still smitten by his wife's charm after all these years, he can do nothing to curb her generous nature, which permits stray humans and animals to find haven in the already crowded house. Thus, when thirteen-year-old Jane, an unwanted child of divorced parents, arrives for a two-week stay, the Rose family's thorough understanding and proper handling gradually win her away from moods of distrust and sullenness, and she becomes a permanent member of the family.

"Poppy" Rose is determined to have nothing more to do with playing godfather to "disturbed" juveniles, but inevitably his wife informs him on the eve of the family vacation, that she has offered a haven to Jimmy-John, a cripple with braces on his legs, who is regarded by the authorities as vicious and mean. Naturally, the Roses meet this challenge, gradually win the boy over, and in a final sequence done with feeling and taste, the boy becomes an Eagle Scout.

## REVIEWS:

*Room For One More* is a delightful domestic comedy, stunningly produced by Henry Blanke, and warmly directed by Norman Taurog.

As the father, Cary Grant offers a sock performance, witty, debonair but always real. Betsy Drake is superb as the young matron, pretty, serious and with a heart that never falters.

*Hollywood Reporter*

*Room For One More* is a wonderful picture for young people because it's close to their own lives. It's full of the fun and heartaches of growing up, of the experiences of young marrieds in establishing a home, and of the warmth of a fine family relationship. All the men will appreciate the witty observations of "Poppy" when he feels he's being neglected by a wife too busy with children and pets.

*Redbook Magazine*

Betsy Drake is not quite like all the other young stars or starlets who adorn the films of Hollywood. She has a charming style of her own—one which has hinted that, given a reasonable role, she may yet prove herself to be a fine actress. Her partner in this film is Cary Grant, a thoroughly experienced player who whenever his films have allowed him, has shown that he can be both funny and pleasant. But this film is too much for them, or at least it is one of those comedies which, however it may seem to an American audience, brings to the European mind, a deep, deep depression. The behavior of American children and the attitude at once maudlin, indulgent, and puerile, which American grown-ups (on the screen) adopt towards their young are subjects which simply should not be allowed to cross the Atlantic.

The familiar and dismal theme as treated in this particular variation upon it concerns a young wife who though al-

With Betsy Drake

With Betsy Drake and Gay Gordon

211

ready possessing three children of her own insists on adopting two more. These two are presented as thoroughly tough cases who under the benign guidance of their adoptive mother, become splendid little specimens of American youth. The father's part, incidentally, is that of genial buffoon; it is not his authority but that of the mother and of course, of the awful children which counts. Is this perhaps an instructive film in the gloomy sense that in its exaggerated way it indicates a real difference between American and European ways of treating children? One would wish desperately to believe that it is wholly misleading, but to believe that is, alas, scarcely possible—if only because the evidence has been corroborated only too often by other American films.

*Manchester Guardian Weekly*

NEWS ITEM

*Room For One More,* Warner's film starring Cary Grant and Betsy Drake, has received a special mention award in the Films for Children Fete at the Venice Film Festival. The picture was cited for its "positive treatment of social problems regarding childhood and adolescence."

*Hollywood Reporter*

With Betsy Drake, Iris Mann, George Winslow, Malcolm Cassell, Gay Gordon and Larry Olson

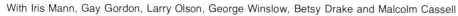

With Iris Mann, Gay Gordon, Larry Olson, George Winslow, Betsy Drake and Malcolm Cassell

212

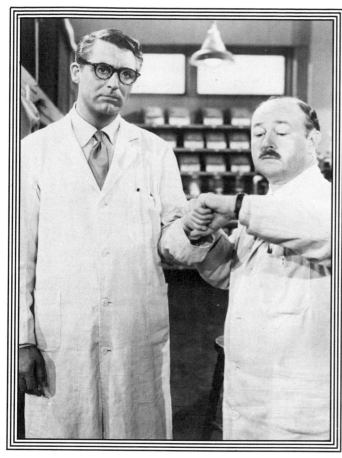
With Henri Letondal

# MONKEY BUSINESS

1952

**CREDITS:**

*Distributing company:* 20th Century-Fox. *Producer:* Sol C. Siegel. *Director:* Howard Hawks. *1st Assistant director:* Paul Helmick. *Screenplay:* Ben Hecht, I. A. L. Diamond, and Charles Lederer. From an unpublished story by Harry Segall. *Cinematography:* Milton Krasner. *Special Photographic effects:* Ray Kellogg. *Editor:* William B. Murphy. *Composer:* Leigh Harline. *Musical direction:* Lionel Newman. *Orchestration:* Earle Hagen. *Art directors:* Lyle Wheeler, and George Patrick. *Set decorations:* Thomas Little, and Walter M. Scott. *Wardrobe direction:* Charles LeMaire. *Costumes by* Travilla. *Makeup artist:* Ben Nye. *Sound:* W. D. Flick and Roger Heman. *Release date:* September 15, 1952. *Running time:* 97 minutes.

**THE CAST:**

| | |
|---|---|
| *Professor Barnaby Fulton* | Cary Grant |
| *Edwina Fulton* | Ginger Rogers |
| *Mr. Oliver Oxly* | Charles Coburn |
| *Lois Laurel* | Marilyn Monroe |
| *Hank Entwhistle* | Hugh Marlowe |
| *Dr. Siegfried Kitzel* | Henri Letondal |
| *Dr. Zoldeck* | Robert Cornthwaite |
| *Mr. G. J. Culverly* | Larry Keating |
| *Dr. Bruner* | Douglas Spencer |
| *Mrs. Rhinelander* | Esther Dale |
| *Little Indian* | George Winslow |

with Emmett Lynn, Jerry Sheldon, Joseph Mell, George

With Charles Coburn

With Marilyn Monroe

With Esther Dale, Ginger Rogers and Hugh Marlowe

Eldredge, Heine Conklin, Kathleen Freeman, Olan Soule, Harry Carey, Jr., John McKee, Faire Binney, Billy McLean, Paul Maxey, Mack Williams, Forbes Murray, Marjorie Halliday, Harry Carter, Harry Seymour, Harry Bartell, Jerry Paris, Roger Moore, Ruth Warren, Isabel Withers, Olive Carey, Dobbs Greer, Russ Clark, Ray Montgomery, Melinda Plowman, Terry Goodman, Ronnie Clark, Rudy Lee, Mickey Little, Brad Mora, Jimmy Roebuck, Louis Lettiere, and Robert Nichols.

## SYNOPSIS:

Dr. Barnaby Fulton, a research chemist, has been working on a formula to regenerate worn-out tissue in the human body. His wife, Edwina, serves him some hot soup, which scalds his mouth, and in doing so solves the formula he has been searching for.

President Oliver Oxly is delighted by Fulton's discovery and due to a number of mix-ups, everyone becomes convinced the formula is working.

Edwina Fulton thinks her husband is becoming too involved with Lois Laurel, a company secretary, and so Edwina takes Barnaby on a second honeymoon. When they return home Barnaby disappears. Edwina finds a child in bed with her and thinks that it is Barnaby regenerated too far. She rushes him to President Oxly's office and after much more confusion, most of the mistakes of the previous weeks are straightened out and everyone returns to normal.

## REVIEWS:

If youth is anything like the nonsense displayed here, maybe it's just as well that nobody has really concocted anything that would force us older citizens back into it.

John McCarten, *The New Yorker*

Grant has never been better than in his part as the absent-minded professor in search of the elixir of youth. His extraordinary agile and amusing performance is matched to the hilt by that of Ginger Rogers as his long-suffering wife. And those who recall that Miss Rogers was once a famous dancing star, will find that she excels in that department. She obviously delights in her part, which is a demanding one.

Throughout, director Hawks has seen to it that *Monkey Business* doesn't become static. Grant's wild car ride with Marilyn Monroe is pure farce in the great tradition of the screen and some other climactic sequences come across with the same explosive effect.

*Motion Picture Herald*

*Monkey Business* is one of the best comedies of the year. Despite the excessive numbers of variations on a single and extremely simple joke, director Howard Hawks maintains a satisfying illusion of sprightliness, and the authors interject any number of unexpectedly sly and nudging spots of dialogue. It would be hard to improve on the cast. Coburn is fine. Miss Monroe has her own special form of eloquence and vice versa, Miss Rogers—as she has demonstrated before—can meet broad comedy head-on without sacrificing either charm or intelligence. And the chances are that only Cary Grant could do Barnaby justice with the underplaying that avoids the mawkish and the silly.

*Newsweek*

Ever "catch" a film comedy that made you double up with laughter even though you knew it was silly, ridiculous and even preposterous? It's a pleasure to report that *Monkey Business,* starring Cary Grant, Ginger Rogers, and Charles Coburn, is just such a movie.

John L. Scott, *Los Angeles Times*

Even so, without becoming at all stuffy about it, *Monkey Business* agreeably reverses the general movie view of life, suggesting that there might be some virtue and dignity in maturity and that the golden dream of eternal youth could have its nightmare aspects. Cary Grant, a polished *farceur,* makes this point with considerable skill and charm.

Arthur Knight, *Saturday Review*

With Henri Letondal and the chimpanzee, Bingo

With Ginger Rogers

# DREAM WIFE

## 1953

With Walter Pidgeon and Deborah Kerr

**CREDITS:**

*Distributing company:* Metro-Goldwyn-Mayer, Loew's Incorporated. *Producing company:* Loew's, Incorporated. *Producer:* Dore Schary. *Director:* Sidney Sheldon. *Assistant director:* Arvid Griffen. *Screenplay:* Sidney Sheldon, Herbert Baker, and Alfred L. Levitt. Based on an unpublished story by Alfred Lewis Levitt. *Cinematography:* Milton Krasner. *Special effects:* A. Arnold Gillespie, and Warren Newcombe. *Editor:* George White. Music by Conrad Salinger. *Art direction:* Cedric Gibbons and Daniel B. Cathcart. *Set decorations:* Edwin B. Willis and Alfred E. Spencer. Women's costumes designed by Helen Rose. Men's costumes designed by Herschel McCoy. *Makeup:* created by William Tuttle. *Hair styles:* Sydney Guilaroff. *Sound:* Douglas Shearer. *Songs:* "Ghi-li, Ghi-li, Ghi-li" and "Tarji's Song" by Charles Wolcott, and Jamshid Sheibani. *Release date:* June 19, 1953. *Running time:* 98 minutes.

216

**THE CAST:**

| | |
|---|---|
| Clemson Reade | Cary Grant |
| Effie | Deborah Kerr |
| Walter McBride | Walter Pidgeon |
| Tarji | Betta St. John |
| Kahn | Eduard Franz |
| Vizier | Buddy Baer |
| Ken Landwell | Les Tremayne |
| Ali | Donald Randolph |
| Charlie Elkwood | Bruce Bennett |
| Henry Malvine | Richard Anderson |
| Mr. Brown | Dan Tobin |
| Rima | Movita |
| Mrs. Landwell | Gloria Holden |
| Mrs. Elkwood | June Clayworth |
| George | Dean Miller |
| Louis | Steve Forrest |

With Deborah Kerr and Betta St. John

With Deborah Kerr and Walter Pidgeon

| | |
|---|---|
| *Sailor* | Jonathan Cott |
| *Pat* | Patricia Tiernan |

**SYNOPSIS:**

Clemson Reade, who wants a wife in the home, not in business, breaks with Effie, a State Department official who is too busy with an oil crisis to have time for matrimony.

Remembering a comely princess, Tarji, whom he met on a trip to Bukistan and the fact that she had been schooled from birth in the art of pleasing men, Reade proposes via cable. Because of the oil situation, the State Department steps in and assigns Effie to see that her ex-fiancé sticks to protocol in his new courtship. The princess comes to the United States, but the feminine craft of Effie soon has Tarji figuring that emancipation is more fun than being a dream wife. Reade sees the mistake he has made and makes up with Effie.

## REVIEWS:

*Dream Wife* as made under the personal supervision of Dore Schary and Cary Grant is on hand to get laughs where it isn't always possible to find them in the script. Nevertheless, this uneven mixture of sophisticated humor and downright slapstick amounts to little more than a fairly amusing comedy.

*Newsweek*

*Dream Wife,* a rather fantastic comedy contrived to allow Cary Grant a field day with his typical facial and vocal tricks, and providing plenty of femme beauty and charm in the persons of Deborah Kerr and newcomer Betta St. John, opened yesterday.

I suppose one could regard this as a "battle of the sexes" story done with tongue-in-cheek and proving eventually that east and west may meet but only in passing. The film has been given first-class production by Dore Schary; and contains comic situations that will bring smiles if not loud laughs.

Cary Grant gives the typical light comedy portrayal for which he is noted. Miss Kerr, beautifully gowned throughout, comes through with a solid performance as the conniving American girl who has lost her man. Miss St. John makes a fine impression in her initial featured film role.

John L. Scott, *Los Angeles Times*

With Betta St. John, Deborah Kerr and Buddy Baer

218

# TO CATCH A THIEF

1955

## CREDITS:

Produced and distributed by Paramount Pictures. *Producer:* Alfred Hitchcock. *Director:* Alfred Hitchcock. *1st Assistant director:* Daniel McCauley. *Screenplay:* John Michael Hayes. From a novel by David Dodge. *Cinematography:* Robert Burks. *2nd Unit photography:* Wallace Kelley. *Technicolor-Vista-Vision Consultant:* Richard Mueller. *Editor:* George Tomasini. *Music:* Lynn Murray. *Art direction:* Hal Pereira, and Joseph MacMillan Johnson. *Gowns for Miss Kelly:* Edith Head. *Sound:* Harold Lewis and John Cope. *Release date:* September , 1955. *Running time:* 103 minutes.

## THE CAST:

| | |
|---|---|
| *John Robie* | Cary Grant |
| *Frances Stevens* | Grace Kelly |
| *Mrs. Stevens* | Jessie Royce Landis |
| *H. H. Hughson* | John Williams |
| *Bertani* | Charles Vanel |
| *Danielle* | Brigitte Auber |
| *Foussard* | Jean Martinelli |
| *Germaine* | Georgette Anys |

with Roland Lesaffre, Jean Hebey, Rene Blancard, Wee Willie Davis, Dominique Davray, Edward Manouk, Russell Gaige, Marie Stoddard, Paul "Tiny" Newlan, Lewis Charles, Aimee Torriani, Frank Chelland, Don Megowan, John Alderson, Otto F. Schulze, Martha Bamattre, Bela Kovacs, Guy Dè Vestel, Leonard Penn, Michael Hadlow, Margaret Brewster, Adele St. Maur, Alberto Morin, Eugene Borden, Donald Lawton, Philip Van Zandt, Steven Geray, Albert Pollet, Ed. LeBaron, Gladys Hollard, Louis Mercier, Manuel Paris, George A. Nardelli, George Paris, Loulette Sablon, Nina Borget, Cosmos Sardo, George Adrian, Barry Norton, and Jeanne Lafayette.

**SYNOPSIS:**

John Robie, "The Cat," a reformed jewel thief, now living on the Riviera, finds the gendarmes looking his way after a series of thefts break out in Cannes. Each has the hallmark of the stealthy, neat style he had perfected years before. To clear his name, he sets out after the real thief, hoping to catch him in the act. To help him, H. H. Hughson, whose insurance company has suffered the financial burden of the robberies, supplies Robie with a list of the company's rich clients who might be on the thief's list. One is Mrs. Stevens, an American, delightfully frank about her recent affluence, who is husband-hunting for her beautiful daughter, Frances Stevens. The story then turns from intrigue to romance as Frances helps Robie catch his thief, and she in turn catches Robie.

**REVIEWS:**

It's been several seasons since Grant has made a film and, while this is no sock vehicle for the screen return, it's not a weak one, either. Grant gives his role his assured style of acting, meaning the dialogue and situations benefit.

*Weekly Variety*

With marquee magic in such names as Cary Grant and Grace Kelly, plus VistaVision and the Alfred Hitchcock reputation, *To Catch A Thief* is bound to open big. Whether its box office will sustain will be a test of the comparative value of a name draw versus story deficiency.

The sad truth is that this film is a disappointment. Billed as a comedy-mystery, it stacks up as a drawn-out pretentious piece that seldom hits comedy level. As a mystery it fails to mystify, although it does confuse. This film won't enhance the prestige of either the stars or the producer-director.

Grant once again demonstrates he is a master of timing, getting laughs where a lesser talent would draw a blank.

*Daily Variety*

What else can I tell you? The dialogue is so bad that Cary looks embarrassed to be saying it, and Hitchcock has been too busy shooting auto chases on the Corniche from an airplane to pay much attention to the suspense, and altogether the picture is a little bit of a mess. Maybe the wise guys on the New York papers will be claiming that somebody stole the jewels that should have been in the dialogue, but it has got Grace Kelly and it has got Alfred Hitchcock and there are 10,000,000 ladies who will give you Albert Schweitzer and Pandit Nehru if they can have Cary Grant.

Lee Rogow, *Saturday Review*

Alfred Hitchcock's latest mystery melodrama is, unlike most of his films, pictorial rather than dramatic, leisurely rather than frenetic, calm rather than energetic.

*Cue*

*To Catch A Thief,* Alfred Hitchcock's new thriller, is not the film it could have been. But most audiences, I am sure, will find it pleasant enough entertainment on most counts.

*Hollywood Citizen News*

Has Alfred Hitchcock over-refined his technique? There are those who will say yes after seeing his *To Catch A Thief,* but this fan is quite happy with Hitchcock as he is. In his latest mystery the emphasis is less on the mystery than on the incidental mechanics that develop it, much as it was in *Rear Window,* though here the plot is even thinner.

Nevertheless, it is a high-polish job, a kind of reversion to the urbanities of a gentleman Raffles, with Cary Grant and Grace Kelly ideal in the romantic leads.

Philip K. Scheuer, *Los Angeles Times*

With Grace Kelly

With Grace Kelly, Jessie Royce Landis and John Williams

With Grace Kelly

# THE PRIDE AND THE PASSION

1957

**CREDITS:**

*Distributing company:* United Artists. *Producing company:* Stanley Kramer Pictures. *Producer:* Stanley Kramer. *Assistant directors:* Alfonso Acebal, Jose Ma Ochoa, and Isidoro Ferry. *Supervising assistant director:* Carter DeHaven, Jr. *Screenplay:* Edna and Edward Anhalt. Based on novel *The Gun* by C. S. Forester. *Cinematography:* Franz Planer. *Associate cameraman:* Manuel Berenguer. *Camera Operator:* Fred Mandl. Technicolor-VistaVision. *Special effects:* Willis Cook, and Maurice Ayers. *Editor:* Frederic Knudtson and Ellsworth Hoagland. Music by Georges Antheil. *Music conductor:* Ernest Gold. *Art direction:* Fernando Carrere. *Associate art director:* Gil Parrondo. *Costumes:* Joe King. *Makeup:* Bernard Ponedel, John O'Gorman, and Jose Ma Sanchez. *Sound:* Joseph de Bretagne. *Sound effects:* Walter Elliott, Bates Mason. Titles designed by Saul Bass. *Production designer:* Rudolph Sternad. *Production manager:* Stanley Goldsmith. *Production supervisor:* Ivan Volkman. *Production Liaison:* Eduardo Maroto, Augustin Pastor, Fernando Navarro, and Hank Werba. *Military Adviser:* Lt. Col. Luis Cano. *Release date:* July 10, 1957. *Running time:* 130 minutes.

**THE CAST:**

| | |
|---|---|
| *Anthony* | Cary Grant |
| *Miguel* | Frank Sinatra |
| *Juana* | Sophia Loren |
| *General Jouvet* | Theodore Bikel |
| *Sermaine* | John Wengraf |
| *Ballinger* | Jay Novello |
| *Carlos* | Jose Nieto |
| *Jose* | Carlos Larranaga |
| *Vidal* | Philip VanZandt |
| *Manolo* | Paco El Laberinto |
| *Enrique* | Julian Ugarte |

| | |
|---|---|
| *Bishop* | Felix De Pomes |
| *Leonardo* | Carlos Casaravilla |
| *Ramon* | Juan Olaguivel |
| *Maria* | Nana De Herrera |
| *Francisco* | Carlos De Mendoza |
| *French Soldier* | Luis Guedes |

and the Spanish People in the tens of thousands who made possible this motion picture.

## SYNOPSIS:

A British naval officer, Anthony, is landed in Spain during the Napoleonic Wars to make contact with what Spanish forces there are. His mission is to locate and prevent from falling into French hands a Spanish cannon, the biggest in the world. Anthony wants to get it out of Spain. But when he meets Miguel, a leader of the guerrilla forces, he is forced to amend his ideas. Miguel has more direct plans. He wants to take the gun to Avila, the French headquarters, and blast the French out of that city, and out of Spain. The plan is fantastic, as Anthony points out, but Miguel's stubborn belief makes the impossibility a probability and finally a reality. Against all logic Miguel and the gun rally the Spanish people and they get it to Avila, attack the city and win the important battle. In spite of the personal conflict between the two men over Juana, they are able to work together to win the military victory.

## REVIEWS:

A movie like Stanley Kramer's *The Pride And The Passion* brings smiles to the faces of motion-picture executives. (Some executives were present at the screening I attended, and I saw them smiling.) They don't always smile, mainly because they are so worried much of the time. The weekly attendance figures for movies have had a way, of late, of swinging wildly to a high point of perhaps 80 million customers around Labor Day to a low of 30

million or so in midwinter. Box-office take for one may amount to $5,000 and for another $500 even though the two might have cost the same amount to make. The executives know that the audience is out there somewhere waiting, like a marvelous fish to be baited, but which hook will it take? Well, when they see something like *The Pride and the Passion* they know they have the answer. No worries. Kramer may have spent $5,000,000, but he came through.

There is daring and creativity and calculation that goes into a movie project like *The Pride and the Passion.* First of all, the possibilities in a fairly obscure, but very good C. S. Forester story, *The Gun,* had to be recognized and assessed. Some of the story was kept, new elements added, most of the history thrown out. Kramer then rounded up a star combination—Cary Grant, Frank Sinatra, Sophia Loren, not only because there were tailored parts for them in the picture, but because the combination guaranteed the financing he needed.

Almost any enterprising, fairly reputable producer could have gotten that far, but the distinctive qualities in Kramer made him go a lot farther. For one thing, he went to Spain for six months where he recruited a virtual army of Spaniards, obtained permission to use historic monuments and shrines for settings, and organized one of the most extraordinary logistical operations in movie history. He, in other words, dragged the big gun over half of Spain, decided that for spectacle one must be truly spectacular—and set up his cameras on carefully scouted vantage points, used helicopters when there was no ideal vantage point, built several replicas of his cannon because of the rigors it would be put through, built a wall in front of the walls of Avila so that it wouldn't be necessary to knock down the real one.

One result of all this effort is that the spectacle in *The Pride and the Passion* looks real, and very much unlike the sleazy effects gotten by DeMille in several of his cardboard and plaster epics. To make peasants look ragged and like peasants, Kramer got the people and clothes dirty. When a monster gun runs wild down a mountainside it is a real effect and not something worked out in a laboratory.

Stanley Kramer began by producing low-budget pictures of quality, but he has been slowly adapting himself to the change in the motion-picture economy, and meanwhile demonstrating that he is not only an astute judge of materials, but a thoroughgoing professional. There were doubts about him as a director, there will be none now.

There is more romance than history in the end-product, and it is an adventure spectacle with an added ingredient —the theme of people rising up from defeat to repel the conqueror. For the latter the big gun serves as an eloquent if rather obvious symbol. As the virtual star the cannon does nobly—if it doesn't exactly out-act the stars, it is usually there, like Everest. While the gun deserves a special Academy Award, Mr. Sinatra must be commended for his restrained and appealing *guerillero* leader, Mr.

Grant for his stalwart, understated British captain, and Miss Loren for her good looks.

Franz Planer's photography is not only superior, but often haunting as it captures something of the look and quality of Spain. And there are Spanish people by the thousands, who, childlike, seem to have done everything Mr. Kramer asked them to do. It's a big package he has put together, and there are a lot of fine things in it, and no one in Hollywood is worried about how big or small the audience is for it, or whether it will make any money. When you make a picture like this, they know these things take care of themselves.

Hollis Alpert, *Saturday Review*

One great advantage that *The Pride and the Passion* has over most epic films is its unity of theme; all action revolves around the gun, the symbol of men fighting for what they believe in. The English captain, skillfully played by Cary Grant, is a trained soldier, an authority on ordnance who has been commanded by his commodore to rescue the giant cannon, which was jettisoned by the fleeing Spanish army, and deliver it to a British warship. The guerrilla leader, colorfully played by Frank Sinatra, is an uneducated, undisciplined patriot determined to deliver his hometown, Avila, from the occupying French. Again and again the two men are contrasted: the smart, immaculately dressed, cold but sentimental English officer versus the emotional, cruel, provincial Spaniard. Each has his big moments: the Englishman muddies his clothes as he assembles the broken cannon and directs its perilous journey, blows up a bridge and even eloquently pleads with the Bishop at the Escorial that the cannon be hidden in the cathedral; with less eloquence but with greater passion, the guerrilla leader persuades a group of townfolk to help drag the cannon out of the river and he effectively commands the peasants who work under him in the long march to Avila. . . .

It is fortunate that producer-director Stanley Kramer stressed the visual aspects in telling his story. The script, written by Edna and Edward Anhalt and stemming from C. S. Forester's novel *The Gun,* is strangely ineffectual; and the dialogue, whether due to the actors' odd mixture of accents or to poor recording, does not come through well. The plot's argument is, therefore, difficult to follow at times; but Kramer has so directed the picture that the visuals succeed in developing the themes with little help from the spoken word. Kramer's film is occasionally reminiscent of *For Whom the Bell Tolls,* another movie in which a foreigner was involved in one particular objective in helping war-torn Spaniards; although the characters in the film made from the Hemingway novel were better drawn and motivated, *The Pride and the Passion* is far superior visually. In magnificent scenes, like those showing the Holy Week procession in the Escorial, the dragging of the cannon through a dangerous mountain pass, the storming of Avila's walls and the routing of the French, Kramer has

Frank Sinatra
and Sophia Loren

used locale and crowds of people superbly, alternating the big panoramic canvas with telling close-ups that are right from Goya. Without minimizing the horrors of war, *The Pride and the Passion* is an epic sung in praise of the triumph of will over all obstacles.

Philip T. Hartung, *The Commonweal*

## ARTICLE:

Writers are notoriously sensitive about strangers monkeying around with their precious commas and semicolons. Accordingly, when we heard by jungle tom-tom that novelist Cecil Scott (*African Queen, Horatio Hornblower*) Forester was in town, we thought we'd check up on how he felt about the giant movie, *The Pride and the Passion,* that is being metamorphosed out of his modest little novelette, *The Gun.*

"Look at it this way," said Mr. Forester, when we cornered him the other day behind coffee and crumpets at the Elysée. "Professional writers (and I consider myself a pro) don't run screaming through the streets when their work is altered, reasonably, to fit another medium. I've written too many scripts myself to worry about changes. They're frequently for the better, anyway."

The Cairo-born, ex-British, long-time resident of Hollywood (who looks more like a happy Rotarian than a fabulously successful novelist) discussed his recent trip to Spain, where producer Stanley (*Caine Mutiny*) Kramer "and about 10,000 actors and horses" were turning *The Gun* into an epic drama of the Spanish War of Independence from the Napoleonic yoke, circa 1810.

Forester's original story told how guerrilleros found a 6,000-pound cannon abandoned by fleeing Spanish regulars and dragged the bronze giant all over the Peninsula, blowing Napoleon's garrisons to smithereens along the way.

'The book had to be altered for filming," said Forester, "and the Anhalts, Edna and Edward, did a good job of

compressing characters, and expanding incidents. The various guerrillero chiefs are now combined into one—Frank Sinatra. And there's a British naval officer to teach them how to handle the big gun—he's Cary Grant. And for love interest (you can't get along without *that* in the movies) there's a girl who fights with the guerrilleros—and, of course, the men fight over her. She's Sophia Loren. Could anyone ask for more?"

Obviously not. "One morning we drove from Madrid to location. From the edge of a cliff I looked down the valley. There, spread out as far as I could see, was the whole blooming Frency Army. An ocean of tents, stacked rifles, regimental banners, equipment, batteries of cannon, rows of tethered cavalry horses and artillery mules, and massed troops. Bugles blew, couriers galloped about—a vast army came to life.

"It was an extraordinary experience! A tremendous, unforgettable impact. As though I'd stepped back through the centuries—back to Spain 146 years ago. I was seeing the cream of Napoleon's army wheel into battle formation, I heard the clang and clatter of their arms, the crackling of their rifles, the thunder of their guns, the screams of the wounded and moans of the dying. Black smoke of 'burning' cities billowed up beyond the horizon—and one could almost feel Napoleon lying in wait across the frontier."

No cameras? "I hardly noticed the cameras," said Forester. "The whole operation was organized like an army on maneuvers—which of course it was—by Mr. Kramer and his 'General Staff.' He seemed to be everywhere. Flying gunpowder set fire to a couple of hayricks—and Kramer directed the fire brigades while he told Cary Grant to get a haircut, ordered 60 stuffed 'dead' horses, and instructed the prop-man to check the firing mechanisms for the 2,000 dummy guns."

Author Forester seemed lost in admiration of producer Kramer, as moviemaker Kramer must undoubtedly have been of novelist Forester. "It's wonderful," he said, "to be able to stand on the sidelines and watch a pro turn a book into a film."

Forester's experience with book-into-film goes back to *Payment Deferred,* a thriller he wrote when he was 24. "It wasn't much of a book," he says happily, "but it gave Charles Laughton his chance at Broadway, and brought both of us to Hollywood."

Jesse Zunser, *Cue Magazine*

With Frank Sinatra

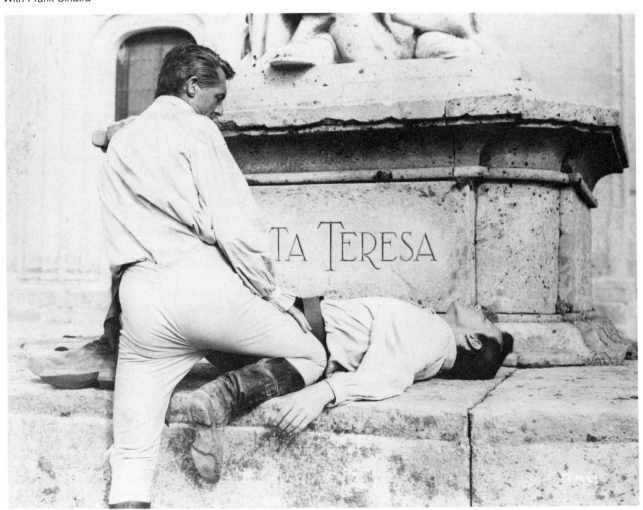

TA TERESA

With Deborah Kerr

# AN AFFAIR TO REMEMBER

1957

**CREDITS:**

*Distributing company:* 20th Century-Fox. *Producing company:* A Jerry Wald Production. *Producer:* Jerry Wald. *Director:* Leo McCarey. *Assistant director:* Gilbert Mandelik. *Screenplay:* Delmer Daves and Leo McCarey. Based on unpublished original story by Leo McCarey and Mildred Cram. *Cinematography:* Milton Krasner. DeLuxe Color and Cinemascope. *Color Consultant:* Leonard Doss. *Special photographic effects:* L. B. Abbott. *Editor:* James B. Clark. Music by Hugo Friedhofer, conducted by Lionel Newman. Orchestration by Edward B. Powell and Pete King. *Art direction:* Lyle R. Wheeler, and Jack Martin Smith. *Set decorations:* Walter M. Scott, and Paul S. Fox. *Executive Wardrobe designer:* Charles LeMaire. *Makeup:* Ben Nye. Hair styles by Helen Turpin. *Sound:* Charles Peck, and Harry M. Leonard. *Songs:* Music by Harry Warren. Lyrics by Harold Adamson, and Leo McCarey. *Title song:* "An Affair to Remember," sung by Vic Damone

Vocal supervision by Ken Darby. *Release date:* July 2, 1957. *Running time:* 114 minutes.

**THE CAST:**

| | |
|---|---|
| *Nickie Ferrante* | Cary Grant |
| *Terry McKay* | Deborah Kerr |
| *Kenneth* | Richard Denning |
| *Lois Clarke* | Neva Patterson |
| *Grandmother* | Cathleen Nesbitt |
| *Announcer* | Robert Q. Lewis |
| *Hathaway* | Charles Watts |
| *Courbet* | Fortunio Bonanova |
| *Father McGrath* | Matt Moore |
| *Mario* | Louis Mercier |
| *Miss Webb* | Geraldine Wall |
| *Miss Lane* | Sarah Selby |

| | |
|---|---|
| *Bartender* | Alberto Morin |
| *Gabrielle* | Genevieve Aumont |
| *Landlady* | Jesslyn Fax |
| *Gladys* | Nora Marlowe |

with Butch Bernard, Theresa Emerson, Richard Allen, Tina Thompson, Scotty Morrow, Kathleen Charney, Terry Ross Kelman, Norman Champion III, Mary Carroll, Suzanne Ellers, Juney Ellis, Don Pietro, Paul Bradly, Tony De Mario, Michka Egan, Bert Stevens, Brian Corcoran, Priscilla Garcia, Marc Snow, Anthony Mazzola, Helen Mayon, Walter Woolf King, Roger Til, Jack Raine, Dino Bolognese, Jack Lomas, Dorothy Adams, Al Bain, Robert Lynn, Danny Scott, Ken Kane, Patricia Powell and Alena Murray.

## SYNOPSIS:

Nickie Ferrante, a notable and faintly notorious bachelor is on board a transatlantic liner enroute to New York via Naples. He plans to marry Lois Clarke, a wealthy heiress who is waiting for him in New York. On board the ship he meets Terry McKay, for whom Kenneth Bradley is waiting in New York. They enjoy each other's company. But when they land, each goes their separate way. Nickie works hard to become a successful painter, and makes several unsuccessful attempts to meet Terry again. Terry is involved in a serious accident and incapacitated for many months. Finally Nickie finds Terry, and they decide to return to Naples to live happily together.

## REVIEWS:

Only sensitive acting by Deborah Kerr and Cary Grant saves this saccharine trifle from suffocating in its sentimental wrappings.

*Time*

To bring back to the screen within twenty years an enormously appealing picture subject, and cause it to appear as effective, if not even better than the original, is a true achievement in film-making. Leo McCarey, a not-too-active director in recent years, has accomplished this both movingly and impressively in *An Affair To Remember*. Results in this heart-interest cinema, which is bound to evoke many tears from its audience, are actually phenomenal and demonstrate that the same victory may be twice won.

*Love Affair* the first picture was produced with Charles Boyer and Irene Dunne in starring parts; the new version spotlights Deborah Kerr and Cary Grant, and they are quite a remarkable couple, considering the important place their predecessors made for themselves about 1939 in identical assignments. Grant, unfortunately, does not suggest the foreign character of his name as did Charles Boyer, because he is not the Latin type. This fundamentally will be a distraction for those who remember the earlier picture. However, *An Affair To Remember* has been sympathetically developed in its new manifestation by Director McCarey, while Miss Kerr, who seems artistically remarkably right for her portrayal, and Grant give their utmost to their assignments.

Edwin Schallert, *Los Angeles Times*

Leo McCarey has had the good sense not to pretend that this romantic comedy is ever anything more than that, meanwhile exploiting a quality so long absent from the screen that it comes through with all the force of a brand new discovery—namely, charm. Jerry Wald, the producer, observed that one reason there were so few real love stories being made any more was because there were so few actors who could play them convincingly. "Today's actors," he said, "either look good and talk lousy or they look lousy and talk good." Well, Cary Grant, an early exponent of cinematic charm, still looks good and talks good—and his graceful performance as a playboy is one good reason for seeing this film.

Arthur Knight, *Saturday Review*

228

With Cathleen Nesbitt and Deborah Kerr

With Deborah Kerr

229

# KISS THEM FOR ME

1957

With Suzy Parker

## CREDITS:

*Distributing company:* 20th Century-Fox. *Producer:* Jerry Wald. *Director:* Stanley Donen. *Assistant director:* David Hall. *Screenplay:* Julius Epstein—from the play "Kiss Them For Me" by Luther Davis, and the novel *Shore Leave,* by Frederic Wakeman. *Cinematography:* Milton Krasner. DeLux Color. *Color consultant:* Leonard Doss CinemaScope. *Special photographic effects:* L. B. Abbott. *Editor:* Robert Simpson. Music by Lionel Newman. *Orchestration:* Pete King and Skip Martin. *Art direction:* Lyle R. Wheeler, and Maurice Ransford. *Set decoration:* Walter M. Scott, and Stuart A. Reiss. *Executive Wardrobe designer:* Charles LeMaire. *Makeup:* Ben Nye. *Hair styles:* Helen Tarpin. *Sound:* Charles Peck, and Frank Moran. *Song:* "Kiss Them For Me," by Carroll Coates and Lionel Newman, sung by The McGuire Sisters. *Release date:* December 10, 1957. *Running time:* 103 minutes.

## THE CAST:

| | |
|---|---|
| *Crewson* | Cary Grant |
| *Alice* | Jayne Mansfield |
| *Gwenneth* | Suzy Parker |
| *Eddie Turnbill* | Leif Erickson |
| *Mac (Lieut. McCann)* | Ray Walston |
| *Mississip* | Larry Blyden |
| *C.P.O. Ruddle* | Nathaniel Frey |
| *Commander Wallace* | Werner Klemperer |
| *Ensign Lewis* | Jack Mullaney |
| *R.A.F. Pilot* | Ben Wright |
| *Gunner* | Michael Ross |
| *Roundtree* | Harry Carey, Jr. |

230

| Neilson | Frank Nelson |
| Debbie | Caprice Yordan |
| Lucille | Ann McCrea |

## SYNOPSIS:

During World War II, Navy hero fliers, Crewson, Mississip, and Mac (who is running for Congress from his home state in New England in absentia) take off for a quick relaxation visit to San Francisco. Public relations officer, Commander Wallace, is forced to tag along as he is responsible for them. They get an entire hotel suite despite the room shortage, and have a party at which they meet Alice and other cuties. Shipbuilder Eddie Turnbill asks them to appear at pep rallies in his yards, but is chased away by Crewson. But Crewson is attracted by Turnbill's fiancee, Gwenneth. The Navy attempts to investigate their visit to San Francisco, but has little luck. Turnbill becomes obnoxious and Crewson knocks him down, after which Gwen breaks their engagement. But when Gwen tries to pin Crewson down to a possible marriage date, he is evasive. Mac learns that he has been elected and that he is automatically out of the Navy. The Shore Patrol takes them into custody. They are freed and plan to return to their ship when they receive news that it has been hit by the enemy. Crewson and Gwen finally come to an understanding.

## REVIEWS:

Cary Grant, whose name virtually assures box office success to any picture in which he appears, stars in this rowdy comedy-drama. Helping the marquee is Jayne Mansfield, just voted one of the Top Ten Stars of Tomorrow, and Suzy Parker, one of the country's top models, who makes her film debut here.

Much of what occurs in the film seems a bit dated now, not because it takes place during the war, but due rather

With Suzy Parker

231

With Jayne Mansfield and Suzy Parker

to the situations involving civilians and servicemen. Despite this, the screenplay by Julius Epstein is loaded with glib lines and farcical circumstances that are quite funny in the main although somewhat bawdy and adult. Too, the picture vacillates from slapstick to satire to sentiment and much of the best of each is lost in the shuffle.

Grant, even though a bit old as a dashing pilot, is wonderful, be he romantic, comic, bitter or sad.

*Motion Picture Herald*

*Kiss Them For Me,* coincidentally enough, is also about some military men intent on staging a party. The party-givers in this case are three naval aviators who arrive in wartime San Francisco determined to devote all their brief French leave from a carrier to wine, women and song.

The color-and-CinemaScope movie is based on a novel written during World War II and made into a (not very successful) play soon after that.

By 1957, its attitudes are curiously dated. For one example, the enemy seems to be the civilian population. For another, the fliers behave alternately like post-adolescent Peck's Bad Boys and like swashbuckling heroes with equally juvenile motivation. Though Cary Grant delivers some sardonic wisecracks very well, he seems a little old to be acting so irresponsibly.

The picture also has leading-woman trouble. Fashion model Suzy Parker, who plays the enigmatic heroine, is lovely to look at but can't act; while director Stanley Donen has allowed Jayne Mansfield, in the role which was Judy Holliday's stepping stone to fame, to be broadly and unamusingly vulgar.

Moira Walsh, *America*

In 1944 Frederic Wakeman wrote a biting cynical novel about war-weary officers on leave. Now translated to the screen, it depicts three blasé officers with four days to kill in San Francisco. They wangle themselves into an ambassadorial suite in the town's best hotel, throw a colossal drinking party, tangle with the Shore Patrol, look for cushy land jobs and make themselves generally what every man in uniform should be proud not to be. A change of heart at the end, which sends them back to active duty, does not in any way redeem them. The immediacy and realism which gave the novel some impact is missing. Cary Grant, poorly made up, flops through the part of Commander Crewson, on beds, on sofas, and on street-cars. Jayne Mansfield, wearing the tightest war-worker's coveralls ever devised, wiggles in and out of scenes, and

Suzy Parker, as the beautiful (but good) girl friend of the ship-building tycoon, freezes everyone for ninety minutes until Crewson's last flop, when she melts in his arms, throws over the tycoon and cries real glycerine tears as the boys sail into the wild blue yonder with a drunken pilot and much under the influence themselves. Pretty dull stuff even for Cary Grant fans.

Mary C. Hatch, *Library Journal*
*Readers' Adviser, New York Public Library*

With Suzy Parker and Jayne Mansfield

# INDISCREET

1958

With Ingrid Bergman

## CREDITS:

*Distributing company:* Warner Bros. Pictures. *Producing company:* A Grandon Production. *Producer:* Stanley Donen. *Director:* Stanley Donen. *Associate producer:* Sydney Streeter. *Assistant Director:* Tom Pevsner. *Screenplay:* Norman Krasna, from his play *Kind Sir*. *Cinematography:* Frederick A. Young. *Camera Operator:* Robert Walker. *Editor:* Jack Harris. *Composer:* Richard Bennett and Ken Jones. Conducted by Muir Mathieson. Song "Indiscreet" by Sammy Cahn and James VanHeusen. *Art direction:* Don Ashton. *Costumes:* Cary Grant's clothes by Quintino. Jewelry by M. P. Greengross. Furs by Calman Links. *Makeup:* John O'Gorman. *Sound recordists:* Richard Bird and Len Shilton. *Sound editor:* Winston Ryder. *Production manager:* Roy Parkinson. *Release date:* May 20, 1958. *Running time:* 100 minutes.

234

## THE CAST:

| | |
|---|---|
| *Philip Adams* | Cary Grant |
| *Anna Kalman* | Ingrid Bergman |
| *Alfred Munson* | Cecil Parker |
| *Margaret Munson* | Phyllis Calvert |
| *Carl Banks* | David Kossoff |
| *Doris Banks* | Megs Jenkins |
| *Finleigh* | Oliver Johnston |
| *Finleigh's Clerk* | Middleton Woods |

## SYNOPSIS:

Anna Kalman, star of the theatre, comes home to her London apartment for a rest. Her older sister, Margaret Munson, and her husband, Alfred Munson, a NATO official, arrive to attend an organization dinner at which the principal speaker is to be Philip Adams, a monetary expert. Anna is impressed with Philip and agrees to attend the dinner. Later she invites him to the ballet. Before accepting, he warns her he is married, separated, and unable to get a divorce. She still agrees to their becoming friends. Philip tells Anna that he has been called to New York for another NATO meeting. Meanwhile Alfred discovers that Philip has never been married, figuring that he can play the field better if no permanent attachments are in mind. Margaret reveals this to her sister. Anna is angered, and she plans to make Philip jealous when he returns. But it backfires, for Philip intended to make a proposal of marriage, but when he sees the butler-chauffeur with Anna in her bedroom, he decides not to. After a while, the matter is cleared up and the pair are reunited.

## REVIEWS:

Norman Krasna's screen adaptation of his 1953 Broadway hit *Kind Sir,* is a vast improvement over the original.

For one thing, the comedy of manners is now set against a posh and technicolored backdrop of London at its loveliest. For another, director Donen's stars are Cary Grant and Ingrid Bergman. Together for the first time since 1946 and *Notorious,* the actors volley Krasna's ebullient dialogue with masterful adroitness and manage romance with a subtlety that detracts not for a moment from its ardor.

*Newsweek*

Trifle, as every visitor to Britain knows, is a light fluffy dessert topped with whipped cream. The new Ingrid Bergman-Cary Grant film, *Indiscreet,* which was filmed largely in London, is a trifle in that as well as the other sense. It is unessential but pleasant. There are two faults. Not enough use was made of the city of London, which is a pity because the color in this Warner Bros. film is good. And Miss Bergman, although she still has the ability to fall in love in a way to make the male viewer jealous of her leading man, is neither a deft comedienne nor convincing as a star of the English theatre. But Cary Grant

With Ingrid Bergman

With Cecil Parker, Ingrid Bergman and Phyllis Calvert

and Cecil Parker are gifted *farceurs,* Phyllis Calvert is a nice peanut-brittle sister to Miss Bergman, and the script by Norman Krasna, from his play *Kind Sir* does adequately what a farce ought to do: it supplies logical surprises both in dialogue and plot.

Stanley Kauffmann, *The New Republic*

*Indiscreet* is an attempt to revive the kind of urbane romantic comedy that was popular some twenty years ago. To qualify for this category it was necessary that the leading characters be rich and handsome and spectacularly well dressed and that they behave in the somewhat irresponsible fashion equated in the mind of the average audience with genuine sophistication. It was also helpful, though not altogether obligatory, to have Cary Grant as the male star.

Cary Grant, as impeccably tailored and deft with a witty line as ever and looking very little older, is on hand in this new one (in fact, with director Stanley Donen he also co-produced it). Playing opposite him is a magnificently gowned Ingrid Bergman.

The film was adapted by Norman Krasna from his play, *Kind Sir.* It was not much of a play and the addition of some clever new dialogue does not make the movie version much better. Even so, the two principals, though a trifle mature for this kind of shenanigans, are thoroughly expert and so are Phyllis Calvert and Cecil Parker. And an ultra-handsome Technicolor production rounds out what I suppose could be called glamorous escapism.

Moira Walsh, *Catholic World*

# HOUSEBOAT

1958

With Sophia Loren

**CREDITS:**

*Distributing company:* Paramount Pictures release of a Paramount Scribe. *Producer:* Jack Rose. *Director:* Melville Shavelson. *Production Associate:* Hal C. Kern. *Assistant director:* Michael D. Moore. *Screenplay:* Melville Shavelson, and Jack Rose. *Cinematography:* Ray June. Technicolor; VistaVision. *Technicolor Consultant:* Richard Mueller. *Special effects:* John P. Fulton. *Editor:* Frank Fracht. Music by George Duning. Songs by Jay Livingston and Ray Evans. Other music by Felix Mendelssohn and Richard Wagner. *Art direction:* Hal Pereira and John Goodman. *Set decoration:* Sam Comer and Grace Gregory. *Costumes:* Edith Head. *Hair style supervision:* Nellie Manley. *Makeup supervision:* Wally Westmore. *Sound:* Hugo and Charles Grezbach. *Process photography:* Farciot Edouart. *Second Unit photography:* Wallace Kelley. *Release date:* November 19, 1958. *Running time:* 112 minutes.

**THE CAST:**

| | |
|---|---|
| Tom Tinston | Cary Grant |
| Cinzia Zaccardi | Sophia Loren |
| Caroline Gibson | Martha Hyer |
| Angelo | Harry Guardino |
| Arturo Zaccardi | Eduardo Ciannelli |
| Alan Wilson | Murray Hamilton |
| Elizabeth Winston | Mimi Gibson |
| David Winston | Paul Petersen |
| Robert Winston | Charles Herbert |
| Mrs. Farnsworth | Madge Kennedy |
| Mr. Farnsworth | John Litel |
| Harold Messner | Werner Klemperer |

with Peggy Connelly, Kathleen Freeman, Julian Rivero, Mary Forbes, Helen Brown, Florence MacAfee, Richard

238

Emory, Larry Carr, Gordon Wynn, Richard Nelson, William R. Remick, Ernst Brengk, Wally Walker, Joe McTurk, Gilda Oliva, Earl Spainard, Bob Scott, Brooks Benedict, Bill Hickman, Pat Moran, and Marc Wilder.

## SYNOPSIS:

When eight-year old Robert Winston slips away from a concert in search of more exciting entertainment, he exhibits intelligence far beyond his years. He meets Cinzia Zaccardi and they enjoy themselves, walking, talking, eating. Tom Winston is a widower who is trying to regain the love of his children after prolonged absences on government work have made him a stranger to them. When Robert brings Cinzia home, or vice versa, Tom persuades her to stay and act as a maid. Since she is having a dull time touring the country with her domineering father, an orchestra leader, she agrees. The children adore her and teach her a few of the necessary arts of housekeeping. Cinzia is interested in Tom, but he is involved in a romance with his wealthy sister-in-law, Caroline Gibson, until he

discovers what has been obvious to Robert all the time: it is Cinzia that he is really in love with.

## REVIEWS:

Grant's performance is just about flawless. With sure artistry, he seems unconscious of the farcical nature of the ridiculous events that overwhelm him. Everything he does is made poignant by the worries of a man wounded by the repudiation of his children. Slowly he learns to love them and his hurt grows deeper. There is one beautiful scene of muted tenderness when he encourages his elder son to teach him to fish. By so doing, he finds out the boy's tendencies toward being a Peeping Tom, a thief and a sneak are all traceable to his worries over his mother's death. With well-concealed parental anxiety and complete absence of theatrical sentimentality. Grant consoles the lonesome child with a quiet and moving discussion of immortality.

Jack Moffitt, *Hollywood Reporter*

With Mimi Gibson, Peggy Connelly, John Litel, Charles Herbert, Sophia Loren, Paul Peterson and Martha Hyer

With Paul Peterson, Sophia Loren, Charles Herbert and Mimi Gibson

With Charles Herbert, Paul Peterson, Sophia Loren and Mimi Gibson

Back in the '30s Hollywood regularly used to turn out a brand of happy family comedies which helped consolidate moviegoing as a weekly family habit. WIth the advent of the war and the end of an era the films turned to other, more serious trends.

They never returned to this type of picture because a new entertainment competitor called television made such types of family comedy its first basic staple and has continued to hold on to them to this day, along with picking up another longtime movie staple—westerns.

TV or no, moviemakers have decided to return to one of their most popular formats after scattered sporadic attempts in the past decade. Amid the mayhem, realism and horror cycle it will be intriguing to see how filmgoers greet the old favorite.

One of the first such excursions is *Houseboat,* a Cary Grant-Sophia Loren romp in color which manages deftly to combine chuckles and corn in the right proportions.

The comedy, an original written by Mal Shavelson and Jack Rose, has its full share of Desi-Lucy brand of corn but it also benefits from bright performances by Grant, Loren and crew. Grant is always perfectly at home in these roles in which, with an exasperated look, head tilt or dryly stated irony, he can put his point across.

Dick Williams, *Mirror News* (Los Angeles)

*Houseboat* is the kind of picture to which you can take your stuffy maiden aunt, your wicked sophisticated uncle, and your ten-year-old child and they will all have a wonderful time.

*Houseboat* is the zaniest comedy, and at the same time, it is real romance. It also has in it, beautifully enunciated by Cary Grant, an essay on life and death. Mr. Grant, as you know, is just about the screen's smoothest, most worldly comedian. That's what he is here—but he gets in that serious moment.

Ruth Waterbury, *Los Angeles Examiner*

With Eva Marie Saint

# NORTH BY NORTHWEST

1959

**CREDITS:**

*Distributing company:* Metro-Goldwyn-Mayer release of a Loew's Incorporated Production. *Producer:* Alfred Hitchcock. *Director:* Alfred Hitchcock. *Associate producer:* Herbert Coleman. *1st Assistant director:* Robert Saunders. *Screenplay:* Ernest Lehman. *Cinematography:* Robert Burks. *Editor:* George Tomasini. *Music:* Bernard Herrmann. *Art direction:* William A. Horning, and Merrill Pye. *Production designer:* Robert Boyle. *Release date:* July 17, 1959. *Running time:* 136 minutes.

**THE CAST:**

| | |
|---|---|
| *Roger Thornhill* | Cary Grant |
| *Eve Kendall* | Eva Marie Saint |
| *Phillip Vandamm* | James Mason |
| *Clara Thornhill* | Jessie Royce Landis |

| | |
|---|---|
| *Professor* | Leo G. Carroll |
| *Lester Townsend* | Philip Ober |
| *Handsome Woman* | Josephine Hutchinson |
| *Leonard* | Martin Landau |
| *Valerain* | Adam Williams |
| *Victor Larrabee* | Edward Platt |
| *Licht* | Robert Ellenstein |
| *Auctioneer* | Les Tremayne |
| *Dr. Cross* | Philip Coolidge |
| *Chicago Policeman* | Patrick McVey |
| *Capt. Junket* | Edward Binns |
| *Chicago Policeman* | Ken Lynch |

with John Beradino, Nora Marlowe, Doreen Lang, Alexander Lockwood, Stanley Adams, Lawrence Dobkin, Harvey Stephens, Walter Coy, Madge Kennedy, Tommy Farrell, Jimmy Cross, Harry Seymour, Frank Wilcox, Robert Shayne, Carleton Young, Ralph Heed, Paul Genge, Robert B. Williams, Maudie Prickett, James McCallion, Haynes

Barron, Doris Singh, Sally Fraser, Maura McGiveney, Susan Whitney, Ned Glass, Howard Negley, Jesslyn Fox, Jock Daly, Tol Avery, Tom Greenway, Ernest Anderson, Malcolm Atterbury, Andy Albin, Carl Milletaire, Olan Soule, Helen Spring, Patricia Cutts, John Damler, Len Hendry, Sara Berner, Wilson Wood, Bobby Johnson, Taggert Casey, Lucile Curtis, Sid Kane, Hugh Pryor, Charles Postal, Anna Anderson, Dale Van Sichel, Frank Marlowe and Harry Strang.

## SYNOPSIS:

Roger Thornhill, a business executive, is mistaken for a secret agent and kidnapped. When questioned by Phillip Vandamm, head of a spy ring, Roger is unable to convince him that he is not an agent. They force him to become drunk, and place him in a car expecting him to have a fatal accident. Instead he is arrested by the police. Neither his mother nor the police believe his story. Roger then goes to the U.N. Building to see the owner of the estate where he was held prisoner. Explaining that he has not been living at his estate, the man falls dead in Roger's arms. Roger now must hide from the police as well as the spy ring. In an effort to find the agent he is being confused with, Roger gets to Grand Central Station and boards a train to Chicago. On the train he meets Eve Kendall, who hides him in her compartment when the detectives search the train. She arranges a meeting between Roger and the agent, sending him to a road-crossing out in open farming country. While waiting there, Roger discovers that a crop-dusting plane is being used to try to kill him. He escapes, returns to the city, where he finds Eve. She tells him they must not see each other anymore. Later he discovers Eve and Vandamm sitting together at an auction. When they leave, Roger realizes he is trapped between two agents who plan to murder him. He makes a scene and the police arrive and take him away. Instead of taking him to the police station, he is taken to the airport, where the Professor, a government agent, explains to him that Eve is also a government agent and that her life is in danger. Roger agrees to assume the role of the nonexistent agent and try to save her life. He is flown to South Dakota where Vandamm is hiding. Finding him there, Eve shoots him with a blank to prove

With Robert Ellenstein, Martin Landau and Adam Williams

With Leo G. Carroll and Eva Marie Saint

her loyalty to Vandamm. Roger is taken to a hospital, although he is not injured; and later goes to Vandamm's house and helps Eve escape. There is a chase across the historical figures carved on Mount Rushmore, during which Vandamm is killed and Roger saves Eve's life.

## REVIEWS:

A new thriller from MGM, *North by Northwest,* convinces me more than ever that when Alfred Hitchcock is at his best it is because his sense of humor is nicely in tune with his material. It ought to be said at once, of course, that *North by Northwest* is much the best Hitchcock that has come along in some years, and it is probably due to the fact that his situation, this time, has allowed him to indulge his fancy for all sorts of playfully macabre moments. If, by the way, you like to take your suspense straight, the movie has all that's necessary to keep you on the edge of your seat, as Cary Grant gets himself into a variety of baffling and dangerous corners; it is only when you adopt the basic premise that Cary Grant could not possibly come to fatal harm that the tongue in Hitchcock's cheek becomes plainly visible.

But the villains are devilish and ingenious. Grant is at the U.N. speaking to an important delegate. The delegate suddenly gasps, and Mr. Grant notices the handle of a knife sticking from his back. What does Hitchcock have him do next? Mr. Grant pulls the knife out from the delegate's vertebrae and, bemused, examines it. Photographers appear and photograph the man with the knife. Grant runs, but the picture appears on the front page of several dozen newspapers, and he has the task not only of finding a villain, a nonexistent double, and the reason for it all, but must run the risk of being instantly recognizable

wherever he goes. The similarity to the running gag of the silent film is unmistakable.

The funniest and most macabre of Grant's trials occurs when he is waiting for his "double" at a barren crossroads in the midst of a vast Illinois cornfield. Someone once said that the most chilling effect can be gotten by placing one's hero in an empty field in bright sunlight. It is afternoon. Grant stands at the edge of the highway, impeccably dressed, waiting. A car appears in the distance. It whooshes by. Another appears. A farmer gets out to wait for a bus. The farmer remarks to Grant on the oddness of a small plane crop-dusting a crop that doesn't need dusting. The whole thing is done with such realism that I suppose it can be called surrealism.

Mr. Hitchcock, no doubt having the time of his life, drags out his yarn a little too long, mainly because his climax occurs on the sculpted monuments to four Presidents on Mount Rushmore, and having gone to all that trouble to get there, he must now make use of this photographic opportunity. These moments are the least suspenseful and also the most obvious in humorous terms. But for the most part he is at the top of his form. His players are perfect: Cary Grant, Eva Marie Saint, and James Mason; also, Jessie Royce Landis, Leo G. Carroll, and Martin Landau. And a complimentary word for Ernest Lehman, who wrote the screenplay. Mr. Lehman not only provided Hitchcock with exactly the right kind of story to take advantage of his skills, but he has written that rare thing these days—a screen original. It is no wonder, then, that *North by Northwest* is all movie, and a delightful treat as well.

Hollis Alpert, *Saturday Review*

If it does nothing else (but it does, it does), *North By Northwest* resoundingly reaffirms the fact that Cary Grant and Alfred Hitchcock are two of the very slickest operators before and behind the Hollywood cameras. Together they can be unbeatable. Each has his own special, career-tested formula. Actor Grant's is a sartorial spiffiness and mannered charm; producer-director Hitchcock's is an outrageously simple yet effective blend of mayhem and humor at mayhem's expense, the whole usually framed by a famous piece of scenery that no one else had ever considered a suitable backdrop for melodramatic shenanigans. The present shiny and colorful collaboration offers Grant as a dapper Madison Avenue advertising executive being chased by foreign agents over the slippery precipices of the Presidential faces carved into Mount Rushmore—a most unlikely bit of contrived suspense, but one that is hypnotizing while it jangles the nerves.

*Newsweek*

Cary Grant performs with the polish that movie-goers have for long come to expect of him.

*Look Magazine*

With Eva Marie Saint

# OPERATION PETTICOAT

1959

**CREDITS:**

*Distributing company:* Universal-International release. *Producing company:* Granart Company Production. *Producer:* Robert Arthur. *Director:* Blake Edwards. *Assistant Director:* Frank Shaw. *Screenplay:* Stanley Shapiro and Maurice Richlin. From an unpublished story by Paul King, and Joseph Stone. *Cinematography:* Russell Harlan. *Color Consultant:* Henri Jaffa. Eastman Color. *Special Photography:* Clifford Stine. *Editors:* Ted J. Kent and Frank Gross. Music by David Rose. *Art direction:* Alexander Golitzen and Robert E. Smith. *Set decorators:* Russell A. Gausman, and Oliver Emert. *Costumes:* Bill Thomas. *Makeup:* Bud Westmore. *Hair stylist:* Larry Germain. *Sound:* Leslie I. Carey, and Vernon W. Kramer. *Release date:* December 2, 1959. *Running time:* 124 minutes.

**THE CAST:**

| | |
|---|---|
| *Sherman* | Cary Grant |
| *Holden* | Tony Curtis |
| *Dolores* | Joan O'Brien |
| *Barbara* | Dina Merrill |
| *Molumphrey* | Gene Evans |
| *Tostin* | Arthur O'Connell |
| *Stovall* | Richard Sargent |
| *Major Edna Hayward* | Virginia Gregg |
| *Henderson* | Robert F. Simon |
| *Watson* | Robert Gist |
| *Hunkie* | Gavin MacLeod |
| *The Prophet* | George Dunn |
| *Harmon* | Dick Crockett |
| *Lt. Claire Reid* | Madlyn Rhue |
| *Lt. Ruth Colfax* | Marion Ross |
| *Ramon* | Clarence E. Lung |
| *Dooley* | Frankie Darro |
| *Fox* | Tony Pastor, Jr. |
| *Reiner* | Robert Hoy |
| *Kraus* | Nicky Blair |
| *Williams* | John W. Morley |
| *Crewman* | William Bryant |
| *Bowman* | Bert Beyers |
| *Fireman 1/c* | Tony Corrado |

with Glen Jacobson, Nino Tempo, Robert Keys, Dale Cummings, Joseph Kim, Leon Lontoc, James F. Lanphier, Alan Dexter, Nelson Leigh, Francis DeSales, Preston Hanson, Hal Baylor, Bob Stratton, Malcolm Cassell, Harry Harvey, Jr., Haile Chase, Vi Ingraham, Vince Deadrick, William Kinney, Alan Scott, Francis L. Ward, William R. Callinan, Gordon Casell, Robert C. Youmons, Howard Venezia, David Meek, Larry Gilliland, Fred Harlfinger, II, Robert Gibson, and Tusi Faiivae.

## SYNOPSIS:

A submarine anchored near Manila is damaged and partly sunk by an enemy air attack. The Navy is prepared to write if off, but Sherman, the skipper is determined to raise her and with the scratch crew left him, sail her to the nearest drydock, Port Darwin, for a complete overhaul. The first tribulation is the assignment to the sub of Holden, an admiral's aide. Although lacking in seagoing knowledge or skills, Holden is worth his weight in gold as a procurement officer, for, assisted by the biggest crook in the Philippines, Ramon, he is able to swipe everything necessary to get the ship on its way. At their first stop, Holden brings a group of nurses aboard including Dolores and Barbara. The ladies cause many problems in the running and the management of the submarine. After Sherman has faced the many challenges of keeping his crew and the nurses safety apart, the submarine is brought to port.

## REVIEWS:

Though he gets many laughs Cary Grant plays an essentially straight part and theatrical pros will recognize it as one of the trickiest acting jobs of his long and brilliant career. Throughout every inch of it, he makes you feel that this is a dedicated captain determined to sail his ship again. He makes all that follows seem funny instead of silly. Curtis has an actor's field day with his flashy part, but under Blake Edwards' skilled direction, all the players make valuable contributions to the general hilarity.

Jack Moffitt, *Hollywood Reporter*

Cary Grant is a living lesson in getting laughs without lines. In this film, most of the gags play off him. It is his reaction, blank, startled, etc., always underplayed, that creates or releases the humor. Tony Curtis is a splendid foil, one of the two or three best young comedians around, and his own style meshes easily with Grant's.

Powe, *Daily Variety*

*Operation Petticoat,* another in the seemingly endless series of comedies depicting military life, is far more in keeping with the season. This is a slick, often hilarious lark about a battered submarine that undergoes a series of misadventures during World War II and winds up, painted an embarrassing pink, busily dodging depth charges sent down by our own Navy. Though much of it is supposedly based on true incidents, the movie seems

With Arthur O'Connell

like outlandish fiction. In any case, the end result is a flock of sight and word gags, some of them forced, others funny indeed. Thus, we get the stock situation of a group of comely nurses disrupting submarine life, side by side with a genuinely amusing sequence in which an officer is forced to dress a stolen pig as a sailor in order to get it past the MPs, a worthy subterfuge that provides a gratifying New Year's dinner for the crew.

The film benefits enormously from the performances. Cary Grant makes a wonderfully befuddled captain, manfully working to make his submarine worthy of the U.S. Navy, while struggling desperately to control the nurses, his madcap sailors, and his supply officer who supplies everything—by stealing it. As the master supply officer, Tony Curtis almost steals the picture as well as the pig.

Dina Merrill and Joan O'Brien are prominently attractive among the nurses, and the Technicolor shots of Key West provide an excellent background for their charms. *Operation Petticoat* is much too long, but the pace is so rapid that if a given moment is dull, you can be sure the next one will be funny.

Richard Marek, *McCalls Magazine*

In fact, it's Grant's cleverness in sustaining restraint in the face of outrageous happenings and his underplaying in the time of perpetual crises, that proves the motivating keynote that holds together the entire movie. And it's a performance that is something to shout about.

Sara Hamilton, *Los Angeles Examiner*

With Arthur O'Connell and Virginia Gregg

With Joan O'Brien

With Tony Curtis and Dick Crockett

# THE GRASS IS GREENER

1961

## CREDITS:

*Distributing company:* A Universal-International release. *Producing company:* Grandon Productions, Ltd. *Producer:* Stanley Donen. *Director:* Stanley Donen. *Associate producer:* James Ware. *Assistant director:* Ray Stevens. *Screenplay:* Hugh and Margaret Williams. From their London play, *The Grass Is Greener*. *Cinematography:* Christopher Challis. Technicolor and Technirama. *Editor:* James Clark. Music and lyrics by Noel Coward. Music arrangements by Douglas Gamley, and Len Stevens. Music conducted by Muir Mathieson. *Art direction:* Paul Sheriff. *Set decorations:* Vernon Dixon. *Costumes:* Miss Kerr's clothes by Hardy Amies. Miss Simmons' clothes by Christian Dior. *Makeup:* John O'Gorman, and Eric Allwright. Hair styles by Gordon Bond. *Sound Supervisor:* John Cox. Main Titles designed by Maurice Binder. *Special Consultant on settings:* Felix Harbord. *Release date:* January 00, 1961. *Running time:* 104 minutes.

## THE CAST:

| | |
|---|---|
| *Victor Rhyall* | Cary Grant |
| *Hilary Rhyall* | Deborah Kerr |
| *Charles Delacro* | Robert Mitchum |
| *Hattie* | Jean Simmons |
| *Sellers* | Moray Watson |

## SYNOPSIS:

Lynley Hall, stately home of Victor, Earl of Rhyall and his wife Countess Hilary, is one of the English mansions thrown open to tourists. One of the sightseers, American millionaire Charles Delacro, invades the private apartments and meets and falls in love with Hilary. Victor gets an old friend of the family, Hattie Durrant to help him make Hilary jealous. There is a duel. Victor misses his shot but is hit in the shoulder. Hilary administers to Victor, and realizes anew his love for her. Hattie departs with Charles.

250

With Deborah Kerr and Robert Mitchum

With Robert Mitchum, Jean Simmons and Deborah Kerr

**REVIEWS:**

*The Grass Is Greener* proves once again how fundamentally even the most talented and glamorous performers are dependent on the words supplied them by a script. This Stanley Donen production for Universal-International, which he also directed, has one of the most glittering casts of the year. But the stars do not glitter or even glow. Instead of being liberated and propelled by the screenplay, they are chained and sunk. It is one of the year's most disappointing films.

James Powers, *Hollywood Reporter*

The best thing about *The Grass Is Greener* is its title, which fits so well an inexplicable set of circumstances. The worst thing about the picture is that producer-director Stanley Donen forgot he was making a movie, and in spite of all its glitter and glamorous cast, this film is awfully static and talky—and no fresher and greener than those comedies that used to turn up on our stages regularly in the thirties.

The script that Hugh and Margaret Williams wrote from their popular London stage comedy is only so-so funny, but Donen has given his picture a handsome production in Technicolor with lovely shots of England and the interior and exterior of Grant's elegant mansion. Brighter than the dialogue is the musical score stemming from Noel Coward's songs. It's too bad Coward couldn't have written the wisecracks too.

Philip T. Hartung, *The Commonweal*

With Robert Mitchum

# THAT TOUCH OF MINK

1962

With Doris Day

**CREDITS:**

*Distributing company:* A Universal-International Release. *Producing company:* A Granley Company-Arwin Productions, Inc.-Nob Hill Productions, Inc. *Producer:* Stanley Shapiro, and Martin Melcher. *Executive Producer:* Robert Arthur. *Director:* Delbert Mann. *Assistant director:* Phil Bowles, and Carl Beringer. *Story and Screenplay:* Stanley Shapiro, and Nate Monaster. *Cinematography:* Russell Metty. Eastman Color-Panavision. *Editor:* Ted J. Kent. *Music:* George Duning. *Art direction:* Alexander Golitzen, and Robert Clatworthy. *Set decorations:* George Milo. *Costumes:* Cardinal clothes for Mr. Grant's Suits; Leo Ritter for Miss Day's Furs. *Makeup:* Bud Westmore. *Hair stylist:* Larry Germain. *Sound:* Waldon O. Watson, and Corson Jowett. *Unit Production Manager:* Norman Deming. *Titles:* Pacific Title. Norman Norell for Special Fashions. *Release date:* July 18, 1962. *Running time:* 99 minutes.

**THE CAST:**

| | |
|---|---|
| *Philip Shayne* | Cary Grant |
| *Cathy Timberlake* | Doris Day |
| *Roger* | Gig Young |
| *Connie* | Audrey Meadows |
| *Dr. Gruber* | Alan Hewitt |
| *Beasley* | John Astin |
| *Young Man* | Richard Sargent |
| *Short Man* | Joey Faye |
| *Showgirl* | Laurie Mitchell |
| *Mr. Smith* | John Fiedler |
| *Hodges* | Willard Sage |
| *Dr. Richardson* | Jack Livesey |
| *Collins (chauffeur)* | John McKee |
| *Millie* | June Ericson |
| *Mrs. Golden* | Laiola Wendorff |

*with the New York Yankee players:* Mickey Mantle, Roger

Maris and Yogi Berra and Art Passarella, Ralph Manza, William Lanteau, Kathryn Givney, Alice Backes, Richard Deacon, Fred Essler, Helen Brown, Nelson Olmstead, Clegg Hoyt, Isabella Albonico, Billy Greene, Melora Conway, Yvonne Peattie, Russ Bender, Jon Silo Tyler McVey, Louise Arthur, John Morley, Edna Bennett, Sally Hughes, William Gleason, Rosalind Roberts, Dorothy Abbott, Cathie Merchant, Barbara Collentine, Jan Burrell, Jack Rice, Suzanne Barton, Bette Woods, Doris Lynn and George Simmons.

## SYNOPSIS:

Philip Shayne is a wealthy bachelor who is not interested in marriage. Cathy Timberlake, a small-town girl working in New York, is on her way to pick up her unemployment check, when Shayne's Rolls Royce splashes water on her coat. A frenzied romance starts, and Philip asks Miss Timberlake to go to Bermuda with him. She accepts, but breaks out with a rash and so cannot go. Sometime later, thinking she has rejected him for another, Philip follows her at his accountant's advice to an Asbury Park motel. However, everything is straightened out, they are married and finally set out for Bermuda.

## REVIEWS:

Comedy, which not so long ago was painfully absent from our screens, is now present, almost equally painfully, in abundance. Stanley Shapiro is perhaps primarily responsible for this state of things. The success of his *Pillow Talk* a few years back undoubtedly inspired the present cycle of frothy, handsomely dressed, and slyly suggestive pictures that seem to be coming at us from all directions—including Mr. Shapiro himself. His current *That Touch Of Mink,* costarring Cary Grant and Doris Day, is a deft reworking of the same basic situations that served him so well in his earlier films, and as such it towers above its contemporaries. Unfortunately, although this is intended as praise for a picture that abounds in bright moments and even brighter lines, it is actually no tribute at all—simply a statement of fact. It is no trick for an average man to tower above midgets.

Arthur Knight, *The Saturday Review*

The recipe is potent: Cary Grant and Doris Day in the old cat-and-mouse game. Pure gag-propelled farce, in which the commercial values tote up in a way that should handily extend the recent continuity of comedic success

at the box office. The gloss of *That Touch of Mink,* however, doesn't obscure an essentially threadbare lining. In seeming to throw off a sparkle, credit performance and pace are the key virtues of this Universal release. The Stanley Shapiro-Nate Monaster screenplay maintains a generally good clip, all to the good, but too often there's a hampering second-hand air about situation and joke. Throughout, it seems, the determination is to keep faith with the American sex mythology at any cost.

Jack Pitman, *Variety*

Going even farther (than *Boys' Night Out*) in its attempt to be daring, *That Touch of Mink* falls even flatter. Cary Grant, still charming although acting as if he'd been through this routine so often he's bored with the whole thing, plays a millionaire bachelor who works harder luring Doris Day to Bermuda and other places than he did to make his millions. Most of the film is thin, unsophisticated stuff—with some handsome color photography that tries to cover up the empty story.

Philip T. Hartung, *The Commonweal*

*That Touch of Mink* stars Cary Grant and Doris Day in a movie identical in almost every respect with *Lover Come Back* (Universal, 1962). *Lover Come Back* was a funny picture and *That Touch of Mink* is a funny picture. Stanley Shapiro was one of the authors and producers of *Lover Come Back* and is one of the authors and producers of *That Touch of Mink.* Mr. Shapiro is not ashamed to repeat himself. Ashamed? Am I kidding? The only significant difference between *Lover Come Back* and *That Touch of Mink* is that in *Lover Come Back* the Cary Grant part was played by Rock Hudson, and in *That Touch of Mink* the Cary Grant part is played by Cary Grant. When it comes to playing Cary Grant, nobody can beat Cary Grant. Go see for yourself.

Brendan Gill, *The New Yorker*

With Louise Arthur, John Marley and Tyler McVey

With Doris Day

With Mickey Mantle

# CHARADE

## 1963

With Audrey Hepburn

**CREDITS:**

*Distributing company:* Universal-International. *Producing company:* A Universal-Stanley Donen Production. *Producer:* Stanley Donen. *Director:* Stanley Donen. *Production Manager:* Leopold Schlosberg. *Production Executive:* Arthur Carroll. *Associate Producer:* James Ware. *Assistant Director:* Marc Maurette. *Screenplay:* Peter Stone. *From published story:* "The Unsuspecting Wife," by Peter Stone, and Marc Behm. *Cinematography:* Charles Lang. *Editor:* James Clark. Music by Henry Mancini. *Title song:* Music: Henry Mancini. Lyric: Johnny Mercer. *Art direction:* Jean D'Eaubonne. *Costumes:* Miss Hepburn's clothes by Givenchy. *Makeup:* Alberto de Rossi, and John O'Gorman. *Sound:* Jacques Carrere, and Bob Jones. Main Title designed by Maurice Binder. *Animation:* Robert Ellis. *Release date:* December 25, 1963. *Running time:* 113 minutes.

**THE CAST:**

| | |
|---|---|
| Peter Joshua | Cary Grant |
| Regina "Reggie" Lambert | Audrey Hepburn |
| Hamilton Bartholomew | Walter Matthau |
| Tex Penthollow | James Coburn |
| Herman Scobie | George Kennedy |
| Leopold Gideon | Ned Glass |
| Inspector Edouard Grandpierre | Jacques Marin |
| Felix | Paul Bonifas |
| Sylvie Gaudet | Dominique Minot |
| Jean-Louis Gaudet | Thomas Chelimsky |

**SYNOPSIS:**

When Regina Lambert returns to her Paris home after a holiday in the French Alps, she finds her home stripped of furnishings and her husband murdered. Peter Joshua, whom she met at the resort, offers to help her untangle the mystery. Her husband had hidden $250,000 somewhere and his ex-cronies want it, and believe that Mrs. Lambert knows where it is. Then it becomes apparent that Peter might be a member of the gang. One by one the members of the gang are murdered and suspicion is pointed at just about everybody. Mrs. Lambert, after a chase through the subways, is about to be killed by a heretofore unsuspected man when she is saved by the quick actions of Peter.

### REVIEWS:

Clues, red herrings, and murders pile up in *Charade* until you begin to suspect the picture is working overtime to keep you mystified. But since producer-director Stanley Donen is also interested in holding your attention with his good cast, engaging shots of off-beat Paris, and amusing give-and-take between Cary Grant and Audrey Hepburn, both of whom are fine in the give-and-take department, the plot becomes secondary, and the film holds you mainly for the ornaments in the charade.

Philip T. Hartung, *Commonweal*

Not since John Huston's *Beat the Devil* has there been such a gay romp as *Charade*. Huston himself recently tried something similar in *The List of Adrian Messenger,* but the comedy thriller is a chancy little form, and he could not duplicate that first brilliant success. More credit, then, to producer-director Stanley Donen who has brought to the screen an absolute delight in which Cary Grant and Audrey Hepburn schottische about with evident glee.

It is characteristic of the generally civilized and witty fun of the entire film, and somehow entirely appropriate that Miss Hepburn should suddenly look into the can of Calox toothpowder and ask Grant if he can tell heroin by its taste. He tastes and says: "Heroin! Peppermint-flavored heroin!" *Charade* merits not merely audiences, but addicts.

*Newsweek*

Imitation Hitchcock seems to be quite the thing this season. Following on Mark Robson's *The Prize,* comes Stanley Donen's obeisance to the old master. As a black comedy *Charade* fails just where *The Trouble With Harry* so triumphantly succeeds, in knitting the comic and the macabre into a stylistic unity. Donen's film tends to splinter up into individual sequences, that one for thrills, this one

With Audrey Hepburn

With George Kennedy

for laughs, with comedy generally working better than the suspense (Donen was, I take it, making macabre comedy rather than a thriller with comic overtones). Neither can Donen share a black humor with Hitchcock, failing to rise to the splendid opportunities inherent in a sequence wherein a collection of screwballs come to pay their last respects, if such they can be called, to a murdered man. Neither would Hitchcock have allowed the comic possibilities of a scene in which a private conversation goes out over the simultaneous translation headphones at an international conference to peter out so fitfully. There is, however, one wonderfully funny and macabre moment when the cameraman is substituted for a corpse in a morgue, and the camera's baleful eye glares up at the world from the slab.

But enough of Hitchcock and invidious comparisons. *Charade,* it is pleasant to record, is the first Donen film since he deserted the musical for those upstage comedies to have any sort of visual style. Part of the credit must go to Charles Lang, Jr.'s imaginative color photography, but the crispness and fluidity are so much due to mise-en-scène as camerawork. The chase sequences, notably Hepburn stalking Grant through the streets of Paris and Grant pursuing Hepburn through the subways, are handled with that old choreographic brio and timing; some of the quieter romantic moments, particularly those in an empty apartment have a beautifully muted dreamlike quality similar to those in the earlier Donen-Hepburn *Funny Face,*

although this time the images are sharp and clear, unlike Ray June's softly diffused vision of Paris in the previous film.

The plot of *Charade* is exactly that, an enigma, in which a word of two or more syllables has to be guessed by a description or representation of the separate syllables and of the whole. In this case Grant is the enigma, and the rest of the cast have to spend the entire film guessing at his function and purpose, for Grant is continually changing his identity to suit the circumstances. Too much cold logic turned on this story riddles it with implausibilities, but as the basis for sophisticated comedy it is eminently serviceable. Peter Stone's screenplay is full of excellent inventions, and his dialogue is barbed with a distinctive wit and style.

Apart from the two stars the actors only have to register baffled menace, which they all do excellently, but Grant and Hepburn foil each other sympathetically. Both employ the stiletto rather than the harpoon as the basis of their comic technique, and their ease and assurance together remind one of the vintage years of Hollywood comedy. Hepburn, an elegant apparition in her Givenchy gowns, gives her usual distinctive performance, but Grant, skillfully handling some of the best material he's worked on in a long time, comes up with one of his happiest high-comedy performances (although even his impeccable comic technique can't carry him through an embarrassingly unfunny bit of mime in a shower). Slick, fast, and funny

260

*Charade* is infinitely superior to Universal's other cash crop of comedies. It may not equal *The Trouble With Harry* but it makes the Ross Hunter confections look like very stale pastries.

Richard Whitehall, *Films and Filming*

One hesitates to be uncharitable to a film like *Charade,* which seeks only to provide a little innocent merriment and make pots of money. One hesitates also to be uncharitable to such affable and graceful performers as Cary Grant and Audrey Hepburn, whose perdurable charms suffuse every frame of this mystery comedy in the Hitchcock tradition. No doubt, a few weeks ago *Charade* could be viewed with relative equanimity. True, its deaths are frequent and violent; but we have grown quite used to that in our pictures—even in our comedies. But that, I fear, is just the point. Our films and our television have made us so familiar with murder that we can laugh about it and shrug it away—until murder walks the streets and lurks in police corridors.

The mass media, like it or not, have a heavy responsibility. They not only reflect our times; they affect them. *Charade,* in which shootings, beatings, and strangulation are played for laughs, is a bit more symptomatic of our times. Certainly no one involved—least of all Mr. Grant—could be accused of a lack of conscience. But they, like most of our picture-makers today, must plead guilty to a lack of awareness that each film that laughs at murder, each film that celebrates violence, each film that makes a hero out of a man with a gun is dehumanizing our society just a little bit more. Of itself, *Charade* is a stylish and amusing melodrama; but in the context of the bloodlust that seems unloosed in our land, it is as sinister as the villains who stalk Miss Hepburn through the cobbled streets of Paris.

Arthur Knight, *The Saturday Review*

With Audrey Hepburn

# FATHER GOOSE

1964

## CREDITS:

*Distributing company:* A Universal-International Release. *Producing company:* A Granox Company Production. *Producer:* Robert Arthur. *Director:* Ralph Nelson. *Assistant directors:* Tom Shaw and James Welch. *Screenplay:* Peter Stone and Frank Tarloff. From an unpublished story by S. H. Barnett entitled "A Place of Dragons." *Cinematography:* Charles Lang, Jr. Technicolor. *Editor:* Ted J. Kent. Music by Cy Coleman. *Music supervision:* Joseph Gershenson. *Art direction:* Alexander Golitzen, and Henry Bumstead. *Set decorations:* John McCarthy and George Milo. *Costumes:* Aghayan. *Make-up:* Bud Westmore. *Hair stylist:* Larry Germain. *Sound:* Waldon O. Watson and William Russell. *Production manager:* Ernest Wehmeyer. *Song:* "Pass Me By," music by Cy Coleman; lyrics by Caroline Leigh, sung by Digby Wolfe. French title for "Father Goose" is "Grand Méchant Loup Appelle," or "Big Bad Wolf is Calling." *Release date:* December 24, 1964. *Running time:* 116 minutes.

## THE CAST:

| | |
|---|---|
| *Walter Eckland* | Cary Grant |
| *Catherine Freneau* | Leslie Caron |
| *Comdr. Frank Houghton* | Trevor Howard |
| *Lt. Stebbins* | Jack Good |
| *Christine* | Verina Greenlaw |
| *Anne* | Pip Sparke |
| *Harriet* | Jennifer Berrington |
| *Elizabeth* | Stephanie Berrington |
| *Angélique* | Lourelle Felsette |
| *Dominique* | Nicole Felsette |
| *Jenny* | Sharyl Locke |
| *Submarine Captain* | Simon Scott |
| *Submarine Executive* | John Napier |

| | |
|---|---|
| Radioman | Richard Lupino |
| Doctor | Alex Finlayson |
| Chaplain | Peter Forster |
| Navigator | Don Spruance |
| Helmsman | Ken Swofford |

## SYNOPSIS:

Walter Eckland lives on a South Pacific Island, alone and some distance from the civilization that he doesn't care for. Australian Navy Commander Frank Houghton needs a lookout for the advancing Japanese forces and persuades Eckland to volunteer, and to use the code name of Mother Goose when he radios his reports.

While attempting to rescue another watcher on another island, Eckland arrives only to find the man dead, and discovers Catherine Freneau, daughter of the French Consul at Rabaul, and seven little girls who were students at the consulate. Eckland brings them to his hut. They take over his home, drive him out, clean up his habitat, and attempt to improve his habits. Catherine and Eckland fall in love and are married by the military radio. He rebuilds a boat to get them off the island, the Japanese endanger them, but an American submarine finally rescues them.

## REVIEWS:

Normally, I am less than enthusiastic about the way fantasy and reality are blended in Hollywood comedies. I must say I found the mixture in *Father Goose* very engaging. The film was co-authored by Peter Stone (who also wrote Grant's recent success *Charade*) and directed by Ralph Nelson (*Lilies of the Field*). Both men appear to have an unusual flair for combining tongue-in-cheek wackiness with honest human insight to produce a very palatable entertainment package.

The difference between Grant and most other old-line movie stars, who also essentially played themselves on the screen, is that he is an extremely accomplished craftsman and also has a highly developed sense of how to choose a script that does well by him and that he can do well by. I thought Miss Caron was delightful in a role that was an off-beat combination of propriety, gumption and earthly good sense.

Moira Walsh, *America*

*Father Goose* is the Hollywood counterpart of the French product—a thickly upholstered, high-powered Cadillac of the love-film business, as against Demy's attempt (*Umbrellas of Cherbourg*—reviewed previously) at a jaunty little Simca. By now Grant is a major minor American industry, and his vehicles have a slight smell of protective oil-film on them when they are uncrated—intricate mechanisms that have been carefully planned on huge drawing boards and constructed just as carefully all the way down the line.

The story, reminiscent of Michener's *Tales of the South Pacific,* takes place in that area in 1941 as the Japanese advance. When the Australians withdraw from the islands, they leave coast-watchers, one of whom is an American ex-professor who had fled there some years before to escape civilization. His code name on the naval radio is Mother Goose. By a series of accidents he becomes the ward of some schoolgirls, escaping with Leslie Caron. Despite this, there are some quite funny lines. Grant makes a strong effort, partly successful to subdue his usual sleek self in the whiskery curmudgeon; even when the gloss shines through, he is still a very skillful performer.

Stanley Kauffman, *The New Republic*

Trevor Howard and Jack Good

Cary Grant, gray now but graceful as ever, wrings whatever there is to be wrung from the role, but never quite enough to conceal the fact that *Father Goose* is a flagrant waste of his talent and the audience's time.

Arthur Knight, *The Saturday Review*

Although by this time *Father Goose* was beginning to sound like many of the movies I saw during World War II and shortly thereafter. As the film progresses, however, it becomes more and more like past successes, particularly *The Pied Piper* and *The Beachcomber*.

Director Ralph Nelson makes some of this tale and its incidental incidents quite amusing. Grant is excellent as the unshaved, Scotch-drinking misanthrope; and his reform, although rather sentimental, is quite convincing. Miss Caron, who looks right in her role, probably sounds right too, but her French-English is sometimes hard to follow.

Philip T. Hartung, *The Commonweal*

There seem to be a notion that by tossing a handful of cute youngsters into a film you come up with what is charmingly called a "family picture." Add such proven box-office stars as Cary Grant and Leslie Caron, and reasoning would indicate a made-to-order Christmas package for the family trade. This probably will be the case for those who adore this type of entertainment. However, the more sophisticated may be bored and exasperated after some of the initial brightness wears off. Grant is properly engaging as a shiftless, selfish character.

*Cue Magazine*

## ARTICLE

Cary Grant, who probably holds all box office records—his name on a film virtually guarantees an opening at the Radio City Music Hall—is placing himself in double jeopardy in his latest film, *Father Goose*. He is shattering his image as the paragon of tailors and barbers and cluttering his scenes with children, the most notorious of scene stealers.

The choices, like most of Mr. Grant's 65 films, are his own. He is regarded in Hollywood as occult in picking scripts. But even Mr. Grant conceded, the other day, in his dressing room at Universal City, that *Father Goose* is unprecedented for him. "I have often played the part of a spiritual bum," he noted. "But I don't think I have ever looked like one."

A couple of generations of females would have been a bit surprised at the appearance of their idol. His graying hair, usually regarded as a mark of his special brand of sophistication, was disheveled. The stubble of beard, a week old, was not typical of his romantic charm. His shirt was rumpled and the jeans well worn. His bare feet were in straw sandals.

Commenting on the movie while a thatched hut was being fitted out with such primitive conveniences as dishes made of coconut halves, Mr. Grant shook off his casual manner and revealed that he had been very deeply involved in this script by Peter Stone for more than a year. When he was first asked by Mel Tucker, a Universal executive, to read the original story by S. W. Barnett, he was still working on *Charade*.

"It's a good basic idea, but it needs a lot of developing," he told Mr. Tucker. But secretly he sent it off to Mr. Stone who had written *Charade*. Mr. Stone told the star he would

With Leslie Caron

like to write this movie. Mr. Grant then informed Mr. Tucker that he had a suspicion Mr. Stone, if approached properly, might agree to work on the project. By this time *Charade* had proven to be a huge success. "This gave Peter a chance to make his own deal," said Mr. Grant with a laugh.

Mr. Grant divulged that like all experienced actors he tried to avoid unnecessary props.

"When you're young, you're insecure," he said. "You hang on to any props you can get your hands on. Some young actors deliver their lines with tosses of the head. Their subconscious objective is to distract you from what displeases themselves."

Murray Schumach, *The New York Times*

With Verina Greenlaw, Sharyl Locke, Nicole Felsette, Laurelle Felsette, Jennifer Berrington, Pip Sparks and Stephanie Berrington

NEWS ITEM

Universal's Cary Grant-Leslie Caron starrer, *Father Goose,* soared to $210,380 for its opening week at Radio City Music Hall to set a new all-time record for a Christmas attraction at the theatre. *Father Goose* topped Universal's *Charade,* the previous record holder, by more than $30,400.

*Hollywood Reporter*

# WALK, DON'T RUN

1966

## CREDITS:

*Distributing company:* Columbia Pictures Corp. *Producing company:* Granley Co. *Producer:* A Sol C. Siegel Production. *Director:* Charles Walters. Production designed by Joe Wright. *Assistant director:* Jim Myers. *Screenplay:* Sol Saks. Based on a story by Robert Russell, and Frank Ross. *Cinematography:* Harry Stradling. Panovision and Technicolor. *Editors:* Walter Thompson and James Wells. Music by Quincy Jones. *Set decorations:* George R. Nelson, and Robert Priestley. *Costume Designer:* Morton Hoack. Hair style by Virginia Jones. *Makeup:* Supervised by Ben Lane. *Sound:* James Z. Floster, and Jack Haynes. *Unit Production Managers:* Russell Saunders and Rusty Meek. *Release date:* July 15, 1966. *Running time:* 114 minutes.

## THE CAST:

| | |
|---|---|
| *William Rutland* | Cary Grant |
| *Christine Easton* | Samantha Eggar |
| *Steve Davis* | Jim Hutton |
| *Julius P. Haversack* | John Standing |
| *Aiko Kurawa* | Miiko Taka |
| *Yuri Andreyovitch* | Ted Hartley |
| *Dimitri* | Ben Astar |
| *Police Captain* | George Takei |
| *Mr. Kurawa* | Teru Shimada |
| *Mrs. Kurawa* | Lois Kiuchi |

## SYNOPSIS:

Visiting Tokyo during the 1964 Olympic games, Sir William Rutland, an English industrialist, is unable to find a room until he talks lovely young Christine Easton into letting him share her apartment. Later, meeting Steve Davis, an American athlete, Rutland sneaks him into the apartment as well. Morning is especially complicated in the tiny apartment, what with breakfast and the bathroom and Christine's irate discovery of Steve's presence. Christine is engaged to Julius Haversack, a British Embassy official, whom Rutland finds a complete bore, especially when he becomes officious after Christine, now sharing her apartment with two men, also is suspected of espionage. Rutland joins Steve in his race through Tokyo streets, in order to persuade Steve to marry Christine immediately after the race and thus protect her good name. Steve is dead-tired at the wedding ceremony that Rutland has arranged. As Christine later learns, Rutland has thoughtfully prepared a solution for that problem too.

## REVIEWS:

If you are getting on in years (or are addicted to watching the Late Show), the plot of *Walk, Don't Run* may strike you as familiar. In 1943, it was called *The More The Merrier* and involved Jean Arthur, Joel McCrea and the late Charles Coburn in the wartime Washington housing crush. The updated version has Cary Grant as a titled British industrialist, Samantha Eggar as a British Embassy secretary and Jim Hutton as an American Olympic athlete, confronting the Tokyo Olympics housing shortage.

Tastes in comic invention have changed in twenty-three years, and the plot limps somewhat by this time. Besides, the Washington housing crisis was a solid and enduring phenomenon around which to build a comedy. A temporary, sports-event jam-up simply does not work as well, and a lot of tedious exposition has to be introduced for the sake of minimal plausibility.

Foremost on the credit side of the film's ledger is Grant himself, who is as deft and winning a light comedian as ever. Intermittently he gets good support from his fellow players, the script writer, the director and the Tokyo backgrounds in color—the authentic locale encourages the inclusion of a few satiric comments on the changing oriental culture. With Grant the picture is more than tolerably amusing. Without him it would probably seem intolerably thin.

Moira Walsh, *America*

Too long as are most comedies today, *Walk, Don't Run* seems to take its title far too literally; but there are several very funny sequences, a jaunty score by Quincy Jones, and the unflawed elegance of Mr. Grant. With a light, bright touch and a debonair smile, he gives the film the happy sheen of a charade that must never be taken seriously. It almost works.

Arthur Knight, *The Saturday Review*

In one of his wonderful dissertations on ancient history, Will Cuppy posed the question of why the pyramids have not fallen down, then supplied the answer. They have not fallen down because it is not in the nature of a pyramid to fall down, he said. A pyramid could not fall down if it tried. The explanation applies equally well to Cary Grant, who could not be unfunny if he tried. Grant has watched the decline of Hollywood comedy at first hand, and in

With Jim Hutton and Samantha Eggar

With Samantha Eggar

*Walk, Don't Run* he tries almost singlehandedly to prevent its complete downfall.

Though set in Tokyo during the 1964 Olympics, *Walk, Don't Run* could just as well be in New York, London or San Diego, since it is a standard one-set farce that serves as meat and potatoes for summer stock and strychnine for Broadway.

What this amounts to is a remake of that famous scene from *It Happened One Night,* stretched thin enough to reach from Tokyo to Osaka. There is a great deal of Japanese bowing and scraping on the bottom of the plot barrel, and a few funny scenes with Grant retrieving his pants and joining the walking race. For the rest, lengthy lapses of ingenuity are broken up by great gaps of invention, the sort of gaps that writer, producer and director hope will be filled in by the performers, who hope and trust that the offending scenes will be left on the cutting-room floor.

Though Grant's personal presence is indispensible, the character he plays is almost wholly superfluous. Perhaps the inference to be taken is that a man in his 50s or 60s has no place in romantic comedy except as a catalyst. If so, the chemistry is wrong for everyone.

*Newsweek*

With Jim Hutton and Samantha Eggar

With Samantha Eggar
and John Standing

268

With Jim Hutton

With Anna Chang in *Singapore Sue*

## OTHER APPEARANCES

### SHORT FILMS AND GUEST APPEARANCES IN FEATURE FILMS

The first short film that Cary Grant made was *Singapore Sue* which was released in the summer of 1932. Three of his full length films were already in distribution. However he had made this short film in New York City. In it he played an American sailor who visits a cafe run by actress Anna Chang. It was probably on the basis of this film that Grant obtained his first five-year contract with Paramount. The film was written and directed by Casey Robinson. The dialogue was staged by Max E. Hayes.

In 1936 Metro-Goldwyn-Mayer released a twenty minute color film entitled *Pirate Party on Catalina Island*. Chester Morris as Master of Ceremonies narrated the film in which the following stars appeared as themselves: Marion Davies, Cary Grant, Virginia Bruce, John Gilbert, Lee Tracy, Errol Flynn, Lili Damita, Sid Silvers, Eddie Peabody,

Leon Errol, Robert Armstrong, Charles (Buddy) Rogers and His Band. The film was Louis Lewyn Production in Technicolor with continuity and dialogue by Alexander Van Dorn, and musical direction by Abe Meyer.

In 1939 United Artists released the Hal Roach presentation of *Topper Takes A Trip* produced by Milton Bren and Directed by Norman Z. McLeod. Originally they had planned to star Cary Grant in this sequel to *Topper,* but Grant was not available and so the script was rewritten and a short clip of footage from *Topper* was used as a story explanation, so that although Grant did not work on this film at all, he does make an appearance by way of a film clip.

In 1944 Warner Brothers made one of several short films for the war effort. The ten-minute long film was called *Road to Victory* and was issued in May. It starred Bing Crosby, Cary Grant, Frank Sinatra, Charles Ruggles, Dennis Morgan, Irene Manning, Jack Carson, Jimmy Lydon, and Olive Blakeney. The trade paper *The Hollywood*

With Anna Chang in *Singapore Sue*

With Carol Burnett and Len Mince in a scene from the stage musical "Golden Dawn"

With Anna Chang in *Singapore Sue*

Lux Radio Theatre presentation of *Theodora Goes Wild,* June 13, 1938, with Irene Dunne and Cecil B. deMille

*Reporter* described the film: *"The Road to Victory* short made by Warner Bros. and produced by Jack L. Warner for the War Activities Committee to boost the forthcoming Fifth War Loan Drive is one of the most entertaining and effective films of its kind yet made. This one actually is worthy of inclusion in any program on its merits as a picture, without reference to its purpose. It opens in an American home in 1951 and by means of the miracles then to be available to all free peoples, it flashes back to 1944 with compelling power, having the happy faculty of combining laughs, good ones, with its serious objective."

Claudette Colbert and John Wayne starred in *Without Reservations* which was released by RKO in 1946. It was produced by Jesse Lasky, and directed by Mervyn LeRoy. Cary Grant made a brief unbilled guest appearance in this film. The reviews were mostly lukewarm. "Surprise walk-ons are spotted in the footage," said weekly *Variety,* "such as Jack Benny approaching Miss Colbert in a railway station and asking for an autograph: Cary Grant dancing with Miss Colbert; LeRoy himself dining with her." Cecilia Ager at the end of her review in PM said: "But if you'd like a quick look at Jack Benny and Cary Grant, or even at Louella Parsons or Mervyn LeRoy, the director himself —they're all in for a fast and private laugh. Showing so briefly they're the best, and except for Mr. LeRoy, the wisest people anywhere near the vicinity of *Without Reservations.*"

In 1963 Robert Youngson wrote and produced a composite film of sequences from famous motion picture comedies. Released by Metro-Goldwyn-Mayer it was called *The Big Parade of Comedy.* Two of the sequences were taken from Cary Grant films: 1. a duel of wits between Jean Harlow and Grant from *Suzy;* and 2. a daffy sequence between Katharine Hepburn and Grant from *The Philadelphia Story.*

## TELEVISION

Like several other major stars, Cary Grant has refused to work on television. Of course, many of his films are shown regularly on television.

The one exception was an unbilled guest appearance. Cliff Arquette and another radio actor, David Willock, had a local television show in Los Angeles in 1950, which they wrote and produced themselves, called *Dave and Charlie,* seen at 8:00 pm each Thursday. Mr. Arquette played Charley Weaver, a character that he had been developing on radio, and Dave played a young friend with a touch of larceny in his heart. Cary Grant so enjoyed this program that he insisted on appearing one night as a hobo passing by Charlie's house which was next to a railroad yard.

Grant of course later appeared "live" as himself rather than playing a character, when he accepted the Academy Award given him, as well as when in 1957 he accepted the Academy Award for Ingrid Bergman for best performance by an actress for her role in *Anastasia.* Grant was also seen on the 1970 Tony Awards presentations.

## RADIO

Beginning in the mid-1930s Grant made appearances on radio shows such as *The Circle,* 1939, a talk show sponsored by Kellogg Corn Flakes, heard over NBC; and on *The Hollywood Guild* sponsored by Gulf Oil, heard over CBS. But perhaps he is best remembered for his performances on *The Lux Radio Theatre* sponsored by Lever Brothers. Cecil B. DeMille directed many of these broadcasts. The date, title, and co-stars of *The Lux Radio*

*Theatre* programs on which Cary Grant was starred are given below.

| | | |
|---|---|---|
| May 5, 1935 | Adam and Eve | Constance Cummings |
| March 8, 1937 | Madame Butterfly | Grace Moore |
| June 13, 1938 | Theodora Goes Wild | Irene Dunne |
| May 28, 1939 | Only Angels Have Wings | Jean Arthur, Thomas Mitchell, Rita Hayworth |
| Sept. 11, 1939 | Awful Truth | Claudette Colbert, Phyllis Brooks |
| Dec. 11, 1939 | In Name Only | Carole Lombard, Kay Francis |
| June 30, 1941 | I Love You Again | Myrna Loy, Frank McHugh |
| Jan. 26, 1942 | Here Comes Mr. Jordan | Claude Rains, Evelyn Keyes, James Gleason |
| July 20, 1942 | The Philadelphia Story (Special Victory Show for the U.S. Government) | Katherine Hepburn, Lt. James Stewart Ruth Hussey, and Virginia Weidler |
| May 17, 1943 | Talk of the Town | Ronald Colman and Jean Arthur |
| Oct. 18, 1943 | Mr. Lucky | Laraine Day |
| Feb. 26, 1945 | Bedtime Story | Greer Garson |
| June 13, 1949 | Bachelor and the Bobby Soxer | Shirley Temple |
| June 27, 1949 | Every Girl Should Be Married | Betsy Drake |
| Oct. 10, 1950 | Mr. Blanding Builds His Dream House | Irene Dunne |
| April 17, 1950 | Every Girl Should Be Married | (Repeat with previous cast.) |
| May 11, 1953 | The Bishop's Wife (repeat of the story previously presented on Dec. 19, 1949 with Tyrone Power playing the Grant role) | Phyllis Thaxter |
| Sept. 21, 1953 | I Confess | Phyllis Thaxter |
| Jan. 25, 1954 | People Will Talk | Jeanne Crain |
| April 5, 1954 | Welcome Stranger | Barry Fitzgerald and Pat Crowley |
| Jan 18, 1955 | Awful Truth | Irene Dunne (This story repeated for the third time, but only twice with Grant.) |
| March 1, 1955 | The Bishop's Wife | (Repeat). |

## THE MONEY-MAKERS

In the 65th Anniversary special issue of *Weekly Variety,* the following Cary Grant films were listed among the All-Time Box-Office Champs. These are the films which have the most successful rental sales for theatrical distribution in the United States and Canada.

| | |
|---|---|
| Operation Petticoat (1960) | $9,500,000.00 |
| That Touch of Mink (1962) | 8,500,000.00 |
| North By Northwest (1959) | 6,310,000.00 |
| Charade (1963) | 6,150,000.00 |
| Father Goose (1965) | 6,000,000.00 |
| Notorious (1946) | 4,800,000.00 |
| The Bachelor and The Bobby-Soxer (1947) | 4,500,000.00 |
| To Catch A Thief (1955) | 4,500,000.00 |
| The Pride and the Passion (1957) | 4,500,000.00 |
| I Was A Male War Bride (1949) | 4,100,000.00 |
| Night And Day (1946) | 4,000,000.00 |
| Walk, Don't Run (1966) | 4,000,000.00 |

The importance that distributors give to films starring Cary Grant is clearly indicated by the fact that twenty-eight of his films have been chosen to play the Radio City Music Hall in New York City, during Christmas week. This is a prime time and place to open a new film.

Lux Radio Theatre presentation of *Madame Butterfly,* March 8, 1937, with Gail Patrick, Bob Cobb, Grace Moore, Cecil B. deMille, Princess Der Ling and Pietro Cimini

Frank Sinatra presents Academy Award

# THE ACADEMY AWARD

During the forty-second annual presentation of awards by the Academy of Motion Picture Arts and Sciences, on Tuesday, April 7, 1970, Cary Grant was given a special award for his achievements in film acting over the past four decades. Although he had received two nominations as best actor for his performance in *Penny Serenade,* 1941; and for his performance in *None But The Lonely Heart,* 1944, he did not win either time. When one considers the fact that the Academy Awards are not always given to the best actor of the year, but more often to the most popular; and also that an actor often wins not for his best work but for the current film, perhaps this award given to Mr. Grant is really more meaningful, for it was given for a career of quality work over the years and did not attempt to select a single performance which might have been debatable.

The inscription on the Academy Award read:

*TO CARY GRANT*
*for his unique mastery*
*of the art of screen acting*
*with the respect and affection*
*of his colleagues*

The following comments in the press reflect the atmosphere surrounding the giving of the award that evening.

A special award, for sheer brilliance in the acting business was presented by Frank Sinatra to Cary Grant, who accepted the statuette, alternating between tears and laughter, following the showing of a montage of clips from his past films.

Ted Thackery, Jr., *Los Angeles Times*

275

And there was Cary Grant, who on film clips and in person, provided by far the most gracious, moving moments of the show. He received his special award for outstanding artistry and memorable performances, and well he deserves it. Frank Sinatra, on hand to present the citation, put it well. "No one has brought more pleasure to more people for many years than Cary has, and nobody has done so many things so well." The film clip sequence which followed, superbly compiled by director Jack Haley, Jr. and Richard Dunlap, showed Cary in unforgettable scenes with unforgettable leading ladies: Mae West, Jean Harlow, Katharine Hepburn, Irene Dunne, Grace Kelly, Eva Marie Saint, to mention a few.

Then Cary, handsome and suave and tasteful as ever, took a standing ovation from the industry audience as he started to make his comments. He thanked the Academy, Sinatra the presenter, his former directors and writers, ending: "Probably no greater honor can come to a man than the respect of his colleagues."

Joyce Haber, *Los Angeles Times*

The most emotional moment came when Cary Grant, sixty-six years old and a star for thirty-three of them, stepped on stage to accept his Special Oscar awarded him by the Board of Governors of the Academy of Motion Picture Arts and Sciences. Many Hollywood pundits and "know-it-alls" predicted Cary Grant would not show up to receive this award. But he did. By so doing, Cary earned and received one of the most thunderous ovations in Oscar history. In fact the entire audience stood up and applauded the man who has starred in very few box-office flops in his career but has never earned an Oscar before.

Yes, Hollywood paid tribute to one of its greatest stars and goodwill ambassadors last night. Long may he remain so.

John Austin, *Citizen News*

Inside the Music Center, the audience proved that they too, had idols as Cary Grant, looking outrageously handsome with gray hair, strode on stage to receive a special Oscar from Frank Sinatra, who flew into town just to make the presentation.

The star-packed audience rose to its feet and tendered Grant a thunderous ovation, and, again, one could almost feel a physical transfer of affection.

Charles Parker, *Herald-Examiner*

Frank Sinatra presented the award to Grant, and said: "It was awarded for sheer brilliance of acting." Then Sinatra added: "Cary has so much skill that he makes it all look easy."

James Bacon, *Herald-Examiner*

Anyone who has been around this business as long as I have could not fail to be deeply moved by the tribute to Cary Grant on Tuesday's forty-second annual Academy Award telecast.

In as much as the favorites romped off with all the prizes, leaving the various races, singularly unexciting, it was the urbane Grant, grown white in service and his age showing around the mouth and eyes—looking a little bit like Cary Grant made up for an old man's role—and the standing ovation they gave him in the Music Center's Dorothy Chandler Pavilion that made the evening.

And like actors have been doing since Oscar was a pup, Cary began thanking directors and writers he's worked with over the years, not apologizing for doing so but saying: "Why not? This is a collaborative medium. We all need each other."

It seemed to me right and proper that this award for long and distinguished achievement to Grant should be bestowed by Frank Sinatra—only a superstar should honor a superstar.

Cecil Smith, *Los Angeles Times*